DATE DUE

AP 17 '97		
JE 11 03		
MY 20 '04		
JE 9 04		
NO 2 0		
AP 2 3 08		

DEMCO 38-296

Moral Wisdom and Good Lives

Also by John Kekes

A Justification of Rationality
The Nature of Philosophy
Dimensions of Ethical Thought (co-editor)
The Examined Life
Moral Tradition and Individuality
Facing Evil
The Morality of Pluralism

MORAL
WISDOM
and
GOOD
LIVES

JOHN KEKES

Cornell University Press

ITHACA AND LONDON

First published 1995 by Cornell University Press.

Printed in the United States of America

♾ The paper in this book meets the minimum requirements
of the American National Standard for Information Sciences—
Permanence of Paper for Printed Library Materials, ANSI Z39.48–1984.

Library of Congress Cataloging-in-Publication Data

Kekes, John.
    Moral wisdom and good lives / John Kekes.
        p.   cm.
    Includes bibliographical references and index.
    ISBN 0–8014–3171–9 (alk. paper)
    1. Happiness.   2. Wisdom—Moral and ethical aspects.   3. Virtues.
4. Prudence.   I. Title.
BJ1481.K36   1995
171'.3—dc20   95–16278

for

J. Y. K.

Contents

Preface

Moral wisdom is a virtue—the virtue of reflection. This book gives an account of what it is, how it differs from other kinds of wisdom, and why it is necessary for living a good life. The book is a contribution to the ancient tradition of eudaimonism, known in contemporary moral thought, not altogether happily, as virtue theory. The essential aim of this tradition is to help reasonable people make good lives for themselves. This is a practical aim, and it is not easy to think of one that is more important. But the achievement of a practical aim as complex and difficult as living a good life requires hard critical thought and a willingness to question much that one has taken for granted. A traditional task of philosophy has until recently been to guide this sort of reflection; part of the purpose of this book is to do so.

It would be absurd to suppose that reflection on the nature of a good life, and on how to live it, is the prerogative of philosophers. It is not absurd but true, however, that such reflection is philosophical. Philosophy may be a useful guide to it because philosophers have been expected to reflect on the topic, as it were *ex officio*, whereas others do it only as need or inclination prompts them. It is a sad admission for a philosopher to have to make that few philosophers have lived up to this expectation since the discipline has become professionalized in this century. It is perhaps not unreasonable to hope that with the renewed interest in eudaimonism the situation may be changing. In any case, this book is meant to help bring about that salutary change.

The book is addressed to readers who may or may not be philosophers. It does not presuppose philosophical expertise, only a willingness and ability to think hard about the difficult questions posed by the subject. The Introduction and the first two chapters provide the background against which the nature and importance of moral wisdom is to be understood. Philosophers knowledgeable about eudaimonism may not find much that is new in them. Subsequent chapters do endeavor to say something new, not, however, by offering original ideas about how to live well, but by calling attention to the hitherto not much noticed significance of some familiar ideas.

The beginning of this book was a short section on wisdom in chapter 5 of *The Nature of Philosophy* (Oxford: Blackwell, 1980). This grew into an article, "Wisdom" (*American Philosophical Quarterly* 20 [1983]: 277–286). It was developed as moral reflection in chapter 8 of *Moral Tradition and Individuality* (Princeton: Princeton University Press, 1989), and developed further as the reflective temper in chapter 11 of *Facing Evil* (Princeton: Princeton University Press, 1990). All these now seem inadequate as accounts of moral wisdom, and they are superseded by the present work.

Parts of the book use material that has been previously published in other forms. Chapter 4 uses material from *The Morality of Pluralism* (Princeton: Princeton University Press, 1993), chapter 3. The discussion of contingency, conflict, and evil in Chapter 4 and later derives from a much fuller treatment of contingency in *Moral Tradition and Individuality*, of conflict in *The Morality of Pluralism*, and of evil in *Facing Evil*. Chapter 7 uses material from *The Morality of Pluralism*, chapter 6. And Chapter 10 uses material from "Moral Depth," *Philosophy* 65 (1990): 439–453. In all these cases, the material has been revised, often substantially.

David Hamlyn and Wallace Matson read and commented extensively on a previous version. Their comments were tough and perceptive, and they resulted in major revisions. Their help has been invaluable, and it is acknowledged with gratitude and pleasure. Two readers, commissioned by Cornell University Press, also made useful suggestions, which have been followed in the final revision. They too are hereby thanked. Roger Haydon has been all an author could wish for in an editor: helpful, efficient, and sympathetic to the work. It has been a pleasure to work with him.

JOHN KEKES

ITHAKA
Charlton
New York

Moral Wisdom and Good Lives

A First Approximation

Moral wisdom is a virtue essential to living a good life. A distinctive type of wisdom, it differs from the wisdom that provides synoptic knowledge of the general structure of reality because knowledge is only one aspect of it, and, moreover, that knowledge is not synoptic but concerned specifically with what human beings should do to live a good life. Moral wisdom is thus practical, but its focus is narrower than that of worldly wisdom. The skilled conduct of human affairs which comes from being wise in the ways of the world may or may not be guided by morality. Moral wisdom, however, concentrates on evaluating human conduct from the perspective of good lives. It also differs from religious wisdom, which combines knowledge of God with the application of that knowledge to human life and conduct. Although moral wisdom is certainly concerned with human life and conduct, being wise about them need not presuppose religious commitment. Moral wisdom thus involves practically oriented knowledge, but the practice is guided by morality, and morality is conceived of in terms of good and evil as they bear on individual human efforts to live a good life.

The possession of moral wisdom is a matter of degree: more of it makes lives better, and less makes them worse. It is reasonable therefore to seek as much moral wisdom as possible. It is unclear, however, what exactly moral wisdom is and how it should be sought. A traditional task of philosophy has been to remove this unclarity. But philosophers have not paid much attention to moral wisdom since the the Middle Ages. Ancient Greek and medieval Christian philosophers, by contrast, were centrally concerned with it. They disagreed about many things, but they shared the assumption that reality is permeated by a moral order and that the good

1

life for human beings depends on living in conformity to it. They took the importance of moral wisdom to be that it provides knowledge of this order and motivation to live according to it.

One main reason for the lack of philosophical attention to moral wisdom in postmedieval times is that we—possessors of a contemporary Western sensibility—have become doubtful about the assumption that so many Greeks and Christians shared: we doubt that there is a moral order in reality. And because we doubt it, we have grown dubious about the traditional conception of moral wisdom. Yet we have not developed an alternative to it, and so, unsurprisingly, we have little to say about moral wisdom. Its importance, however, is not diminished by our doubts. We need a conception of moral wisdom that is independent of dubious assumptions and yet recognizes the importance of moral wisdom to living a good life. It is such a conception that will be formulated in this book.

Just as there are different conceptions of wisdom, so also there are different conceptions of moral wisdom. Philosophical world views, ideological systems, and the moral traditions of enduring cultures explicitly or implicitly endorse a conception of moral wisdom that is embedded in their favored conceptions of a good life. The point of view from which wisdom will be understood in this book is *eudaimonistic.* This point of view is secular, anthropocentric, pluralistic, individualistic, and agonistic. *Secular* because good lives are taken to depend on human effort, and because no supernatural assistance is relied on in trying to achieve them. *Anthropocentric* because the central concern is with good lives for human beings, which are ranked as having the highest value. *Pluralistic* because good lives and the values they embody are assumed to take many irreducibly different forms. *Individualistic* because good lives are interpreted to be for individuals as such, rather than as members of cultures, traditions, societies, or other groups. And *agonistic* because living a good life is recognized as being hard, requiring constant struggle against serious adversity.

Eudaimonism itself has several versions. The ancient Greeks, Montaigne, Spinoza, Hume, and John Stuart Mill, among others, can be interpreted as having developed notable historical instances of it. On the contemporary scene, what is now called "virtue theory" is in the same tradition. The present version of eudaimonism is Aristotelian in that it is more strongly influenced by Aristotle than by other thinkers. It must be emphasized, however, that it is *Aristotelian*, not Aristotle's. It follows Aristotle on several crucial points, but on other equally crucial ones it disagrees with him. The discussion of this version will be restricted to outlining an approach to good lives in which a contemporary account of moral wisdom can be formulated and defended. Its aim is thus not to give a scholarly account of Aristotle's views about good lives and wisdom, although, since Aristotle's contributions to these subjects are most important, it is worth paying attention to what he has to say.

The argument begins then in Chapter 1 with the formulation of a eudaimonistic point of view and the place of moral wisdom in it. This point of view is developed further in Chapter 2, where it is found to encounter very serious difficulties. These difficulties are explored in Chapter 3, which shows that a more thorough understanding reveals them to be far more significant than mere objections to a particular version of eudaimonism. They are, in fact, adversities inherent in the human condition, and they render the achievement of good lives deeply problematic. The importance of moral wisdom is that it provides a reasonable attitude to this lamentable fact about our condition. The attitude concerns increasing our control in order to cope with these adversities, and the possibility of doing so is shown to be connected with the improvement of our judgment. These matters are the topic of Chapter 4. Good judgment is identified with a particular kind of reflection, whose objects are the inward and the outward manifestations of the adversities that stand in the way of good lives. The inwardly directed modes of reflection are moral imagination, discussed in Chapter 5, self-knowledge, discussed in Chapters 6 and 7, and moral depth, discussed in Chapter 8. The mode of reflection directed outward concerns a reasonable attitude toward the inevitable imperfections of justice, and this is the subject of Chapter 9. The last chapter provides an overall view of moral wisdom and of the improvement its possession might make toward coping with the adversities inherent in the human condition.

This approach involves the description of certain reflexive inner processes. Singling out features of our inner life for description is inevitably a matter of selection. The selection is not arbitrary, however, because it is guided by the overall goal of formulating a conception of moral wisdom as an essential constituent of good lives. The relevance of the selected processes, as well as the irrelevance of others, is established by the role they play in making moral wisdom centrally important to good lives. The aim of these descriptions is not to reveal something hidden, but to call attention to generally evident and readily accessible features of our inner life. The descriptions therefore are not discoveries of new aspects of our inner life, but reminders of the significance of well-known aspects. And the reminders are needed because through inattention to moral wisdom we have allowed knowledge of them to fall into desuetude.

The descriptions will serve their purpose if they produce a certain sort of recognition. It is natural to turn to literature for help with this task, specifically to the tragedies of Sophocles. They are works whose moral significance will be shown to be comparable to that of the works of Plato and Aristotle. The descriptions derived from the plays are meant to prompt recognition of and inspire further attention to several significant inner processes and make clear why it is reasonable to cultivate them. These descriptions, therefore, carry considerable evaluative force. They are not meant to be uncommitted accounts of some aspects of the inner lives of human beings offered from a neutral perspective. They are, in current jargon, normative rather than meta-ethical. The justification for this approach is the importance of moral wisdom to living a good life.

WHAT THE DICTIONARIES SAY

The *Oxford English Dictionary* (1989, 2d ed.) gives as the first two definitions of "wisdom": "1. Capacity of judging rightly in matters relating to life and conduct; soundness of judgment in the choice of means and ends; sometimes, less strictly, sound sense, esp. in practical affairs: opp. to folly. 2. Knowledge (esp. of a high or abstruse kind); enlightenment, learning, erudition; in early use often = philosophy, science." According to *The Random House Dictionary* (1987, 2d ed.), the two preferred senses of "wisdom" are: "1. the quality or state of being wise; knowledge of what is true or right coupled with just judgment as to action; sagacity, discernment, or insight. 2. scholarly knowledge or learning." Unlike the second meaning provided by both dictionaries, the first one does not make wisdom dependent on scholarship or erudition, although, of course, it allows that wisdom may accompany such learning. Wisdom in the first sense is essentially connected with judgment, but the judgment does not presuppose a great deal of education. People of average intelligence and education, therefore, are not disqualified from having wisdom in the first sense, although they are disqualified in the second sense. Moral wisdom is a version of wisdom in the first sense.

Moral wisdom is thus a "capacity" to judge, but the mere capacity is not sufficient because the judgment needs to be "right," "sound," or "just." Even if this capacity were inborn, moral wisdom would still have to be acquired, since the capacity would need to be developed to a sufficient extent to make the resulting judgments reliable. Its development is desirable because the judgment it yields concerns "life and conduct" and "what is true or right . . . as to action." It may be thought that these descriptions are so general as to exclude nothing, yet this would be an uncharitable reading of them. The descriptions are certainly general, but their generality intends to signify that the object of sound judgment involved in moral wisdom is to evaluate what is true or right from the perspective of life as a whole. The generality is that of a reflective overview, a distancing of the judgment from the immediate pressures of its context, rather than that of portentous imprecision. A central question that the judgment should be interpreted as answering is one that reflective people cannot avoid putting to themselves: What should I do in this concrete situation, given my overall view of what a good life should be?

This question incorporates a double "should." The first concerns means and the second ends. Sound judgment must consider both, for, as the *OED* says, it is about "the choice of means and ends." The question, therefore, is not merely about the appropriate means for the achievement of some ends but also about the appropriateness of the ends themselves. This may be expressed by saying that the judgment associated with moral wisdom evaluates both means and ends on the basis of their likely contribution to making life better rather than worse. And it does so not from the point of view of what would be true or right momentarily, but from that of the long run. Because only fools would not be concerned with arriving at sound judgments about such matters, moral wisdom is desirable, and its opposite, folly, is not.

Moral wisdom as judgment has two logically distinguishable but actually inseparable aspects: theoretical and practical. The first concerns primarily "knowledge of what is true or right," and the second concentrates mainly on "sound sense . . . in practical affairs." Moral wisdom is not merely disinterested knowledge of what is true or right; it requires also that the knowledge should actually be used for making good lives for ourselves. Moral wisdom, however, is not purely practical either, since what it aims at is not just a good life pure and simple, but one that is pursued through choices of both means and ends, informed by knowledge of what is true or right. The theoretical aspect of moral wisdom therefore involves a kind of knowledge, and its practical aspect involves a kind of good. Both aspects are evaluative through and through, for both the knowledge and the good are sought in order to make life as a whole better.

The dictionaries thus direct us beyond themselves because they identify but leave unexplained such essential constituents of moral wisdom as sound judgment, the objects of the required knowledge, the conceptions of a good life worth aiming at, and the evaluations implicit in the conception of what would make life good.

MORAL WISDOM AS A CAPACITY

A capacity is the power to do or to undergo something. Moral wisdom is the capacity to judge rightly what should be done in particular situations to make life better. Because moral wisdom presupposes choice, deliberation, and being guided by some conception of what would be better or worse in the long run, and because, as far as we know, only human beings possess what moral wisdom presupposes, it may be identified as a human capacity. Moreover, it is a psychological capacity, rather than a physical or physiological one. This contrast is not meant to suggest that psychological capacities are not analyzable in physical or physiological terms. The point is rather that psychological capacities typically involve higher mental processes, while physical and physiological capacities typically do not. Higher mental processes are no doubt made possible by a nervous system of sufficient complexity. What matters, however, is not the physical or physiological prerequisites of moral wisdom, but that moral wisdom enables those who have it to judge rightly in important matters. Because this human psychological capacity, once developed, is likely to be lasting and important, it can be identified as a character trait.[1] And because it is a desirable, prized, and admired character trait, the reference to it may be further narrowed by identifying it as a virtue.

The possession of virtues, of course, is a matter of degree, not an all-or-none affair. Most people have some moral wisdom, since most people act wisely at least some of the time in matters affecting the goodness of their lives. But this is not enough for ascribing moral wisdom to them. Their morally wise actions may be rare, or if they are frequent, so are their foolish actions. There is no precisely definable line on one side of which there is moral wisdom, while on the other it is lacking. It is reasonable to ascribe a character trait to people if their psychological portraits would be seriously incomplete without it. We can say, therefore, that people have moral wisdom if they regularly and predictably act wisely in the appropriate situations and if so acting is an enduring pattern in their lives.

It is tempting to try to refine this characterization of moral wisdom by saying that it is a disposition, but this would be too quick. "The term has become something of a catch-word. As catch-words generally, it can mean almost anything—and therefore often means nothing."[2] The warranted ascription of a disposition requires both a general description of the appropriate type of action and it being true that if the circumstances are normal and the people have an opportunity to act so as to exemplify the type, then they will do so. To say that people are courageous or temperate is to say that they typically tend not to allow their fear of danger to deter them from doing what they think they should or that they typically tend not to overindulge in the pleasures they desire to have. This implies a subjunctive conditional, such as, "If a person were afraid of telling the truth when it was difficult to do so, he or she would nevertheless normally do so," or, "If a person desired to drink too much on a pleasant social occasion, he or she would nevertheless normally refrain from it." To have a disposition,

---

[1] For an analysis of character traits, see Richard B. Brandt, "Traits of Character: A Conceptual Analysis," *American Philosophical Quarterly* 7 (1970): 23–37.

[2] Georg Henrik von Wright, *The Varieties of Goodness* (London: Routledge, 1963), 142.

then, is for a person's actions to form a lasting pattern that makes true the appropriate subjunctive conditionals.

This analysis fits many virtues and vices, but, as it stands, it does not fit moral wisdom. In the case of courage and temperance, to continue with the preceding examples, there is a specific type of action which would exemplify the virtue: for courage, it is controlling one's fear of danger, and for temperance, it is controlling one's desire for excessive pleasure. For moral wisdom, however, there is no analogous specifiable type of action. To act in a morally wise way is to act on the basis of sound judgment about what would make life better. The specific type of action this requires, however, will systematically vary with the countless situations in which people are called upon to exercise such moral wisdom as they have. The reason why moral wisdom is unlike courage and temperance in this respect is that it is not associated with the expression or the control of some perfectly natural human tendency, such as fear of danger or desire for pleasure. There *is* something that makes actions morally wise, but it is not the presence of some specific property intrinsic to the action.[3]

Consider some reasons in support of this claim. First, there is no obvious candidate for a specific type of action which always or even normally would qualify as being morally wise. For instance, acting on considered judgment is not such, since the considered judgments of many people are bad; and acting on sound judgment involves a great variety in the types of action which may exemplify it. Nor would prolonged reflection on the matter at hand qualify, since moral wisdom often shows itself in immediate insight or discernment, which is precisely what the unwise lack.

Second, the claim is not weakened by the fact that it is often possible to identify foolish actions that conspicuously exclude moral wisdom. Even if there were reliable criteria for identifying actions as foolish, they would still not help identify morally wise actions, since actions that are not foolish need not be morally wise.

Third, the generalization from specific actions that have been shown to be morally wise to other actions of the same type is illegitimate, because the same type of action performed in the same type of situation may be morally wise for one person and morally unwise for another. Whether an action is morally wise depends also on what the agents bring to the judgments they make, such as their particular conception of what would make life better. An action being morally wise depends therefore not just on the nature of the action and the situation, but also on the agent, and this invalidates generalizations about moral wisdom which ignore the character and beliefs of the agents.

[3] This account is indebted to Wright, *Varieties of Goodness*, chap. 7.

Fourth, that moral wisdom is not connected with a specific type of action is not an idiosyncratic feature of this one virtue. Kant distinguished between perfect and imperfect duties on analogous grounds.[4] Perfect duties require specific types of action, such as keeping the promise one has made, while imperfect duties, such as beneficence or gratitude, do require action, but not any specific type. Moral wisdom may be thought of analogously as an imperfect virtue, in contrast with courage and temperance which might be thought of as perfect ones.

The lack of a noncontingent connection between moral wisdom and any specific type of action is important to understanding moral wisdom. It may be true that all virtues are alike in being dispositions, but they are not alike in being the same kind of dispositions. The agents' performance of a specific type of action for many virtues is prima facie evidence for their possession of the corresponding virtue. In the case of moral wisdom this is not so. One implication of this is that the most straightforward approach to understanding moral wisdom cannot be followed. That approach would be to begin with many examples of morally wise actions and then go on to ask: What is it about the actions that makes them morally wise? But this cannot be done if the component that makes the actions wise is not intrinsic to the actions. Whatever makes morally wise actions morally wise is not to be found merely by examining the actions themselves. The proper approach to understanding moral wisdom, therefore, is to begin by clarifying what the component is that makes an action morally wise and why it is that some instances of the same type of action have it, while others lack it.

This makes it difficult to understand moral wisdom. One sign of the difficulty is that examples of morally wise people do not readily come to mind. History, literature, and personal experience provide countless examples of people who were or are courageous, just, honest, or loyal. It is possible to look at their actions, see that they form a pattern, and ascribe the virtue to the agents. But who are the candidates for moral wisdom? Socrates? The extraordinarily able advocacy of Plato shows only that his teacher did not share the foolishness of the people whom he engaged in discussion. What were Socrates' morally wise actions? His recognition of his own and especially of others' fallibility did save him from certain kinds of error. But not to err is not yet to be morally wise. And was his acceptance of the injustice his fellow Athenians did to him a sign of moral wisdom? Why? And if it was, is it always or most of the time morally wise to resign oneself to injustice? It is not enough, therefore, to be told that Socrates, or anyone else, was morally wise; it needs also to be shown what

---

[4] See Immanuel Kant, *Groundwork of the Metaphysics of Morals*, trans. H. J. Paton (New York: Harper, 1964), chap. 2.

made that person so. (These questions about Socrates will be taken up in Chapter 2.) And what other candidates can be put alongside Socrates? The scarcity of examples, however, need not betoken the rarity of moral wisdom—it may suggest instead that it is not through examples that moral wisdom should be understood.

MORAL WISDOM AS A SECOND-ORDER VIRTUE

Two kinds of virtues are needed for living a good life: virtues that direct perfectly natural and normal human tendencies and virtues that direct the development of other virtues. The former, first-order virtues, are among the legislative powers of our character, while the latter, second-order virtues, are among its judicial powers. The former prompt action according to certain conceptions of what life and conduct ought to be; the latter prompt the examination of the conceptions that guide the actions.[5]

It would be a misunderstanding to characterize this distinction as holding between action-guiding and what might be called directing virtues. Both first- and second-order virtues are both action-guiding and directing; it is only that they guide and direct different actions in different ways. Examining a conception of what life and conduct ought to be is as much an action as refraining from overindulgence, holding one's fear in check, or giving people their due. But whereas the immediate object of the action toward which first-order virtues guide us is what our responses should be in the concrete practical situations that confront us, the immediate object of actions prompted by second-order virtues is the development of our character in a desirable direction by strengthening or weakening some of our dispositions. First-order virtues guide our actions in view of what we think of as a good life; second-order virtues guide our actions with a view of developing the kind of character that reflects a reasonable conception of a good life.

A way of deepening the understanding of moral wisdom as a second-order virtue is to recognize that it is reflexive. The subject who has the virtue is the same as the object toward whom the appropriate actions are directed. In terms of an often-used but clumsy and potentially misleading distinction, it may be said that moral wisdom is a self-regarding, as opposed to an other-regarding, virtue. The first is thought to affect primarily

---

[5] Several authors have written illuminatingly about the importance of second-order activities, although none has suggested its connection with wisdom. See, for instance, Stuart Hampshire, *Thought and Action* (London: Chatto & Windus, 1960), Harry G. Frankfurt, *The Importance of What We Care About* (Cambridge: Cambridge University Press, 1988), and Charles Taylor, "Responsibility for Self," in *The Identities of Persons,* ed. Amélie Rorty (Berkeley: University of California Press, 1976).

agents themselves, while the second is supposed to affect mainly others. Temperance is said to be self-regarding, and benevolence other-regarding. But whatever may be said in favor of applying this distinction to other virtues, it does not fit moral wisdom. It is true that by being reflexive moral wisdom has its primary effect on the agents who are moved by it. The effect it has, however, is to direct the development of the agents' other virtues, including both self- and other-regarding ones. If moral wisdom leads us to consider, for instance, the respective importance that such other-regarding virtues as justice, benevolence, and loyalty should have in our life and conduct, then it is odd at best and more likely to be misleading to describe this activity as self-regarding. Certainly our own activities are being directed, but the direction may well concern activities whose objects are other people. That moral wisdom is a reflexive virtue, therefore, should not lead to the supposition that it is restricted to the fine-tuning of our soul while disregarding the effects of our actions on others.

That moral wisdom is a second-order and a reflexive virtue means that it involves the direction of first-order virtues. The direction, however, may be motivated by various reasons, such as cultivating artistic creativity, hastening the revolution, serving others or God, contemplating nature, wielding power, and so forth. Sometimes we pursue such goals because we believe that their achievement would make our life good. But this is by no means always the case. We often aim to live in ways that involve the customary or the deliberate subordination of our welfare to the welfare of other people or to the defense of some cause. And we would live in these ways even if we were convinced that it would not make our life good because we value some other goal more than our welfare. We may be motivated by humility, fanaticism, selfless love, resentment, pity, a strong sense of duty, rage at injustice, or by some mixture of these and similar passions. Coming to live in these ways requires second-order and reflexive activities. Moral wisdom, however, must still be distinguished from these other second-order activities. And as that distinction is drawn, so another crucial component of moral wisdom emerges.

The primary motivation behind the second-order and reflexive activities prompted by moral wisdom is the desire to make our lives better. We can do so, however, only if we have some conception of what a good life would be. The aim that governs our exercise of moral wisdom must therefore be the realization of our conception of a good life. The reason for directing our first-order virtues is to improve our lives by transforming our characters so as to improve the chances of achieving what we regard as a good life.

This valued conception of a good life, however, may or may not be reasonable. Since moral wisdom is concerned not merely with means but also with ends, it has among its tasks the critical scrutiny of the conception of a good life which motivates us to act according to moral wisdom. Moral wisdom aims further than the transformation of our character; it aims as well at the development of a conception of a life which not only seems to us to be good but which is good. And the character that we desire to have is not just an instrumental good whose possession would be conducive to the achievement of this genuinely good life; it is also an intrinsic good, because having the sort of character that our conception of a genuinely good life requires is an essential part of the conception. For a conception of a good life guides us to live in a certain way; living involves acting; and we normally act in characteristic ways, that is, according to our character.[6]

It is for the evaluation of both first-order virtues, which prompt one's actions as means, and the conception of the good life, which serves as the overall end, that moral wisdom requires knowledge of what is worth valuing and what is worth doing to achieve what we rightly value. The reason why moral wisdom also requires sound judgment is that that is the form in which this type of evaluative knowledge comes to be expressed and comes to control our actions. An acceptable account of moral wisdom, therefore, essentially depends on an account of conceptions of a good life and of the appropriate type of knowledge, evaluation, and judgment.

APPROACHING MORAL WISDOM

It is now possible to strengthen two previously advanced claims about moral wisdom. The first is about the misleading classification of it as a self-regarding virtue. Once the classification is accepted, suspicion about the moral status of any virtue booked as self-regarding is never far. The thought that motivates this suspicion is that since morality is concerned with the welfare of other people, and since self-regarding virtues further our own welfare, they do not seem to be moral virtues. Moreover, since concentration on our own welfare is likely to divert our attention and energy from others and focus them on ourselves, the suspicion is that the effort to develop moral wisdom, as well as other self-regarding virtues, tends to be not only a nonmoral activity but also one that moves us in the direction of the immorality of self-centeredness. Gregory Vlastos, for instance, thinks it necessary to seek "a release from that form of egocentricity which is endemic in . . . all eudaemonism. In that theory the good for each of us is unambiguously our own personal good: the happiness which is the final reason for each of our intentional actions is our own happiness."[7]

---

[6] For a perspicuous analysis of character, see Joel Kupperman, *Character* (New York: Oxford University Press, 1991).

[7] Gregory Vlastos, *Socrates, Ironist and Moral Philosopher* (Ithaca: Cornell University Press, 1991), 177.

This is a misplaced observation, however, and the line of thought behind it is mistaken. Whether or not moral wisdom encourages self-centeredness depends on the end toward which it directs our first-order virtues, several of which, of course, directly affect other people. The end is a conception of a good life. Moral wisdom requires that these conceptions should not merely seem to be good to us but that they should be genuinely good. Since it is undoubtedly true that genuinely good conceptions of life include caring about the welfare of other people and exclude self-centeredness, moral wisdom will lead us to do so. Hence, even if in some sense it can be said that moral wisdom is a self-regarding virtue, no moral taint attaches to it on that account.

The second claim mentioned above arises out of the difficulty of the ascription of moral wisdom. The simplest approach to understanding moral wisdom would be to reflect on the lives of morally wise people in order to discover what makes them morally wise. But since morally wise people can be identified only by observing their actions and finding them preponderantly morally wise, there must be a way first of identifying morally wise actions. This, however, is formidably difficult, because there is no one specific type of action which is identifiably morally wise. Two of the reasons for this have already been provided. Morally wise actions direct first-order virtues, and what this requires varies with the particular first-order virtue in question, with the context, and with the reason the need for direction arises in that case. Furthermore, the direction is motivated by our conception of a good life, and these conceptions vary with individuals. But now that moral wisdom has been seen as a second-order and a reflexive virtue, it is possible to add a very powerful third reason why the identification of morally wise actions is difficult. The reason is that they are inaccessible to direct observation by people other than the agents themselves and because such indirect evidence as may be available is systematically ambiguous and liable to misinterpretation.

The direction moral wisdom provides takes the form of us *not* doing what we are motivated to do and of making an effort *to* do what we are insufficiently motivated to do. Both the weakening and the strengthening of our motivation are dictated by our conception of a good life. Neither of these activities, however, is among our overt actions. No witness or video-camera could register their occurrence. Moreover, even if it could be ascertained that we were initially motivated to do what we did not do or that we were not motivated to do what we ended up doing, this would be insufficient to serve as evidence for moral wisdom. Moral wisdom requires being moved by our conception of a good life, but it is an open question whether we go against our initial motivation because we are morally wise or for some other reason. Perhaps we are convinced that following our initial motivation would contribute to the goodness of our lives, but we do not follow it out of fear, laziness, hypocrisy, or because we regard some other consideration as more important. It looks, therefore, that what is needed for the identification of morally wise actions is autobiographical evidence. Such evidence, however, is rarely available; and what there is of it is notoriously unreliable because of self-deception, the desire to present ourselves in a favorable light, and lack of self-knowledge. Even if these obstacles were overcome in exceptional cases, what would warrant the ascription of moral wisdom is not isolated examples but an enduring pattern of morally wise actions. The availability of reliable evidence for such patterns, however, is even more exceptional. This is why it is an unpromising approach to understanding moral wisdom to try to begin with concrete examples and then generalize from them.[8]

In the light of this, the procedure that suggests itself is to begin with the dictionary meaning of "wisdom." This meaning merely catalogues the intuitive understanding of the term that competent users of the language possess. An analysis of this intuitive understanding will require going beyond intuitions because the complexities involved in moral wisdom cannot be understood otherwise. To have more than a superficial grasp, it must be analyzed what is meant by such components of moral wisdom as a conception of a good life and the judgment, knowledge, and evaluation relevant to it. The analysis will then proceed by trying to understand the role these components play in reasonable conceptions of good lives.

It must be remembered, however, that accounts of moral wisdom and its place in good lives are bound to begin as analyses of the intuitive understanding of their subject matter. This means that, if successful, analyses will provide a better, because deeper, account of the superficial intuitive understanding with which they begin. They will show in considerable and illuminating concrete detail just what is involved in the conception of a good life, knowledge, evaluation, and judgment, which are the key components of moral wisdom. But very strong arguments are needed to support the results of analyses if they are inconsistent with the intuitive understanding whose analysis they intend to be. Analyses normally explain, reveal the complexity of, and disclose the component parts of their subject matter; they do not show that the intuitive understanding with which they began is erroneous. They could do so by showing that the intuitive understanding is incoherent or defective in some way other than being superficial. It is therefore possible, although unlikely, that an account of moral wisdom would contradict the intuitive understanding cata-

---

[8] This is the reason why psychological studies of wisdom are so singularly unpromising. For a collected sample of them, see Robert J. Sternberg, ed., *Wisdom: Its Nature, Origin, and Development* (New York: Cambridge University Press, 1990).

logued by dictionaries. One way of proceeding then with the analysis of moral wisdom is to ask whether the analysis succeeds in deepening our intuitive understanding. If it does not because it regards the intuitive understanding as faulty, then the supporting arguments given for this conclusion must be examined. But regardless of whether the analysis deepens or corrects the intuitive understanding with which it starts, this approach involves a constant comparison of intuitive understanding and analysis. This approach has been in conscious use at least since Aristotle, but recently it has been given the name of "reflective equilibrium."[9]

CONCLUSION

Moral wisdom is a human psychological capacity to judge soundly what we should do in matters seriously affecting the goodness of our life. The judgment is made in the light of our conception of a good life, but it concerns the evaluation of both the actions that exemplify the conception and the conception itself. Moral wisdom is thus sound judgment involving the application of knowledge of good and evil to the evaluation of both the means to and the ends constitutive of good lives. It is a character trait that different people possess to different degrees, but insofar as we aim to live a good life, reason dictates that we should aim also at developing moral wisdom, because it is indispensable to living such a life. This is why moral wisdom is a morally important character trait, hence a virtue.

Moral wisdom is a disposition, but unlike many other dispositions it is not connected with the performance of any specific type of action. What makes actions morally wise depends not just on the properties and context of the action but also on the character of the agent and the conception of a good life the agent has. That this is so makes both the identification of morally wise actions and the subsequent ascription of moral wisdom difficult. The most important reason for this is that moral wisdom is a second-order and reflexive disposition, which, by its nature, is not in the public view. Moral wisdom guides action and directs conduct not by focusing on actions directly, but by concentrating on the development of our character from which our actions normally follow. And moral wisdom does this by strengthening or weakening our first-order virtues and vices in the light of the evaluations suggested by our conception of a good life.

Both the approach to be employed and the questions to be answered in order to achieve a better understanding of moral wisdom follow from this account. Since moral wisdom is not identifiable through morally wise ac-

[9] John Rawls, *A Theory of Justice* (Cambridge: Harvard University Press, 1971), 48–51.

tions, it is necessary to give first a general description of it. This description begins with our intuitive understanding and is deepened by analysis. The next step is to consider in greater detail the conceptions of a good life, and the knowledge, evaluation, and judgment that constitute moral wisdom.

CHAPTER ONE

A Eudaimonistic Conception
of Good Lives

This chapter is about eudaimonism, but only insofar as it is relevant to moral wisdom. The intention behind it is not to present a full-scale moral theory, but only the barest outline of one. It concentrates on a eudaimonistic conception of good lives, and so it may be viewed as having one of the four components of moral wisdom as its subject matter. The other components—knowledge, evaluation, and judgment—will be discussed here only briefly; detailed accounts follow in subsequent chapters.

The version of eudaimonism discussed in this chapter and the next, although presented in positive terms, has serious problems; the problems will be addressed, and the conception of eudaimonism will be reformulated in later chapters.

THE HUMAN POINT OF VIEW

Aristotle distinguishes between philosophical and practical wisdom (between *sophia* and *phronesis*). Philosophical wisdom aims at truth, while practical wisdom aims at action.[1] The truth philosophical wisdom aims at is "that which causes derivative truths to be true" (*Meta.* 993b26–27). These are "the principles of eternal things [which] must be always true" (*Meta.* 993b27–28), and so they may be called "first principles" (*Meta.* 982b1–2). Philosophical wisdom, therefore, involves knowledge of first principles, which are necessary and cannot be otherwise.[2] Practical wisdom, by contrast, is "to be able to deliberate well about what is good and

---

[1] Aristotle, *Metaphysics*, 993b20–21.
[2] Aristotle, *Nicomachean Ethics*, 1140b1–2.

expedient . . . about what sort of things conduce to the good life in general" (*NE* 1140a26–29). Deliberation, however, is "about what can be otherwise" (*NE* 1140b27). It concerns those aspects of concrete situations that can be changed so as to make life better. The knowledge practical wisdom yields is thus of how to improve human lives in general and one's own life in particular. In a later idiom, philosophical wisdom can be said to seek knowledge and truth *sub specie aeternitatis*, while practical wisdom does so *sub specie humanitatis*.

Moral wisdom should not be identified with either philosophical or practical wisdom, although it embodies parts of each. Moral wisdom is like philosophical wisdom in seeking knowledge of first principles, but the principles are only those that bear on living a good life. This is what makes moral wisdom moral. Furthermore, because living a good life requires action, and the contexts of actions are always changing, moral wisdom is practically and contingently oriented, while philosophical wisdom is not.

Moral wisdom, however, is not to be identified with practical wisdom either because practical wisdom is concerned only with what is contingent in human life, while moral wisdom takes into account both contingency and necessity. Moral wisdom thus focuses on the nature of good lives for human beings, and, since good lives have both necessary and contingent features, it views good lives both *sub specie aeternitatis* and *sub specie humanitatis*. Its scope, however, is at once narrower and wider than either philosophical or practical wisdom's because it includes both the necessary first principles and the contingent aspects of good lives.

It remains nevertheless important to distinguish between good lives understood from the human point of view, *sub specie humanitatis*, and good lives understood not from any particular point of view, unless it were God's, but as they are in themselves, uncolored by specifically human concerns, *sub specie aeternitatis*.[3] The first yields anthropocentric, the second non-anthropocentric knowledge. Both are partial, however, and in need of the other. Knowing the facts that have human significance depends on knowing the facts. Anthropocentric knowledge must be continually corrected, therefore, in the light of non-anthropocentric knowledge. But non-anthropocentric knowledge is sought by human beings, for human purposes, and seeking it presupposes the motivation and resources that only the satisfaction of anthropocentric interests can supply. The distinction between these two points of view is thus epistemological, not metaphysical: it concerns two interdependent types of knowledge, not two areas or levels of reality.

---

[3] A contemporary study of these two points of view is Thomas Nagel's *The View from Nowhere* (New York: Oxford University Press, 1986).

One of Aristotle's enduring achievements is that he recognized the epistemological importance of the distinction, but, unlike numerous philosophers before and after him, he resisted the metaphysical interpretation of it. His view was that what makes a particular thing good depends on the nature of that thing. This may seem so obvious as to be hardly worth saying, unless its significance is appreciated in contrast with what it denies. It denies, among other things, that the good of the thing in question is the realization, or at least the approximation, of some ideal that exists independently of it. This was Plato's view. According to Plato, the ideal for good human lives is set by the Form of the Good. Aristotle thought that good lives involve the development of potentialities inherent in human nature, and he had no use for any external ideal, and certainly not for a metaphysical one.

Eudaimonism follows Aristotle in approaching the nature of good lives through human nature. Human nature may be thought of as comprising universal, constant, and invariable characteristics shared by normal human beings. A reasonable conception of a good human life must depend on human nature, because what would be a good life for beasts or angels will not suit us. But this line of thought suggests that because a good human life depends on human nature, and because human nature is uniform, the good life will also be uniform for all human beings. Readily available evidence, however, seems to be inconsistent with the expected uniformity. Historical, ethnographic, and literary sources, as well as our personal experience, reveal great human diversity, a multiplicity of radically different conceptions of a good life, and many different good lives that people have actually succeeded in living. How can this apparent plurality be reconciled with the expected uniformity?

The eudaimonistic answer is that human nature sets necessary requirements that any reasonable conception of a good life must meet, but meeting them is not sufficient for a good life. The expectation of uniformity is indeed reasonable, insofar as the necessary requirements are concerned, while the appearance of plurality is a reliable indicator of the different forms good lives may take beyond the necessary requirements. Good human lives are alike in ways determined by human nature, and they are different in ways that depend on the variousness of individual human character and circumstance. Good lives are both uniform and plural, according to eudaimonism, and this leads to no inconsistency provided the proper sphere for each is recognized. There will be goods and evils within each sphere, and they will make their appropriate contributions and present their threats to each reasonable conception of a good life.

The task of moral wisdom then is to acquire knowledge of these goods and evils, to evaluate situations encountered in the course of trying to live a good life in the light of that knowledge, and to judge well in situations whose evaluation is difficult. The exercise of moral wisdom presupposes, however, that the goods and evils are known. The next step, therefore, is to consider them.

THE VALUES OF A GOOD LIFE

According to the eudaimonistic interpretation of reasonable conceptions of a good life, values in general are benefits and harms, whose possession makes a life better than it would be without them and whose infliction makes a life worse than it would otherwise be. We may regard something as a value and be mistaken because having it would not benefit us, nor would exposure to it be harmful. There is a difference, therefore, between something being a value and something being valued. The essential point about values is that they are connected with benefits and harms. We may be mistaken in valuing something if we are mistaken about what we regard as beneficial or harmful. The key to values, therefore, is understanding the benefits and harms upon which they depend.

The first step is to distinguish between *primary* and *secondary* values. Primary values are based on benefits and harms that must count as such for all reasonable conceptions of a good life, while secondary values derive from benefits and harms that vary with conceptions of a good life. The idea behind primary values is that human nature dictates that some things will normally benefit all human beings and, similarly, that some things will normally harm everyone. These universally human benefits and harms are "primary goods" and "primary evils." Correspondingly, "secondary goods" and "secondary evils" are benefits and harms that derive their status from historically, socially, and culturally variable aspects of a good life.

The distinction between primary and secondary values is drawn by appealing to human nature. The following account of human nature merely repeats what everybody knows anyway. But the repetition has a point because the moral significance of these commonplaces tends to be overlooked. Human nature, then, is composed of universally human, culturally invariant, and historically constant characteristics. The obvious place to start looking for them is the body. Physiology imposes requirements on all human beings: nutrition, oxygen, and protection from the elements are necessary for survival; rest and motion, maturing and aging, pleasure and pain, consumption and elimination, sleep and wakefulness form the rhythm of all human lives; uninjured members of our species perceive the world in the same sense modalities, and, within a narrow range, are capable of the same motor responses. Part of human nature is that all healthy members of the species have many of the same physiological needs and capacities.

These truisms may be enlarged by noticing that there are also psychological similarities shared by all human beings. We do not merely want to satisfy our physiological needs by employing our capacities; we want to do so in particular ways. These ways differ, of course, from person to person, culture to culture, age to age. But there is no difference in the psychological aspiration to go beyond necessity and enjoy the luxury of satisfying our needs in whatever ways happen to count as civilized. We all know the difference between a primitive state characterized by doing what is necessary for survival and a civilized one in which we have leisure, choices, and the security to go beyond necessity. And we all prefer the civilized state to the primitive one. Furthermore, we are alike in our capacity to learn from the past and plan for the future; we have a view, perhaps never clearly articulated, about what we want to make of our lives; we have likes and dislikes, and we try to have much of the former and little of the latter; we have the capacity to think, remember, imagine, to have feelings, emotions, moods, ambitions, to make efforts, go after what we want, or restrain ourselves.

These truisms concern only human beings considered individually. It is possible to go still further in describing obvious features of human nature because contact with others is also an inevitable part of human lives. We are born into small human groups, usually families, and we depend on them for the first few years of our lives. We live in a network of close relationships with our parents or guardians, other children, and later with our sexual partners; and we extend our relationships when we enter the larger community of which the small one is a part. We acquire friends and enemies; we cooperate, compete, look up to, patronize, teach, learn from, imitate, admire, fear, envy, and get angry at people we come to know. We share the griefs and joys of those close to us; we have various positions in life which others recognize; we love and hate others; and we are made happy and sad by them.

Beyond these are the facts of human vulnerability, scarce resources, limited strength, intelligence, energy, and skill, which force cooperation on us. Social life exists because only within it can we satisfy our physiological and psychological needs in the ways we want and establish close relationships. The form social life takes is the establishment of some authority, the emergence of institutions and conventional practices, and the slow development and the deliberate formulation of rules; and all these demand conformity from members of a society. This imposes restrictions on what we can do and provides forms for doing what we want and society allows. Different societies have different authorities, institutions, conventions, and rules. But no society can do without them, and we cannot do without some participation in social life, provided we seek the satisfaction of our physiological and psychological needs.

This list of truisms is the evidence that supports the conclusion that there is a universal and unchanging human nature, composed of the commonplaces just enumerated. And if human nature is understood in this way, then it makes possible the identification of many benefits and harms that will be the same for everyone, always, everywhere, in normal circumstances.

Primary goods are the satisfactions of needs by exercising the capacities included in the description of the facts of human nature. They are universally good because it is good for all human beings to have the capacity to satisfy and to satisfy the physiological and psychological needs just enumerated. These may be called "the goods of the self." It is also good for everyone to be able to establish and actually to establish close personal relationships with some other people and thereby enjoy "the goods of intimacy." And it is similarly good for all of us to live in the kind of society in which the enjoyment of these goods is not only possible but also welcome, thus to have "the goods of social order." It is obviously and clearly true that any human life is better if it possesses the goods of the self, intimacy, and social order, and worse if it does not. The primary goods of the self, intimacy, and social order then define some of the necessary requirements of all good lives. They are necessary, however good lives are conceived, because they are required for the satisfaction of needs that all human beings have. Primary evils, then, are the frustration of those needs and the injury of the capacities required for satisfying them.

Yet, although this account provides some understanding of the nature of values by understanding human nature, it does not go very far. It is possible to derive from human nature primary values, but not all values required by good lives are primary. Various traditions and conceptions of a good life aim at values produced by the particular historical, cultural, and psychological conditions that prevail in some contexts but not in others. Furthermore, although human nature makes it a universal and unchanging truth that the goods of the self, intimacy, and social order are reasonably sought, and the accompanying evils are reasonably avoided, these primary values may take different forms in different contexts.

There are no variations, however, in the desirability of primary goods and in the undesirability of primary evils. This is one universal element present in all cultures. Variations concern, among other things, the conventionally recognized *forms* of primary values. But the variations among these forms, great as they are, do not extend so far as to call into question the truism that some of the necessary requirements of all good lives are set by primary values. One aim of these variable conventional forms is indeed to safeguard those requirements. Murder, social ostracism, and anarchy, for instance, are recognized in all conventional contexts as violations of primary values. Variations concern such questions as what sort of killing murder is, what kind of exclusion ostracism is, and what sort of tearing of the social fabric anarchy is. The existence of such variations, however, is symptomatic of deeper similarities. The differences merely betoken different ways of interpreting the same primary values. If the primary values of the self, intimacy, and social order were not appropriately recognized in these different contexts, then there would be no need to interpret them, and hence there would be no scope for differences in their interpretations.

It must be recognized, therefore, that in addition to universal primary values derivable from human nature, there are also secondary values whose identity varies with social and personal circumstances. Good lives depend on both primary and secondary values. Calling them "primary" and "secondary" is not intended to imply that the latter are dispensable. The implication is rather that secondary values depend on the primary ones, and that primary values are the same for everyone, while secondary values vary with traditions and conceptions of a good life.

One way in which secondary values depend on primary ones is that some secondary values are the particular forms in which primary values are interpreted in some context. For instance, the primary value of the self requires an interpretation to specify the acceptable forms that pleasure, the satisfaction of physiological needs, and the employment of capacities may take; the primary value of intimacy must similarly involve the specification of what kinds of sexual practices, child-rearing arrangements, and friendship are regarded as appropriate; and so also the primary value of social order must be spelled out in terms of concrete institutions, rules, and practices customary in particular contexts.

Another way secondary values depend on primary ones is that some secondary values enrich life by representing possibilities beyond the requirements set by primary values. Such secondary values are desirable professions, prized talents, the acceptable balance between political involvement and private life, work and leisure, competition and solidarity, the value attributed to independence, creativity, honor, comfort, success, privacy, and so on. These secondary values also depend on primary values because their realization is possible only if the necessary requirements set by primary values are first satisfied. If people are hunted or starving, if they are deprived of companionship, affection, or the concern and appreciation of others, if they live in a lawless anarchic society, then they must concentrate on survival and on escaping lasting damage, and they will have little time or energy left to seek the enjoyments derivable from leisure, privacy, or creative participation in art or science.

It is a consequence of the dependency of secondary values upon primary ones that the two kinds of value play different roles in morality in general, in particular traditions, and in individual conceptions of a good life. One of the chief aims of morality is to define a framework within which individuals can live in accordance with primary and secondary values. Particular traditions go beyond general moral requirements by developing and maintaining a framework that safeguards both the primary and the secondary values recognized in that context. Morality normally appears through the mediation of a particular tradition. A tradition usually contains a much richer inventory of secondary values than any individual belonging to it could reasonably pursue in a lifetime. We have the task, therefore, of constructing out of them some conception of a good life for ourselves. This conception will aim to combine in a coherent framework the primary values with such secondary values as we ourselves favor. These secondary values will translate into our individual terms some of the secondary values our tradition makes available: a way of earning a living, political allegiance, aesthetic sensibility, attitude toward sex, having children, social life, and so on. Such a coherent individually constructed framework is a conception of a good life.

The movement from the generalities embodied in morality to the concrete values of individual conceptions of a good life, brings with it a shift of emphasis from uniform primary values to plural traditional and individual secondary values. The former define a grid within which human beings must endeavor to make a good life for ourselves, while the latter provide the ways in which individuals fill in the grid. Both are necessary for living a good life, but the first must be in place before the second can be.

The resulting conception of a good life is a complex mixture within which the uniformity and plurality of values, the limits and the opportunities which define the boundaries of human lives, the requirements of tradition and of individuality, in short, the area of moral necessity and the area of moral possibility are recognized and given appropriate weight. It is a moral ideal because it represents to us, as we act as individual agents, how we should proceed, given our character and circumstances, if we want to make a good life for ourselves. And since no reasonable person will fail to want that, the ideal is bound to appeal to all who understand it and are in a position to pursue it.

Its actual pursuit involves living according to primary and secondary values. In a sense, both are given, and the moral task is to find out what they are and to conduct ourselves according to them. Primary values are discovered by attending to uniform human needs; while secondary values are formed by the reciprocal adjustment between our moral tradition and individuality. The tradition presents a plurality of secondary values, and part of the process of finding secondary values is to grow in our appreciation of these traditional possibilities. This involves coming to see them as possibilities that we may ourselves seek to make actual in our lives. But another part of finding secondary values is to evaluate the possibilities they represent in the light of what we take our character to be and what we would like it to become. That forward-looking evaluation, however, already involves a choice of some secondary values in terms of which we assess our character as it presently is and as we want it to become. At the same time, the choice of secondary values depends on such evaluations of their suitability to our character and circumstances as are already in place. In this way, by a process of reciprocal adjustments, increasingly finer assessments of our character, interdependent interpretations and reinterpretations of the nature and suitability of our possibilities, we make what we believe is a good life for ourselves. The making and the living of it, however, are not two processes, but one. We make a good life by living well, and we live a good life only if we make it good.

To all this, individual effort is crucial. We cannot make that effort effectively, however, unless we have moral wisdom. It is through it that we find out about the appropriate values toward which our efforts ought to be directed, the right way of making reasonable choices among the possibilities secondary values represent, and the reciprocal adjustments between our individual conceptions of a good life and traditional possibilities, which make some efforts suitable and others not. The first is achieved through knowledge of good and evil, the second through using that knowledge to evaluate particular situations, and the third through judgment. It is in this manner, therefore, that the four components of moral wisdom—a conception of a good life, knowledge, evaluation, and judgment—are interpreted within eudaimonism.

THE NEED FOR JUDGMENT

The eudaimonistic conception of a good life is not to be understood as the endorsement of a particular form of life. It is rather a regulative ideal that specifies some general conditions to which all good lives must conform. These conditions involve the enjoyment of the same primary goods and the avoidance of the same primary evils, as well as the enjoyment of some secondary goods and the avoidance of some secondary evils, although secondary values vary from life to life. As a result, knowledge of good and evil cannot be sufficient for a good life. Judgment is also needed because we must answer such questions as which among the secondary goods available to us would best suit our character and circumstances, what respective importance should we assign to the secondary goods we have come to regard as choiceworthy, and how much evil should we risk and tolerate in order to enjoy the goods we want. Judgments of this sort cannot be a matter of general knowledge because they involve filling in the grid of general knowledge with the concrete details of our character and circumstances, and these differ from individual to individual. Furthermore, we differ not only in the concrete details of our lives but also in our evaluations of those details. The plurality of values, therefore, bears a multiple responsibility for the plurality of good lives: the totality of secondary values constitutes a pool from which different values for different lives may be chosen; the respective importance of secondary values may be evaluated differently in different lives; and the acceptable balance of good and evil may vary with conceptions of a good life. These pluralities would remain even if the identity of all the primary and secondary values were agreed upon.

According to this eudaimonistic conception of a good life, primary values may be thought of as establishing the moral limits and secondary values as establishing the moral possibilities that define good lives. The limits are a matter of moral necessity. They are moral because their central concern is with living a good life. And they are necessary because, given human nature, we cannot live a good life unless we enjoy the primary goods and avoid the primary evils. The possibilities are for moral progress toward living a good life. They are created by our character and circumstances, both interpreted in a broad sense. Our character establishes our individuality: the qualities, traits, formative experiences, talents and weaknesses, capacities and incapacities, virtues and vices, and their combinations, which distinguish us from one another. Our circumstances include the political, cultural, economic, historical, technological, personal, religious, and aesthetic influences on us whose joint forces create the context in which we live.

The role of moral wisdom is to acquire general knowledge of good lives and to go beyond it by bringing the general to bear on our particular character and circumstances. The component of moral wisdom that makes this possible is judgment. There is thus a complex connection between the relevant knowledge and judgment. If the knowledge involved in moral wisdom were not general but knowledge of a specific way of life, then the more there was of it, the less need there would be for judgment. For if it were known what specific goods are to be sought and what specific evils are to be avoided in all particular situations, then a good life would require only the translation of that knowledge into action. The need for judgment, then, would indicate a kind of ignorance; judgment would be an expedient needed to take up the slack created by insufficient knowledge. The kind of knowledge that is constitutive of moral wisdom, however, is general, not specific. It is not knowledge of *the* good life, but knowledge of the conditions to which all the many different forms of good lives must conform. If there are many good lives and if they are made good by the enjoyment of some among the plurality of values, then judgment is not a second best after knowledge, but as indispensable a constituent of moral wisdom as knowledge itself is. For it is through judgment that reasonable choices among various conceptions of a good life and the plurality of available values can be made.

It is unclear how much support for this pluralistic view eudaimonism could derive from Aristotle. He may be read as regarding the contemplative life as the best and highest, while reluctantly acknowledging that human frailty makes its pursuit unrealistic for most people. But there is also textual support for reading him as a critic of Platonic monism and as a realistic advocate of a plurality of morally acceptable ways in which human potentialities can be realized. There is no need to decide this exegetical issue here. One point, however, is clear: Aristotle stressed the central importance of judgment to living a good life.

Judgment makes it possible "to deliberate well about what is good and expedient . . . not in some particular respect . . . but about what sort of things conduce to the good life in general."[4] Judgment need not be restricted to oneself because people who possess it "see what is good for themselves and what is good for men in general" (*NE* 1140b9–10). Judgment concerns neither "things that cannot be otherwise," nor "things that it is impossible . . . to do" (*NE* 1140a32), but "what can be otherwise" (*NE* 1140b27). This might be expressed positively by saying that to judge well is to be good at discerning those aspects of concrete situations that can be changed so as to make life better. Put negatively, judgment is not concerned with specific individual states or capacities, unless they contribute to improving life; nor is judgment concerned with the unalterable aspects of concrete situations, since it is impossible to do anything about them. Judgment, therefore, concerns conduct solely with a view of making life better. It "is concerned with things human . . . [with] a good that can be brought about by action" (*NE* 1141b8–12); it is "practical, and practice is concerned with particulars" (*NE* 1141b15–16).

Judgment, then, can be represented in the form of a syllogism, called "practical" because its conclusion is an action. The major premise contains a good the agent wants to achieve. The minor premise contains the description of a concrete situation facing the agent. The conclusion is the action the agent should take in the concrete situation viewed from the perspective of the good that is wanted. Judgment is a process, therefore, by which a decision is reached about what to do or not to do, given the good the agent wants to achieve and the agent's concrete situation.

[4] Aristotle, *Nicomachean Ethics*, 1140a27–29.

In some situations, judgment is easy and making it is barely noticeable, but in others, it is difficult and complicated. If the nature of the good that is wanted is clear, simple, and consciously articulated, and if the concrete situation is so straightforward as to admit of only one reasonable description, then what we ought to do follows as a matter of course. A mother and her child go to swim in the ocean, and the child develops cramps. The mother pulls the child to safety. Such cases are simple moral situations. Not all moral situations, however, are like these. Complications may occur for various reasons. First, the good wanted may be unclear: the mother knows that she wants her child to have a happy life, but she is unclear about what a happy life is. Second, she is fairly clear about what a happy life is, but she is unclear about how to make her child's life happy, given the child's specific character and their circumstances. Third, she finds herself under a great deal of pressure in her job, and she is taxed, tired, and short-tempered. Should she interpret her situations as concerning mainly her career, her parenthood, her responsibilities, her ambitions, the welfare of her child and herself, or of the institution where she works and to which she feels allegiance? How should she identify, combine, and weigh the various considerations that constitute her situation? When questions of this kind occur, and the contents of both the major and the minor premise become controversial, and, consequently, what we ought to do is unclear, then the moral situation is complex.

In simple moral situations judgment is easy because finding the right means to achieving the good wanted is straightforward. This is not so in complex situations because finding the means requires clarity about the good, as well as about the assessment of the situation. Judgment in such situations is difficult because the required clarity and the appropriate assessment are hard to achieve. In complex situations, judgment requires what David Wiggins calls "situational appreciation." He says that what "we should look for may be . . . a conceptual framework which we can apply to particular cases, which articulates the reciprocal relations of an agent's concerns and his perception of how things objectively are in the world; and a schema of description *which relates the complex ideal the agent tries in the process of living his life to make real to the form that the world impresses, both by way of opportunity and by way of limitation, upon that ideal.*"[5] In coming to form this situational appreciation, however, we cannot rely on "maxims or precepts. . . . In no case will there be a rule to which a man can simply appeal to tell him what to do. . . . The man may have no other recourse but to invent the answer to the problem."[6]

[5] David Wiggins, "Deliberation and Practical Reason," in *Needs, Values, Truth* (Oxford: Blackwell, 1987), 237.
[6] Ibid., 236.

It will be seen in later chapters that the "invention" of an answer is not an arbitrary process because there is much that can be done to improve our situational appreciation, to improve, that is, our judgment about complex moral situations. But the discussion of this possibility must be postponed until the impediments to such improvements are considered in Chapter 3. In the meantime, the aim of judgment may be described as the transformation of complex moral situations into simple ones. The sign of its success is that the question of what we should do in a particular situation will seem to have an obvious answer.

OBJECTIVITY AND ANTHROPOCENTRICITY

The eudaimonistic conception of moral wisdom and a good life combines the objectivity of good and evil with an anthropocentric interpretation of them. It approaches values from a human point of view, and yet it is also committed to their objectivity. The objectivity of primary values, on this conception, depends on its being a factual question what benefits and harms are derivable from human nature. Primary values are objective because their status is independent of what anyone believes about them. Everybody may believe that something affecting human beings is beneficial or harmful, and everybody may be mistaken. But the objectivity remains anthropocentric because what actually is beneficial or harmful depends on human nature, and not on some value external to it. Primary values are implicit in human nature, and they are derivable from it. If there were no human beings, therefore, then primary values would cease to exist as well. Propositions, statements, or beliefs about primary values are true or false, but their truth or falsehood depends on human nature's being what it is. The objectivity and anthropocentricity of primary values are consequently inseparable, according to the eudaimonistic conception.

The objectivity of secondary values is more complicated, but no less anthropocentric. As the objectivity of primary values depends on human nature, so the objectivity of secondary values depends on individual character and circumstances. But, while human nature is uniform, character and circumstances are variable. This results in a disanalogy between reasonable judgments about primary and secondary values. If something is a bona fide primary value, there is a presumption in favor of being committed to it, and this presumption holds for all reasonable human beings. There is no such presumption, however, in the case of bona fide secondary values, because there are two further questions that need to be answered before commitments to them can be reasonable. One is whether the secondary value is choiceworthy, given the character and circumstances of particular individuals. Because individuals differ in their character and circumstances, this question will be answered differently by different people. Assuming, however, an affirmative answer, there arises another question regarding the choiceworthiness of the secondary value. It is not about the secondary value itself, but about its importance vis-à-vis other secondary values available to the agent in the same context. And, once again, different individuals may answer that question differently, depending on their evaluations of the available secondary values. Assume that this question is also answered.

Can objectivity be assigned to such judgments about the choiceworthiness of a particular secondary value for a particular individual in a particular circumstance? It can be, because the judgment is either reasonable or unreasonable. The status of the judgment does not depend on whether others agree or disagree with it, since their positions are *ex hypothesi* different, but whether living according to that secondary value would help or hinder the chooser's effort to live a good life. The reasonability of such judgments, having to do with the choice of profession, life-style, friends, surroundings, long-term plans, and so forth, is often very difficult to evaluate, and the evaluation may have to wait until death, when no new facts could invalidate it. But its difficulty does not undermine its objectivity any more than the difficulty of some economic or political analyses, historical explanations, legal rulings, medical diagnoses, criminal investigations, or attributions of works of art undermines the objectivity of the resulting judgments. And, of course, the objectivity of such judgments is compatible with, indeed it presupposes, the possibility that reasonable judgments may be mistaken.

The objectivity and anthropocentricity of both primary and secondary values, therefore, reinforce in yet another way the necessity of moral wisdom to living a good life. For it is moral wisdom that provides both the required general knowledge of values and the capacity to evaluate moral limits and possibilities in the light of that knowledge. The exercise of that capacity, however, depends on judgment, which connects the general knowledge to our character and circumstances.

CONCLUSION

Eudaimonism derives its conception of a good life from human nature, not from any value external to it. The goods, whose enjoyment makes a life good, and the evils, whose infliction prevents a life from being good, are interpreted anthropocentrically as benefits and harms for human beings. The eudaimonistic conception, therefore, regards values as objective, but it combines their objectivity with anthropocentricity.

Eudaimonism conceives of good lives in pluralistic terms. In some ways, set by human nature, good lives are uniform. But there is nevertheless a plurality of good lives because satisfying the uniform requirements of shared human nature is only necessary, and not sufficient, for living a good life. The uniformity of primary values coexists with the plurality of secondary values.

Eudaimonism regards moral wisdom as essential to living a good life. For moral wisdom combines knowledge of good and evil, the motivation to evaluate moral situations in the light of that knowledge, and good judgment connecting the general knowledge to particular situations. Knowledge and evaluation are not by themselves sufficient because the plurality of reasonable conceptions of a good life and the plurality of secondary values make many situations morally complex.

The emerging conception of moral wisdom and good lives involves, however, a crucial ambiguity, which centrally affects how good lives and the role of moral wisdom in them are to be understood. Are lives good on account of their moral worth or on account of the satisfaction they provide? Does the importance of moral wisdom derive from its contribution to moral betterment or to greater satisfaction? The next chapter addresses these questions.

CHAPTER TWO

The Socratic Ideal
and Its Problems

Good lives may be understood as lives of moral worth, or as lives of satisfaction, or as lives combining moral worth and satisfaction in some proportion. These alternatives will be called "virtuous," "satisfying," and "balanced" lives. If good lives were identified with virtuous lives, then such lives may lack satisfaction. In that case, however, it becomes a serious question why reasonable people would accept the considerable hardships involved in living that way. If, on the other hand, good lives were identified with satisfying lives, then the absurd conclusion would follow that good lives may be either virtuous or vicious, depending on what happens to give satisfaction to particular agents. There is much to be said, therefore, for the identification of good lives with balanced ones. But if the goodness of lives is taken to depend on the balance of virtue and satisfaction, then the previous question would still have to be answered: Why would reasonable people seek to add virtue to the satisfaction they already have? Why is satisfaction not enough?

How these questions are answered has a decisive influence on how moral wisdom is understood. Moral wisdom has been argued to consist of a reasonable conception of a good life, knowledge of good and evil, evaluation of situations in which the agent must act, and judgment exercised in the more complex of these situations. The significance of these questions is that they call for an explanation of what the good and evil that make or break a life are taken to be, and thus of how the situations agents face are to be evaluated and judged. Is the good that moral wisdom yields virtue or satisfaction or both? And what is the reason for seeking moral wisdom beyond the satisfaction it yields?

The plan for answering these questions is to consider in this chapter the first eudaimonistic attempt to answer them: Socrates'. His answer will be found to be vulnerable to serious objections. The next chapter will explore the fundamental doubts these objections raise about the possibility of good lives. The objections are nevertheless constructive because they suggest what an improved eudaimonistic answer may be. Subsequent chapters will develop this answer—one that hinges on the right understanding of moral wisdom.

THE SOCRATIC CONCEPTION OF A GOOD LIFE

To begin with a terminological point: the views of Socrates come to us largely through Plato. These views, however, change gradually through the early to the middle Platonic dialogues. The Socratic conception of a good life, therefore, has an earlier and a later version. The differences between the two versions are irrelevant to the present discussion, except on one important point, which will be noted later.[1]

Socrates says: "The really important thing is not to live, but to live well. . . . And to live well means the same thing as to live honorably or rightly."[2] A just and honorable life is lived according to virtue, and Socrates recognizes five virtues required by such a life: temperance, courage, piety, justice, and what is meant here by moral wisdom. He held that these virtues are related to each other more intimately than parts are related to a whole, for "a man who possesses one of them possess[es] them all," although "wisdom is the greatest of the parts."[3] A good life, therefore, is a virtuous life,

---

[1] For the distinction between them see Gregory Vlastos, *Socrates, Ironist and Moral Philosopher* (Ithaca: Cornell University Press, 1991). The distinction is based on two claims. First, the dialogues of Plato may be divided into four groups: (a) the early elenctic dialogues, including *Apology, Charmides, Crito, Euthyphro, Gorgias, Hippias Minor, Ion, Laches, Protagoras,* and *Republic* I; (b) the transitional dialogues between Plato's early and middle period, including *Euthydemus, Hippias Major, Lysis, Menoxenus,* and *Meno;* (c) middle dialogues, including *Cratylus, Parmenides, Phaedo, Phaedrus, Republic* II–X, *Symposium,* and *Thaetetus;* and (d) late dialogues, including *Critias, Laws, Philebus, Politicus, Sophist,* and *Timaeus.* If a view is earlier, it appears in (a) or (b), while if it is later, it appears in (c) or (d). See Vlastos, *Socrates,* 46–47.

Second, there is a sharp contrast between the earlier and later views. The early Socrates is exclusively a moral philosopher; he advances no metaphysical theory; he seeks knowledge elenctically and he denies that he has any; he does not hold the tripartite model of the soul; he has no interest in science or mathematics; and his conception of philosophy is egalitarian. The later Socrates has a moral philosophy that is infused with metaphysics; he seeks demonstrative knowledge and is confident that he finds it; he accepts the tripartite model of the soul; he is a master of science and mathematics; and his conception of philosophy is elitist. See Vlastos, *Socrates,* 47–49. The whole of Vlastos, *Socrates,* chapter 2 supports this distinction. Vlastos refers to "Socrates" and to "Plato," rather than to "earlier" and "later" Socrates. The latter usage is preferable, since Plato attributes all the relevant views to Socrates, and that is why it is adopted here.

[2] Plato, *Crito,* 48b.

[3] Plato, *Protagoras,* 329e.

and the chief virtues whose possession and exercise make a life virtuous form a unified whole. Moral wisdom is thus the most important of the unified virtues that make up a virtuous life.

What exactly is the relation between a good life and a virtuous life according to Socrates? There are three possibilities.[4] First, a virtuous life may be the *means* to a good life, which is the end. This is not Socrates' view, as he makes clear in the *Crito*.[5] He could have fled from his death sentence and thereby saved his life, but because it would have involved acting contrary to virtue, Socrates refused to do it. He did not want life unless virtue was part of it. According to Gregory Vlastos, "The central theme of . . . [Socrates'] 'philosophizing' is that for each and every one of us . . . the perfection of our soul must take precedence over every other concern: money, power, prestige, and all the non-moral goods are trivial by comparison with the awful importance of reaching that knowledge of good and evil which is the condition of moral excellence and therewith the condition of [a good life]."[6]

The second possibility is that a virtuous life is *a necessary part* of a good life but that a good life also has other parts. This will ultimately turn out to be the only defensible possibility, but much needs to be said before this claim can be substantiated. The third possibility is that a virtuous life is both necessary and sufficient for a good life because a virtuous life *constitutes* a good life: if one lives virtuously, then one lives a good life. The key to understanding Socrates' conception of a good life is to understand the sense in which the virtuous life may be said to constitute it.[7]

According to Vlastos, Socrates' claim that "not life, but a good life, is to be chiefly valued . . . and a good life is equivalent to a just and honorable [that is, a virtuous] one" may be interpreted as expressing either the identity or the sufficiency thesis. The identity thesis is the prevalent interpretation, but it leads to an indefensible position, and, Vlastos believes, it is not Socrates' view. The thesis is that "for Socrates, as for all Greek moralists the . . . [good] and virtuous forms of life are identical, that is to say, that the form of life we call ['good'] . . . (the most deeply and durably satisfying kind of life) is *the same form of life* we call 'virtue' . . . (the just, brave, tem-

---

[4] Vlastos, *Socrates*, 204.

[5] For a dissenting view, see Terence Irwin, *Plato's Moral Theory* (Oxford: Clarendon Press, 1977), and for a criticism of Irwin, see Vlastos, *Socrates*, and subsequent references.

[6] Vlastos, *Socrates*, 110. In place of the bracketed phrase, Vlastos has "happiness." Both "happiness" and "a good life" are approximations of the Greek "eudaimonia." "A good life" serves the present purposes better, and it will be substituted for Vlastos's "happiness" throughout the discussion. For disagreement, see Vlastos, *Socrates*, 201–203.

[7] See Vlastos, *Socrates*, chapter 8.

perate, pious, wise way to live)." Virtue is "the only thing that makes life good and satisfying."[8]

Part of the trouble with the identity thesis is that it is too strong. It does more than what is required for understanding how the virtuous life "constitutes" the good life. As Vlastos puts it, the identity thesis "oversatisfies" that requirement.[9] If we are confronted with a choice between two actions, one of which accords with virtue and the other contrary to it, then those seeking a good life will choose the virtuous action, as Socrates is shown to do in *Crito*. But not all choices that have a bearing on the goodness of one's life are between virtuous and vicious actions. We often have to make choices whose outcome affects the goodness of our life, yet our virtues are not involved, or the alternatives facing us are equally virtuous.

Suppose that I have to choose, for instance, between practicing medicine or doing important medical research, and I have the talent and the opportunity to do either. Given the identity thesis, it is a matter of indifference for the goodness of my life which I choose. Suppose further, however, that I would regard my life as impoverished without frequent contact with patients, and that being shut up in a laboratory doing experiments, no matter how beneficial, does not appeal to me at all. The choice I make under these circumstances surely has a bearing on the goodness of my life. Similarly, how I choose in trivial matters of taste has no effect on how virtuously I live. But if I systematically choose to go against what I like, it will make my life less good than it would otherwise be. So, while it may be true that a good life is virtuous, there is more to it than living virtuously. The identity thesis is mistaken, therefore, in regarding them as the same.

This leads Vlastos to propose an "alternative to the Identity Thesis which would provide a ground for rational preference between courses of action indistinguishable in respect of virtue but differing materially in other ways."[10] The alternative is the sufficiency thesis: "Keeping virtue in its place as the sovereign good, both necessary and sufficient for . . . [a good life], let us allow . . . [a good life] a multitude of lesser constituents in addition to virtue. . . . *In disjunction from virtue each would be worthless.* But when conjoined with virtue . . . they would enhance . . . [the goodness of a life]."[11]

The fundamental difference between the two theses may be expressed by saying that the identity thesis is committed to a monistic view of good lives, whereas the sufficiency thesis is committed to a pluralistic one.[12] The

---

[8] Vlastos, *Socrates*, 214.

[9] Ibid.

[10] Ibid., 216.

[11] Ibid.

[12] Vlastos says that one thesis accepts "a unicomponent model" and the other "a multicomponent one" (*Socrates*, 217).

two theses are alike in regarding a virtuous life as constitutive of a good life. But they differ because the identity thesis denies and the sufficiency thesis asserts that there is more to a good life than being virtuous. It is crucial to see, however, that according to the sufficiency thesis, the additional elements can only enhance the goodness of a virtuous life; they are neither independent of nor on an equal footing with virtue.

The additional elements may be identified by distinguishing between internal and external goods. Internal goods are goods of the character, in particular the five most important Socratic virtues: justice, temperance, courage, piety, and moral wisdom. External goods are either physiological, such as health and strength, or psychological, such as security and respect, or political, such as peace and order.[13] The additional elements, recognized by the sufficiency thesis, but ignored by the identity thesis, are the various external goods. In Vlastos's words, they are "subordinate . . . and conditional goods. . . . But goods they are . . . [and] we shall . . . [have a better life] with them than without them, but only if we use them aright, for they are not 'good just by themselves'."[14]

The plurality of goods the sufficiency thesis recognizes as constituting a good life includes, therefore, both internal and external goods, although the latter are conditional on being enjoyed virtuously. By contrast, the identity thesis holds the monistic view that there is only one form that good lives can take: it consists of internal goods, which involve the possession and the exercise of the five Socratic virtues. The chief reason for accepting the sufficiency thesis and rejecting the identity thesis, according to Vlastos, is that on the latter "we would have no rational ground for preference between alternatives which are equally consistent with virtue—hence no rational ground for preference between states of affairs differentiated only by their . . . [external] values. And if this were true, it would knock out the bottom from [Socrates'] eudaemonism as a theory of rational choice."[15]

Consequently, of the three interpretations of the relation between a good and a virtuous life, only the third is correctly attributable to Socrates. But its claim that a good life is constituted of a virtuous life should be interpreted according to the sufficiency thesis, and not the identity thesis. Socrates' reason for rejecting the first interpretation—according to which a virtuous life is instrumental to a good life—is that internal goods are necessary parts of a good life, not means to them. Socrates' reason for rejecting the second interpretation—which regards internal goods as necessary

[13] The distinction between external and internal goods is Aristotle's, and it will be discussed in Chapter 3. It is useful to introduce it here because it helps clarify the difference between the identity and sufficiency theses.

[14] Vlastos, *Socrates*, 231.

[15] Ibid., 225.

parts of a good life, but a good life is supposed by it also to require external goods—is that Socrates denied that external goods could contribute to a good life unless their enjoyment is governed by virtue.

If a good life is identified with a virtuous life, and if a virtuous life is understood in accordance with the sufficiency thesis, then what happens to the other possible component of good lives, namely, the satisfaction that agents may derive from their lives? Perhaps the most attractive feature of Socrates' conception of a good life is the answer it gives to this question. His view of a good life is an instance of the balanced view: in good lives both virtue and satisfaction are present. And the reason for that is that virtuous lives are satisfying. The two components of good lives, virtue and satisfaction, are, according to the Socratic conception, not discrete and unrelated, but inseparably connected with each other. Virtuous lives are satisfying *because* living virtuously is satisfying; and satisfying lives are virtuous *because* the extent to which a life lacks virtue is the extent to which dissatisfaction enters into it.

The reason Socrates gives for the inseparability of virtuous and satisfying lives, and thus for good lives being balanced, derives from his understanding of knowledge of the good. According to Socrates, everyone wants to live a good life. People understand different things by it, however, because they lack knowledge of the goods whose achievement would make a life good. Those who have that knowledge will be guided by it because, being reasonable, they will want to make their lives good. If they know the good, and if they are guided to achieve it, then their lives will be satisfying simply because people take satisfaction in the enjoyment of what they regard as good. But if they habitually act in accordance with their knowledge of the good, then they act virtuously. And this is why knowledge of the good is the key to both virtuous and satisfying lives, and this is also why good lives will be balanced by being composed of both virtue and satisfaction.

Socrates realizes, of course, that many people do not live according to this conception of a good life. They take satisfaction in vice, and they regard virtuous conduct as a grim business requiring them to forego satisfactions. Such people are ignorant of the good; they misunderstand its nature. If they were to understand what the good is, then they would act virtuously and find it satisfying. According to Socrates, therefore, knowledge of the good produces virtue and satisfaction, while ignorance of the good is responsible for vice and dissatisfaction.

Socrates lived his thought, and the result is that "in the whole corpus of Greek prose or verse, no happier life than his may be found."[16] Socrates really meant it when he told the Athenians who were about to sentence him

---

[16] Ibid., 234.

to death: "Discussing goodness . . . and examining both myself and others is really the very best thing that a man can do, and . . . life without this sort of examination is not worth living."[17] At the forced end of his examined life, "quite calmly and with no sign of distaste, he drained the cup [of poison] in one breath."[18] And Vlastos comments: "Is this surprising? If you say that virtue matters more for [the goodness of] your own [life] . . . than does everything else put together, if this is what you say and what you mean—it is for real, not just talk—what is there to be wondered at if the loss of everything else for virtue's sake leaves you light-hearted, cheerful? If you believe what Socrates does, you hold the secret of . . . [good life] in your own hands. Nothing the world can do to you can make you . . . [have a bad life]. In the quest for . . . [a good life] the noblest spirits in the Greek imagination are losers: Achilles, Hector, Alcestis, Antigone. Socrates is a winner. He has to be. Desiring the kind of . . . [good life] he does, he can't lose."[19]

No one will doubt the nobility of Socrates' ideal of a good life and the successful experiment in living he conducted to achieve it. But we may legitimately inquire whether there is any reason *for us* to live as Socrates did and as he thought others should. This question brings us to Socrates' view of moral wisdom. According to Socrates there is such a reason: Moral wisdom compels those who aspire to it to live a life of virtue.

THE SOCRATIC CONCEPTION OF MORAL WISDOM

Socrates regards moral wisdom as superior to all other virtues because it provides the knowledge upon which all virtuous action rests. As Socrates says to Protagoras: "I have nothing else in view but my desire to learn the truth about virtue and what it is in itself. . . . [V]irtue turns out to be, as a single whole, knowledge. . . . Everything is knowledge—justice, temperance, and courage alike."[20] Moral wisdom, for Socrates, is inseparable from the other virtues, because no action can be virtuous unless it is based on the knowledge moral wisdom gives. Furthermore, moral wisdom exercises extremely tight control over other virtues, according to Socrates, because its knowledge of what makes life good necessarily guides action. Everybody wants a good life, and since moral wisdom is knowledge of how to get it, once moral wisdom is acquired, nothing can defeat its motivational force.[21] Vlastos rightly says that provided that "Socrates' assumptions

[17] Plato, *Apology*, 38a.
[18] Plato, *Phaedo*, 117c.
[19] Vlastos, *Socrates*, 235.
[20] Plato, *Protagoras*, 361a–b. See also Plato, *Meno*, 87–89.
[21] For the difference between the earlier and later Socrates, see Irwin, *Plato's Moral Theory*, 200–202.

are correct . . . [if we] understand our good we shall be bound to pursue it: our own desire for the good will drive us to it. . . . [D]oing the worse while knowing the better . . . will then be a psychic impossibility."[22]

One consequence of this view is that in Socrates' account of moral wisdom judgment plays a negligible role. Judgment is needed when we have to decide among different courses of action each of which is backed by prima facie reasons. We judge by weighing the comparative strengths of these reasons. If their strengths were obvious, there would be no need for judgment. And this is exactly the situation Socrates envisages. Those who possess moral wisdom need only be aware of possible courses of action to know which would be better and which worse. For such people, nothing could come between their knowledge and their action.

Socrates recognizes, of course, that people may act contrary to the requirements of a good life. But he thinks that this must be due to their lack of moral wisdom. If they have moral wisdom, they will act on it; and if they act contrary to it, it must be because they are ignorant of the requirements they violate. "Those who suppose evil things bring advantage . . . don't recognize evils for what they are. [They] don't desire evil but what they think is good, though in fact it is evil. . . . [T]hrough ignorance [they] mistake bad things for good . . . [although they] obviously desire the good."[23] And "wisdom everywhere makes men to have good fortune. For wisdom . . . could never make a mistake, but must always do right and have right fortune, or else it would not be wisdom any longer."[24]

Socrates thinks that living a good life, and hence possessing moral wisdom, is within everybody's reach because there is a method available for everybody by which this knowledge could be reached. This is the method of Socratic questioning, the *elenchus*. When he says to his judges that without "discussing goodness . . . and examining both myself and others . . . life . . . is not worth living,"[25] what he means by "discussion" and by the "examination" is engagement in the elenchus. The point of this kind of questioning, which has come to be Socrates' trademark, is not sociability, intellectual stimulation, or deflating the pretensions of conventional authorities or of sundry sophists peddling their trade. The point is to obtain moral wisdom and a good life. By engaging in elenctic discourses, Socrates seeks knowledge of the good both for himself and for others. And because he thinks that the unexamined life lacks it, it could not be good, and that is why it is not worth living.

---

[22] Vlastos, *Socrates*, 88.

[23] Plato, *Meno*, 77d–e. See also Plato, *Protagoras*, 358, and *Gorgias*, 468.

[24] Plato, *Euthydemus*, 280a.

[25] Plato, *Apology*, 38a.

The elenchus enables its practitioners to progress from a special kind of ignorance—foolishness—to a special kind of knowledge—moral wisdom. There are three stages involved in this progression.[26] The first is the stage from which we all normally start. We are born into a society, and as we grow up we imbibe its conventions and customs, its notions of the good, and its ideals of a good life. To take these for granted is foolish. We have not bothered then to find out whether the conventional notions of the good by which we allow ourselves to be guided are indeed good. What makes us foolish at this stage is not merely ignorance of the good, but our ignorance of our ignorance. We think we know because we have been brought up in a certain way, but we do not know because we have not examined our conventional opinions. The reason for examining them is not to challenge the status quo, but to find out for ourselves whether the life we are aiming at is good. We may find, if we inquire, that the conventional opinions are correct, or we may come to see their defects. What matters, however, is to find out for ourselves. And that we cannot do, cannot even want to do, unless we realize our ignorance.

The great service Socrates performs for those who are willing to engage in elenctic discourse is to help them progress beyond this first stage. Time and time again, he shows his readers that they only think that they know, that they are actually ignorant. He puts them on the road to moral progress, not by giving them knowledge of the good, but by motivating them to search for it themselves. The key to doing that is to make them realize their ignorance and feel its burden.

It would be a misunderstanding, however, to interpret Socrates' thought as aiming merely at being of service to others. He does aim at that, but this aim is inseparable from his own progress toward moral wisdom and a good life. He also learns from teaching others. Socrates is a lover of moral wisdom; this means for him that he pursues it because he wants it and he thinks that he does not have it. He certainly reaches thereby the second stage of elenchus, up from ignorant ignorance to Socratic ignorance. This stage involves the realization of one's ignorance of the good, one's lack of moral wisdom, and the motivation to overcome it. As Socrates says, an impulsive disciple of his "went to Delphi and asked this question of the god . . . whether there was anyone wiser than myself. The priestess replied that there was no one. . . . When I heard . . . I said to myself, What does the god mean? . . . I am only too conscious that I have no claim to wisdom, great or small."[27]

---

[26] This discussion is indebted to Alan R. Drengson, "The Virtue of Socratic Ignorance," *American Philosophical Quarterly* 18 (1981): 237–242.

[27] Plato, *Apology*, 21b.

This is a queer thing for Socrates to say since he makes many claims about the good, which imply that he knows them to be true, and, since, according to him, knowledge of the good is moral wisdom, these claims imply that he has moral wisdom. He claimed, for instance, that the unexamined life is not worth living, that the good life is a virtuous life, that there are five important virtues, and that moral wisdom is the most important among them. Socrates' disavowal of his possession of moral wisdom has often been interpreted as a rhetorical pose intended to entice people into elenctic engagement. But it is more reasonable to suppose that what he means is that he has not attained moral wisdom, that he remains merely a lover of it, seeking possession without being able to claim attainment.[28]

As it has been perceptively noted by Gabriel Marcel: "Wisdom, considered not from the outside but from the point of view of someone seeking it, can never be looked upon as acquired. If a man were to say of himself 'I am a sage', he would at once make himself ridiculous. Is this because a sage is expected to be falsely, hypocritically, modest? I do not think so, I think it is because we know that if wisdom became complacent, it would immediately get stiff in the joints and in the end fall into decay. It does seem in the last analysis that, for the seeker, wisdom is in a sense indistinguishable from the pursuit of it."[29]

Be that as it may, what is clear is that Socrates is unwilling to rest at the second stage, the stage of Socratic ignorance, and he means to progress beyond it. His elenctic engagements have persuaded him that the oracle was right, for Socrates has found no one wiser than himself. But he realizes that this amounts to very little, since he knows how far short he falls of moral wisdom. He is, therefore, in the following quandary. He realizes his ignorance; he is motivated to overcome it; he is unlikely to receive help from others who are even worse off than he is; so where could he look for the knowledge he needs? And the answer he arrives at is the discovery of the reflexivity of moral wisdom: The knowledge he seeks turns out to be self-knowledge.

MORAL WISDOM AND SELF-KNOWLEDGE

The third stage of the elenctic progress toward moral wisdom and a good life, therefore, involves coming to know oneself in a certain way. There is considerable agreement among commentators that this is what Socrates was after. I. G. Kidd writes: "Socrates advocated the Delphic motto

---

[28] Vlastos, *Socrates*, chap. 1.
[29] Gabriel Marcel, *The Decline of Wisdom* (London: Harvill, 1954), 40.

'Know thyself' and suggested that introspection showed how man achieves
. . . the . . . realization of his being (arete). . . . Happiness (eudaimonia),
then, depends . . . on knowingly acting rightly."[30] Alan Drengson thinks
that the "knowledge that we need is . . . self-reflexive. . . . [I]ts excellence
is expressed as intelligent action which grows out of the open wakefulness
to which Socratic philosophising leads, when it frees us from . . . our prejudices, . . . erroneous habits of thought and the like. . . . Thus, for Socrates
philosophy was . . . a realization of human excellence. . . . The examined
life is . . . brought to flower out of our own need as a love for that which we
lack, viz. wisdom."[31] According to Laszlo Versenyi, "The only knowledge
that makes man good, i.e. makes him fulfill his nature and attain *eudaimonia*, is the knowledge of good and evil. This is what Socrates calls *sophia*,
phronesis, the only truly practical knowledge—wisdom. . . . Unless a man
knows what . . . he is, what his needs and talents are, and wherein he is deficient, i.e. unless he knows himself, he does not know what is really good
and evil. . . . [Hence] wisdom, or the knowledge of good and evil, can be
defined as self-knowledge."[32]

With his customary penetration, Vlastos articulates the assumption underlying the connection between moral wisdom and self-knowledge. This
assumption is that at the third and final stage of the elenchus, its participants find "that side by side with all their false beliefs . . . [they] always
carry truth somewhere or other in their belief system."[33] Elenctic inquiry
reveals an inconsistency among our own beliefs; it spurs us to remove it,
and that involves ridding ourselves of the "prejudices" and "erroneous
habits of thought" to which we find ourselves committed, and which obscure the truth from us.

The search for moral wisdom, therefore, leads inward; knowledge of the
good turns out to be self-knowledge; and the key to a good life is the examination of our own life in which moral wisdom, through the elenchus,
frees us from internal obstacles to living as we should. Socrates thinks that
in respect to the capacity and the opportunity to follow the elenctic procedure, and thus to acquire moral wisdom and a good life, we are all
equal. This, then, is the background against which we should interpret
Socrates' claims that "whoever has [moral wisdom] . . . needs no more

---

[30] I. G. Kidd, "Socrates," in *The Encyclopedia of Philosophy*, ed. Paul Edwards (New York:
Macmillan, 1967), 484a.
[31] Drengson, "The Virtue of Socratic Ignorance," 239–240. The quoted passages are
widely separated in the text.
[32] Laszlo Versenyi, *Socratic Humanism* (New Haven: Yale University Press, 1963), 85–86.
See also Helen North, *Sophrosyne: Self-Knowledge and Self-Restraint in Greek Literature* (Ithaca:
Cornell University Press, 1966) for tracing this theme in Greek thought.
[33] Vlastos, *Socrates*, 113–114.

good fortune than that" and "[moral] wisdom is good, and ignorance bad."[34]

Perhaps the dominant motive behind the Socratic quest for moral wisdom and a good life is the goal of self-sufficiency. To achieve it, we are urged to turn inward, to control ourselves, not the world. The goodness of our lives is taken to depend on our knowledge of the good, on applying that knowledge reflexively to motivate all of our conduct and to control those aspects of our character which impede our moral progress. We thereby make ourselves our own masters. We teach ourselves to be invulnerable to the harm others may cause us, not by becoming indifferent, insensitive, or selfish, but by committing ourselves to a hierarchy of values in which the external goods, over which we have inadequate control, are ranked very low and the internal goods, whose achievement depends only on ourselves, are ranked very high. According to the Socratic conception, therefore, moral wisdom is a second-order reflexive disposition involving the application of our knowledge of the good to our own dispositions in order to control our character and actions. And the motive for doing so is to live a good life. The natural and universal human desire for such a life supplies the evaluative dimension of moral wisdom.

There is, however, an obvious problem with the Socratic view. Even if it is true that knowledge of the good motivates reasonable people, why should that be the only source of motivation? Or, granted that the virtuous life is satisfying, why should virtue be the only source of satisfaction? The earlier Socrates does not deal with these questions adequately, but the later one endeavors to do so. His later view allows that the desire for pleasure and strong emotions may also motivate reasonable people. It recognizes, furthermore, that the motivational force of pleasure and emotions may conflict with and prevail over the motivational force of knowledge of the good. It can thus recognize the complexity of human motivation, because it subscribes to the tripartite division of the soul, while earlier he lacked this important resource.

According to Irwin's perspicuous reconstruction, this difference between the earlier and later Socrates turns on the understanding of desires: "[Earlier] Socratic desires . . . are concerned with goods, and they are rationally concerned with them, so they seek the over-all good. . . . [The later Socrates] recognizes desires which are, and desires which are not, rational and good-dependent in the Socratic way: . . . 1. The appetitive part; entirely good-independent and non-rational, uninfluenced by beliefs about goods. 2. The emotional part; partly good-dependent, influenced by be-

---

[34] Plato, *Euthydemus*, 280b and 281e.

liefs about some kinds of goods. 3. The rational part; entirely good-dependent and rational, influenced by beliefs about the over-all good."[35]

It emerges, therefore, that although the earlier and later Socrates agree about regarding moral wisdom as the most important virtue, they nevertheless disagree about what makes it so. The earlier Socrates holds moral wisdom supreme because it provides the knowledge on which all virtuous actions have to rest. The different virtues are merely different ways of applying knowledge of the good in different moral situations. By contrast, the later Socrates, having accepted the tripartite division of the soul, attributes the supremacy of moral wisdom to its being the virtue of the highest—the rational—part of the soul.[36]

One consequence of this difference is that the earlier Socrates sees moral wisdom as inseparable from the other virtues, whereas the later Socrates thinks of it as merely controlling the other virtues, which would go astray without it. To the earlier Socrates it is inconceivable that if moral wisdom were present, we would not act on it, whereas the later Socrates could allow for the obvious possibility that we may know what the good is and yet not act on it because moral wisdom's control over the lower parts of our soul has slipped. For the earlier Socrates, moral wisdom is necessarily action-guiding, whereas the later Socrates recognizes that our appetites and passions may interpose themselves between our knowledge of the good and appropriate action.[37]

The later Socrates could therefore go some way toward accounting for the complexity of human motivation, because he could acknowledge that appetites and passions may motivate us; nevertheless he could still insist on moral wisdom's having control over them. He describes a person who succeeds in this as "master of himself . . . [who] puts things in order, is his own friend, harmonizes the three parts. . . . He binds them all together, and himself from a plurality to a unity. . . . [H]e thinks the just and beautiful action, which he names as such, to be that which preserves this inner harmony and indeed helps to achieve it, wisdom to be the knowledge which oversees this action, an unjust action be that which always destroys it, and ignorance . . . which oversees that."[38]

It may be asked, however, "Why is it impossible, when in possession of all this wisdom to act with evil . . . intent?" And the later Socratic answer, according to Georges Grube, is that if a person "has this knowledge of real values, if he knows what is true and good . . . he cannot act against his own

---

[35] Irwin, *Plato's Moral Theory*, 192. The order of the first two sentences has been reversed.

[36] Ibid., 191–195.

[37] Plato, *Phaedrus*, 246–on.

[38] Plato, *Republic*, 443d–e.

ends. . . . He cannot but desire that the world of sense should approach the Ideal . . . he now contemplates, and he must needs do what he can towards its realization. Living above petty interests in the loving adoration of supreme truth, himself a harmonious being who has risen above all conflict in his soul, the Platonic philosopher will inevitably seek everywhere to impose harmony on chaos, which is to change evil into good. His knowledge is goodness indeed."[39]

To move from knowledge to goodness, however, an intermediate step is necessary: we must make ourselves into "a harmonious being who has risen above all conflict in his soul." Achieving that is also a function of moral wisdom. The later Socratic view, therefore, identifies two ways in which moral wisdom may guide us. The first motivates us to act according to our knowledge of the good, and the second controls the unruly elements of our soul by subordinating them to this higher purpose. "It is fitting," according to the later Socrates, "that the reasonable part should rule, it being wise and exercising foresight on behalf of the whole soul, and for the spirited part to obey and be its ally. . . . These two parts, then . . . will exercise authority over the appetitive part which is the largest part in any man's soul and is insatiable. . . . They will watch over it to see that it . . . [will not] upset everybody's whole life."[40]

The tripartite division of the soul contributes, therefore, both constructively and critically to the understanding of moral wisdom. Each of the three parts motivates us, but morally untrained souls are motivated in conflicting directions. Part of the role of moral wisdom is to put an end to this "civil war of the soul" (*Republic* 440e) by making us realize that "it is fitting that the reasonable part should rule" (*Republic* 441e). Another part is that since moral wisdom "possesses the knowledge of what is beneficial to each part, and of what is to the common advantage of all three" (*Republic* 442c), it provides the goal toward which we should move and the motivation to move toward it.

But what kind of knowledge is it that, according to Socrates, moral wisdom provides? The knowledge is self-knowledge.[41] He disdained the "crude science" that means to reduce everything "to the standards of probability." "I myself," he said, "have certainly no time for the business, and I tell you why . . . I can't as yet 'know myself' as the inscription at Delphi enjoins, and so long as that ignorance remains, it seems to me ridiculous to inquire into extraneous matters. Consequently I . . . direct my inquiries . . .

[39] Georges M. A. Grube, *Plato's Thought* (Boston: Beacon Press, 1964), 258.

[40] Plato, *Republic,* 441e–442b.

[41] For an exploration of this theme, see Charles Griswold, *Self-Knowledge in Plato's Phaedrus* (New Haven: Yale University Press, 1986). See also Cedric H. Whitman, *Sophocles: A Study of Heroic Humanism* (Cambridge: Harvard University Press, 1951), chap. 1.

rather to myself."[42] This self-knowledge is knowledge of how the three parts of the soul motivate us and of how their often conflicting directives can be controlled.

The motivating and controlling aspects of moral wisdom are thus intertwined with self-knowledge. For moral wisdom's motivation derives whatever force it has from our conception of a good life, but that can motivate us only if we know what it is. Knowledge of it need not be conscious, articulate, or propositional, but it must inform both our spontaneous and deliberate conduct, since our conduct is a tacit expression of what we think of as good that should be pursued and as evil that should be avoided. Moral wisdom's control is also inseparable from self-knowledge, since we can control only the motives we are aware of having, and we can resolve only those conflicts within us that we know are taking place.

It is readily understandable, therefore, why Socrates thinks that it is "ridiculous to inquire into extraneous matters" so long as one's self-knowledge is deficient. For self-knowledge motivates us to seek what is good and avoid what is evil, and we learn from it that we must control those aspects of our character which undercut this motivation. Inquiry into extraneous matters is ridiculous, if it is not motivated by what we regard as good and if it is not the result of conduct that we control.

A word of caution, however, is in order. Moral wisdom is essentially connected with self-knowledge, but they are not identical. There is more to moral wisdom than self-knowledge, although Socrates sometimes leads one to suppose otherwise. Knowledge of the good cannot be merely the result of an inwardly directed inquiry because there is a difference between what is good and what we think is good. Self-knowledge may reveal what we think is good, but we need also to know whether what we think is good is indeed good. That knowledge, however, cannot be self-knowledge, and yet it is essential to moral wisdom. Not even perfect self-knowledge can, therefore, be identified with moral wisdom.

DOUBTS ABOUT THE SOCRATIC IDEAL

The Socratic ideal is a version of the eudaimonistic, balanced view of good lives. The ideal is of a life that is both virtuous and satisfying. Living virtuously is living in accordance with the good, and the good is what really satisfies. Those who understand this will be motivated to seek a life that is truly good, not one that merely seems so, and they will try to control the various elements of their character to make them conducive to living a good life. The control involves developing the virtues and suppressing the

---

[42] Plato, *Phaedrus*, 229e–230a.

vices, and the motivation involves forming a reasonable conception of a good life and living accordingly.

No matter how attractive this ideal is, we, possessors of a contemporary Western sensibility, do not find it acceptable. We agree that virtue and satisfaction ought to go together in a good life, but we believe that they nevertheless often diverge. We recognize and we mind that the virtuous may have unsatisfying lives and the vicious may have satisfying ones. For Socrates this is impossible; he denies that virtue and satisfaction could diverge. He would have said that our failure to recognize that virtue is bound to provide satisfaction and that vice cannot do so is a moral failure. The very supposition that virtue may not be satisfying or that satisfaction may accompany a vicious life shows, according to Socrates, a grievous lack of moral wisdom. He would have granted that it may *seem* that some vicious lives are satisfying and some virtuous lives devoid of satisfaction, but these appearances, according to him, deceive only those who are foolish. Virtuous lives *cannot* lack satisfaction and vicious lives *cannot* be satisfying because virtue *is* satisfying and vice *is* its opposite. To think otherwise is to be ignorant of good and evil.

But we do think otherwise, and we refuse to attribute it to our ignorance. Our disagreement with the Socratic ideal hinges on what moral wisdom teaches about the good. Socrates thinks that the key to a good life is moral wisdom, for moral wisdom is knowledge of how to act virtuously. He also thinks that everyone has the capacity and the opportunity to act virtuously because everyone can have the appropriate knowledge and live according to it. Because a virtuous life is satisfying, everyone has the capacity to live a satisfying life. We think, by contrast, that we may have the appropriate knowledge and still lack the capacity to live a good life, and even if we have the capacity, we may still not have a satisfying life. We thus disagree with Socrates about the facts of moral life. This disagreement brings to attention several of the deepest problems about the human prospect.

One of these is the problem of contingency. It arises because the internal goods represented by virtuous action can be obtained only if we possess first the appropriate external goods. These external goods, it will be remembered, are political: an acceptable level of peace, security, and justice in the society in which we live; psychological: the possession of at least average cognitive, emotional, and volitional capacities; and physiological: the absence of extreme deprivation, debilitating illness, disabling accidents, or serious handicaps. These and similar external goods are necessary for living a good life. If we are temporarily deprived of them, as in concentration camps and other extreme situations, the habits of our previous existence may persist; temporary deprivation need not make lives bad. But the deprivation has to be temporary, and good lives are possible under adverse conditions only if those conditions had been preceded by a sufficiently long period during which a virtuous character could be formed.

The implication of the dependence of internal goods upon external ones is that the Socratic ideal is mistaken in supposing that we could control all the important aspects of our lives, since we often have no control over the external goods we require for living a good life. Moral wisdom, for instance, is unattainable in the absence of at least average cognitive, emotive, and volitional capacities, but their possession depends on genetic inheritance, not on our efforts. Similarly, the supposed equal capacity to live a good life assumes that we all start in the same initial position. But we differ greatly in the conditions of our birth and upbringing, so our chances of living a good life and developing moral wisdom are also going to be different. This cannot but affect the efforts we can make to live according to the Socratic ideal.

The problem of contingency is that we do not have adequate control over the goodness of our lives because we do not have control over the external goods required to live such a life. It may be true that an unexamined life is not worth living, but whether an examined life is worth it depends not merely on our own efforts, but also on political, psychological, and physiological conditions, which strongly influence both the nature and the outcome of the efforts we are capable of making. We may have some control over these conditions, but it is very much less than what we need to live according to the Socratic ideal. Genetic inheritance and countless episodes in our environment often render us passive subjects of obstructive influences, which we have neither cooperated in producing, nor can resist, alter, or otherwise mitigate.

Another problem that arises for the Socratic ideal is conflict. There is both a plurality of conceptions of a good life and a plurality of ways in which goods could be ranked in them. These conceptions and rankings conflict with each other. Such conflicts reveal alternatives to the Socratic ideal, but the Socratic ideal lacks the resources for resolving conflicts between itself and these alternatives to it.

The importance of individuals is central to the Socratic ideal. It is individuals who make good lives for themselves through their individual efforts; individuals derive personal satisfaction from the way they live; and it is individuals again who decide to include concern for the welfare of other individuals among the goods they seek. One alternative to the Socratic ideal involves a downgrading of this orientation. People may conceive of themselves primarily as members of a community and only secondarily as individuals. The focus of their attention is not concentrated on themselves and on a few select others, but on the community of which they see themselves as inseparable parts. As Socrates sees external goods as subordinate to internal goods, so these people see personal goods as subordinate to communal goods. They recognize individual effort and achievement, but they rank them low in their hierarchy of goods. They prize cooperation, fellow-feeling, humility, obedience, loyalty, and self-sacrifice, and the Socratic virtues are much less important in their conception of a good life.[43]

Consider another possibility. In the hierarchy of Socratic virtues, moral wisdom stands highest. But why does it have to rely on the kind of knowledge Socrates depicts? Why does the knowledge have to be a cognitive achievement that comes to people after prolonged elenctic engagement? Why could it not be a nonanalytical, nondiscursive loving awareness that lovers, intimate friends, long-married couples, and close brothers or sisters may have of each other? Or why could it not be the uncorrupted expression of the simple natural goodness of not particularly intelligent people who respond to others with spontaneous good will? Or again, why could virtuous actions not be based on a simple unquestioning conformity to the conventions of a benign moral tradition?[44]

Yet another alternative to the Socratic ideal involves external goods beyond those Socrates considered. Among them are goods connected with religious and mystical practices, scientific or artistic creativity, adventure and exploration that challenge recognized limits, and participation in a practice devoted to sharing and perpetuating some morally neutral tradition, such as playing chess, listening to music, being a baseball fan, gardening, or collecting the sort of oddities that so many people so passionately collect. When people's lives center on such external goods, they derive much of the meaning, purpose, and enjoyment of their lives from these goods. The Socratic ranking of them as worthless unless informed by the virtues of temperance, courage, piety, justice, and moral wisdom is quite hard to accept. The point is not that lives centering on these not ignoble external goods involve the violation of the Socratic virtues; it is more likely that in such lives there will be a much-reduced scope for their exercise. Lives of this sort are shaped very

---

[43] For a study of this contrast, see Arthur W. H. Adkins, *Merit and Responsibility: A Study in Greek Values* (Oxford: Clarendon Press, 1960), as well as recent communitarian criticisms of liberalism, for instance, Michael Sandel, ed., *Liberalism and Its Critics* (Oxford: Blackwell, 1984). For liberal responses, see Nancy L. Rosenblum, ed. *Liberalism and the Moral Life* (Cambridge: Harvard University Press, 1989).

[44] This is one theme in Nietzsche's complex attitude to Socrates. See *The Birth of Tragedy* and *Ecce Homo*. See also Walter Kaufmann, *Nietzsche* (Princeton: Princeton University Press, 1974), chap. 13, and Alexander Nehamas, *Nietzsche: Life as Literature* (Cambridge: Harvard University Press, 1985), 24–34. For an interpretation that would make this not an alternative to Socrates' view but his own, see Wallace I. Matson and Adam Leite, "Socrates' Critique of Cognitivism," *Philosophy* 66 (1991): 145–167.

differently from the Socratic ideal, and they require different virtues and different rankings of the same virtues.[45] The reason for calling attention to these alternatives is not to deny that the Socratic ideal is worth prizing, but to challenge the claim that the Socratic ideal is superior to them. Conceptions of a good life and the rankings of goods in them conflict with each other. If one of these conceptions or rankings is claimed to be superior to the others, then the claim must be supported by argument. The argument must somehow show, on grounds independent of any particular conception of a good life or ranking of goods, why the conflicts should be resolved in favor of the Socratic ideal. Such an argument, however, has not been given.

A further problem for the Socratic ideal is evil. Any view of human motivation that attributes a dominant role to the good owes an explanation of how evil can exist if the good is so desirable. The more realistic the explanation is in acknowledging the existence of evil, the greater will its difficulty be in maintaining the motivational force of the good. And the further the explanation goes in denying the reality of evil, the less plausible it will be in giving an account of the obvious facts of moral life.

The Socratic ideal must face the problem of evil because it supposes that human beings are naturally motivated to live a good life. But if the good dominates in human motivation, then how can human beings routinely perform evil actions? The Socratic answer is that no one does wrong knowingly. It acknowledges the existence of evil, but it attributes it to ignorance of the good. If people know the good, they will act accordingly. And if people fail to act according to the good, it must be because they do not know what it is.

But is it plausible to suppose that all evil actions are due to ignorance of what an alternative good action would be? The reason for doubting the affirmative answer is that the desire to act in ways we know are evil is also part of human motivation. We often deliberately do not do what we know is good, and we also deliberately choose to do what we know is evil in preference to what we know is good. Why should we think, then, with the earlier Socrates, that all evil is due merely to a failure to know the good, or, with the later Socrates, that evil is merely the failure to subordinate our desires and passions to our knowledge of the good? Why should we not recognize that hostility, greed, anger, envy, jealousy, aggression, and selfishness also

[45] The literature on pluralism is recent and rapidly growing. For some statements of it, see Isaiah Berlin, *Four Essays on Liberty* (Oxford: Oxford University Press, 1969); Stuart Hampshire, *Morality and Conflict* (Cambridge: Harvard University Press, 1983); John Kekes, *The Morality of Pluralism* (Princeton: Princeton University Press, 1993); Michael Stocker, *Plural and Conflicting Values* (Oxford: Clarendon Press, 1990); and Bernard Williams, *Moral Luck* (Cambridge: Cambridge University Press, 1981).

motivate us? Why could evil not be an active force in our character, standing in conflict with the similarly active force of the good? Why should we suppose that our knowledge of the good motivates us to achieve it, but our knowledge of evil motivates us only to resist it? Why could we not, as a matter of conscious policy, pursue evil and resist the good? Why should moral wisdom connect us only to the good and ignorance only to evil? To these questions the Socratic ideal provides no answers.

CONCLUSION

That the Socratic ideal lacks the resources to deal with the problems of contingency, conflict, and evil does not mean that the eudaimonistic conception of good lives as balanced is itself a failure. It is possible to go beyond the Socratic ideal, while adhering to eudaimonism. The first step in that direction is to appreciate just how very deep are the problems presented by contingency, conflict, and evil. This is the topic of the next chapter.

CHAPTER THREE

Permanent Adversities

Contingency, conflict, and evil are adversities that stand in the way of our efforts to live good lives. Socrates recognized their existence, but he supposed that we can eliminate them by being sufficiently virtuous. He was mistaken about this. Contingency, conflict, and evil are *permanent* adversities, and no effort of ours can eliminate them. Good lives require that we come to terms with them, and it is through moral wisdom that we may do so. The nature of these adversities is the topic of this chapter; how moral wisdom makes it possible to come to terms with them is discussed in subsequent chapters.

CONTINGENCY AND THE GOODS OF GOOD LIVES

Shakespeare's *King Lear* presents the problem of contingency with great force.[1] Lear acted foolishly in dividing his kingdom, trusting his wicked daughters, and disowning Cordelia, who truly loved him. Lear's judgment was impaired by his character defects: pride, vanity, and impetuosity. The play shows Lear paying for them in the currency of his own suffering, brought about precisely by the vices that were responsible for his foolish decisions. But he did pay. And not only did he pay, but as he was doing so, his character improved. He came to understand what he had done and how his actions followed from his defective character. As he lost all he valued, as he endured gross humiliations, as he was deprived in his old age of civilized comforts, so he discovered and began to cultivate in

---

[1] The discussion in this section draws on John Kekes, *Facing Evil* (Princeton: Princeton University Press, 1990), chap. 1.

himself gentleness, pity, and remorse for what he was and had done. Then he is reunited with loving Cordelia, who has, of course, forgiven him, and we expect Shakespeare to provide the happy ending they, and we, deserve. What we get, however, is the shocking execution of blameless Cordelia, the broken heart and death of Lear, not to mention the unmerited misfortune of the faithful Fool and the decent Gloucester. We learn that life is contingent, goodness may lead to suffering, moral growth need not be rewarded, and people come to undeserved harm.

The profoundly depressing suggestion of the play is that the scheme of things may be indifferent to human merit, that there may be no cosmic justice, and so the deserving may suffer and the undeserving may flourish. And the books may not be balanced even in the long run because there is no superhuman accounting agency. We are forced to consider that the scheme of things is contingent, not moral. It is not evil, rather than good, nor is it Manichean. It may just be indifferent. Indifference is worse than neutrality, for the latter implies the presence of an umpire, or perhaps some spectators, who are there as witnesses but stand above the tumult and remain uncommitted. That would be of some relief, for we could say that they at least know that injustice occurs, and, perhaps, if things were really bad, their neutrality would be temporarily suspended. But if there is nobody overseeing the fortunes of humanity, then there is no reason to suppose that what happens to us is or ever will be proportional to our merit.

Common experience confirms this. Vicious dictators live out their lives in comfort, continuing to wield their evil power, amid the adulation of people they have duped. Good causes supported by good people lose out to unscrupulous defenders of deplorable conditions. Crimes, accidents, and disease befall us regardless of our merit. Living a reasonable and decent life is of no avail against the contingency of nature. As Mill clearly saw: "The dictum that truth [and, we may add, goodness] always triumph over persecution is one of those pleasant falsehoods which men repeat after one another till they pass into commonplaces, but which experience refutes. History teems with instances of truth [and goodness] put down by persecution. . . . It is a piece of idle sentimentality that truth [and goodness have] . . . any inherent power denied to error [and evil]."[2]

Contingency may be understood as the non-anthropocentric truth about the segment of reality we occupy that our welfare is often at the mercy of conditions we have neither created nor can decisively influence. These truths are non-anthropocentric in the sense that they would be apparent to God, or to any other sufficiently intelligent being who has the capacity to entertain them. Alternatively, contingency may be understood

---

[2] John Stuart Mill, *On Liberty* (Indianapolis: Hackett, 1978), 27–28.

anthropocentrically as the morally significant truth about us that no matter how virtuously we try to live a good life, we are not masters of our fate. No doubt, striving after virtue may make our lives better than they would be otherwise. But it is an illusion to suppose that even the achievement of perfect virtue would guarantee a good life. It becomes, therefore, a major task for moral wisdom to explain why it is reasonable to be motivated by a conception of good life if contingency puts its achievement beyond our control.

Following the line of thought in Chapters 1 and 2, contingency may be attributed to our insufficient control over external goods. Since external goods are required for good lives, the extent to which we lack control over them, is the extent to which the goodness of our lives depends on conditions we cannot alter. These conditions constitute the contingency from which no human life can be free. To appreciate the seriousness of the adversity contingency presents, it is necessary to understand more precisely what external goods are.

Aristotle says that a good life "is active in conformity with complete [virtue] and is sufficiently equipped with external goods, not for some chance period but throughout a complete life."[3] This implies that complete virtue, that is, a virtuous life, is insufficient for a good life, unless it is accompanied by a lifelong supply of external goods. To what, then, are these goods external? Two answers are implicit in Aristotle, and he vacillates between them.[4] In the first, he contrasts external goods with the goods of the soul, which include the virtues, and the goods of the body, such as health. External goods, therefore, are external to both the body and the soul (for "soul" read "mind and character").[5] The second answer includes the goods of the body with external goods and contrasts both with the goods of the mind and character (*NE* 1098b32–1099a8). External goods will here be understood in the second sense, including all the goods we need for a good life, except those of the mind and character. Examples of external goods are some degree of prosperity, security, freedom, education, prestige, status, respect, friendship, good upbringing, as well as health, acceptable physical appearance, and adequate physical and psychological energy. Aristotle's claim is that a good life must be a virtuous life *and* it must be equipped with a steady supply of external goods.

In contrast to external goods, the goods of the mind and character are internal. Aristotle vacillates about them too, and he sometimes counts the

---

[3] Aristotle, *Nicomachean Ethics*, 1101a14–16. The bracketed "virtue" appears as "excellence" in the text.

[4] See John M. Cooper, "Aristotle on the Goods of Fortune," *Philosophical Review* 94 (1985), esp. 176–177.

[5] Aristotle, *Nicomachean Ethics*, 1098b12–14.

goods of the body also as internal.[6] He never waivers, however, in regarding the goods of the mind and character as internal. The most characteristic internal goods are the virtues and the enjoyment derived from living according to them. The internal goods derivable from the possession and exercise of moral wisdom are understanding the scheme of things and our place in it, being sufficiently clearheaded about and sensitive to the complexities of concrete situations to judge them well, and knowing how to make a good life for ourselves in the particular context in which we live. There are, of course, internal goods derivable from the other virtues as well.

The general point is that internal goods are enjoyments derived from successful engagement in the activities central to our conception of a good life, while external goods are both the enjoyment of favorable conditions, which facilitate our engagements, and the rewards we receive from others, which indicate that our activities are appreciated. External goods therefore may be thought of both as means and as rewards.

A central assumption of the Socratic ideal is that good lives depend on our own efforts. We and only we can make a good life for ourselves, and whether we succeed or fail depends on how virtuous are the efforts we make toward the achievement of that end. But the Socratic ideal stands merely at the beginning of a long tradition, which includes the Stoics, Epicureans, Spinoza, Kant, and Kierkegaard. What unites these disparate thinkers is their agreement about the central place our efforts have in making a good life for ourselves and the corollary point that contingency plays at most a negligible role in the outcome of our efforts. This corollary has entered into contemporary discussions under the intriguing label of "moral luck."[7]

There is a good reason, however, for not adopting this label. Writing of luck, Martha Nussbaum says: "I do not mean to imply that the events in question are random or uncaused. What happens to a person by luck will be just what does not happen through his or her agency, what just *happens* to him, as opposed to what he does or makes."[8] The trouble with this is that what does not happen through our own agency need not happen by luck. "Luck" denotes chance events (see any dictionary), and events that happen to us independently of our own agency need not be chance

---

[6] Aristotle, *Rhetoric*, 1360b25–27.

[7] See Thomas Nagel, "Moral Luck," in his *Mortal Questions* (Cambridge: Cambridge University Press, 1979); Martha C. Nussbaum, *The Fragility of Goodness: Luck and Ethics in Greek Tragedy and Philosophy* (Cambridge: Cambridge University Press, 1986); Bernard Williams, "Moral Luck," in his *Moral Luck* (Cambridge: Cambridge University Press, 1981); and John Kekes, *Facing Evil* (Princeton: Princeton University Press, 1990). A historical survey of the ideas is in Vincenzo Cioffari, "Fortune, Fate, and Chance," in *Dictionary of the History of Ideas*, ed. Philip P. Wiener (New York: Scribner's, 1973).

[8] Nussbaum, *Fragility of Goodness*, 3.

events. They may seem so to us, and we may call them "lucky" or "unlucky," but only because we lack understanding and control over them. It is more perspicuous, therefore, to speak of "contingency," as will be done here.

The assumption underlying the tradition that ties good lives to our efforts and denies the relevance of contingency to them is that good lives depend on the enjoyment of internal goods and that, in turn, depends solely or largely on our efforts. It is acknowledged that external goods are contingent, and hence often beyond our control. But that is taken to show only that they are false or unimportant goods, actually endangering good lives, or, if not that, then quite dispensable to them. The more worldly thinkers in this tradition may even go so far as to regard the moderate enjoyment of external goods as pleasant and harmless, much like that of spices, but even they insist that good lives are possible without them.

This assumption, however, is mistaken. It is undoubtedly true that our efforts play a crucial role in the activities on whose success the enjoyment of internal goods depends. We must strive to develop our virtues, cultivate our talents, work hard at our chosen projects, and discipline ourselves to become proficient at the skills required by our conception of a good life. Internal goods are the results of these and similar efforts. They do not come to us, if they come, from the outside. They are the products of our own endeavors. If we possess and enjoy them, our felicity cannot but be deserved because it is due to the success of our own efforts. When technique becomes effortless for violinists, when historians become so familiar with their period as to make it seem like lived-through experience, when mothers, through loving attention, become intuitively attuned to the needs of their children, when teachers communicate to their students the importance, excitement, and complexity of their subject, then, through their successful efforts, some of the internal goods necessary for making their lives good are indeed present.

The fact remains, nevertheless, that even the most successful of our efforts can only be necessary and never sufficient for good lives. For whether we can make successful efforts depends on the possession of external goods. Both internal and external goods are required, therefore, for a good life. The lack of internal goods indicates one of two things. It may be that we cannot engage, or engage successfully, in the activities central to our conception of a good life: thus we are not living the life we want to live. Or it may be that, although we are engaged in the activities, contrary to our expectations we do not find them enjoyable: thus we are mistaken in wanting to live the way we do. Lives are made good partly by the agents' enjoyment of the activities that are characteristic of the lives: musicians of making music, administrators of organizing, teachers of teaching, athletes of disciplined exertion, and so forth. The enjoyment is a sign that the agents' efforts have been well-directed and sufficient to achieve the appropriate internal goods. The absence of enjoyment indicates, on the other hand, that, for one reason or another, the efforts have failed.

One reason for such failures is the lack of external goods. External goods as means are necessary for a good life because they play an essential role in the acquisition and exercise of the virtues on which the achievement of internal goods depends. Consider first situations in which we possess the relevant virtues to a sufficient extent, but we are prevented from exercising them by debilitating poverty and hunger, long-term illness and chronic pain, confinement to a society ruled by terror and brutality, or by rejection and ridicule due to our racial, religious, or ethnic identity. To be sure, these adverse conditions need not prevent occasional virtuous actions, but they will certainly restrict their scope. If the exercise of a virtue requires appropriate action in the appropriate situations, then the rarity of the appropriate situations will be an obstacle to living a virtuous life just as much as is the insufficient development of the virtue. And what makes appropriate situations rare is the scarcity of the external goods, which the exercise of the virtue requires.

Consider next cases in which we lack the virtues through no fault of our own. The acquisition of the virtues depends, among other factors, on innate capacities and suitable early conditions for their development. Average intelligence, adequate span of attention, hormonal balance, sufficient nurturing during infancy, the mastery of a language, an acceptable level of nutrition, health care, and scope for motor and sensory development are among the minimum conditions required for normal functioning as an adult. If we innately lack or if we are deprived in early childhood of the necessary external goods, we cannot go on to develop the virtues, and our subsequent lack of them is often irremediable.

But external goods are not merely necessary means to a good life, they are also intrinsically enjoyable rewards for living it. If we have security, prestige, respect, influence, prosperity, and so forth, our lives are better, and if we do not have them, our lives are worse. Poor education, recurrent physical or psychological terror, systematic discrimination, soul-destroying work, and similar external evils may make it impossible to live a good life, even if we succeed, in the face of considerable odds, in living virtuously. These are some of the reasons, then, for Aristotle's claim that a good life must not only be virtuous, but that it must also be equipped with a sufficient supply of external goods. The problem of contingency is that we often have no control over assuring that sufficient supply.

One of the many merits of this view of contingency is that it can readily explain why the Socratic ideal has been found to be so attractive by so many thinkers. The truth in the Socratic ideal is that good lives are possible without external goods as rewards. But this does not mean, as it has been mistakenly assumed, that good lives are possible without external goods as means. We can indeed live enjoyable and morally meritorious lives without basking in the wealth, respect, status, prestige, and influence that a more just distribution would bestow on us. And it is also true that many otherwise good lives have been ruined by the resentment, anger, envy, jealousy, and bitterness produced by the frustrated expectation of just rewards. Defenders of the Socratic ideal are surely right to warn us against this danger.

Nevertheless, social instability, physical insecurity, extreme poverty, ill health, personal misfortune, and so forth, do jeopardize and often make impossible the possession and enjoyment of external goods. The external goods that these adversities deprive us of are often beyond our control, yet they are necessary means to internal goods, and thus to good lives. It is this feature of them, rather than that of being a possible source of a corrupt worldliness, that was and is being missed by defenders of the Socratic ideal.

The eudaimonistic approach to the problem of the contingency of external goods that is defended here looks to moral wisdom for help in coping with it. This approach should be viewed in contrast to, and as an improvement over, the Socratic approach, which unsuccessfully looked to moral wisdom not to cope with but to eliminate contingency. The discussion so far has merely diagnosed the source of the problem. It is yet to be seen, of course, whether the eudaimonistic approach can actually provide the help we obviously need.

CONFLICT AND THE PLURALITY OF VALUES

It has been argued in Chapter 1 that eudaimonism is not committed to there being a specific conception of a good life that all reasonable people should aim at.[9] The eudaimonistic conception is rather a regulative ideal to which all the various specific conceptions of a good life must conform. The necessity is based on certain truisms about human nature, not on ineluctable logical or moral principles. Just as living a healthy life is possible only if certain requirements are met, so living a good life requires living in conformity to some specific conditions. The eudaimonistic conception spells out what these conditions are, but it insists on there being a plurality of ways of conforming to them. Quite different conceptions of a good life, therefore, may conform to the eudaimonistic regulative ideal.

[9] The discussion in this section draws on John Kekes, *The Morality of Pluralism* (Princeton: Princeton University Press, 1993), chap. 2.

Looking at good lives in this pluralistic way has a liberating influence, especially in contrast with the rigidity of the single visions various monistic thinkers have advocated. Whatever may be the attractions of this conception, however, there is a central difficulty that must be faced by its defenders. If there is a plurality of reasonable values, a plurality of reasonable ways of ranking them, and a consequent plurality of reasonable conceptions of a good life, then how can conflicts among them be settled in a reasonable manner?

That there is a plurality of values is a clear implication of the version of eudaimonism defended here. Values may be primary or secondary. Primary values may be the goods and evils of the self, intimacy, and social order. Secondary values may be either the specific forms primary values take in particular contexts or goods and evils beyond primary ones, which follow from individually, socially, culturally, and historically variable conceptions of a good life. Moreover, values may also be external or internal. And this latter distinction cuts across the distinctions between and within primary and secondary values.

The first step toward appreciating why conflict is a permanent adversity is to realize that if values are plural, then they will conflict with each other. We must often choose between two different things we regard as good because if we have one, we cannot have the other. We cannot live an independent, unencumbered, self-reliant life in which we are accountable only to ourselves and have a large family and a close marriage. Ambition, competitiveness, commitment to some discipline, profession, or institution cannot coexist with the bemused, distant, uninvolved perspective of an observer. Life in politics does not go with a life of contemplation and privacy. A risk-taking adventurous life excludes the peace of mind which derives from cautiously cherishing what one has. Breadth and depth, freedom and equality, solitude and public-spiritedness, good judgment and passionate involvement, love of comfort and love of achievement, ambition and humility, justice and mercy—all exist in a state of tension, and the more we have of one, the less we can have of the other.

These conflicts are not due to unfortunate circumstances pitting normally compossible values against each other. It is not as if we had to choose between our money and our life at the behest of an armed robber. For there is no inherent reason that would prevent the possession of both. Many conflicts among values, however, are inherent in the conflicting values, and when we face this type of conflict, a change in the surrounding circumstances cannot resolve the conflict. The choice forced on us by such conflicts need not be all-or-none. We can try to compromise and strike a balance. Whatever we do, however, it remains a fact of life that as we gain one of two conflicting values so we lose out on the other.

The sense of loss, therefore, is a frequent experience in our lives. It need not be due to our having made a choice that we come to regret. We often feel that we have lost something important even if we are convinced that we have made the right choice, and that if we had to, we would make the same one again. If the loss is accompanied by regret, the regret is about life being such as to exclude the realization of all the goods we value.[10]

The frequent conflicts we experience, however, are not only on account of possibilities we value, for morally deplorable possibilities may also conflict. It often happens that we have to choose between courses of action that morality prohibits. Overall commitment to a good life routinely requires us to choose the lesser of two evils. The choice is nevertheless between evils. We can hide the incompetence of an unfortunate colleague or we can worsen his misfortune. We can hypocritically defend our friend's inexcusable conduct or we can hasten her downfall. We can sacrifice innocent people for the common good or we can worsen the conditions upon which depends the welfare of people we are committed to protecting. We can lower standards by which performance is judged and thereby betray our responsibility or we can uphold the standards but endanger the context in which the standards may prevail. We can collaborate with unsavory people in power or we can withdraw and thereby remove yet another curb on their power.[11]

In each of these situations, the conflict forces on us the choice of a normally immoral course of action. We may claim that what we have done was the best under the wretched circumstances, yet the burden of having violated our moral convictions has still to be borne, even if it is lightened somewhat by the context in which the violation occurred. We would think ill of people who did not have scruples about doing the normally immoral thing they resolved they had to do. We may understand and even approve of a politician for telling a public lie, but it would be a sign of corruption if the politician did not mind having to do so.

[10] Conflict and consequent loss is a constant theme in the writings of contemporary pluralists. For some notable examples, see Stuart Hampshire, *Morality and Conflict* (Cambridge: Harvard University Press, 1983), chaps. 6 and 7; and Michael Stocker, *Plural and Conflicting Values* (Oxford: Clarendon Press, 1990), chaps. 4, 6, and 8.

[11] Much has been written recently about such conflicts under the description of moral dilemmas or situations involving dirty hands, a name derived from Sartre's play of the same name. See the anthology of representative writings and bibliography in Christopher Gowans, ed. *Moral Dilemmas* (New York: Oxford University Press, 1987); as well as Walter Sinnott-Armstrong, *Moral Dilemmas* (Oxford: Blackwell, 1988); and Stocker, *Plural and Conflicting Values*, chaps. 1 and 2. For a discussion of the plurality of values and conflicts in Aristotle, see Stocker, *Plural and Conflicting Values*, chap. 3, and William F. R. Hardie, *Aristotle's Ethical Theory* (Oxford: Clarendon Press, 1980), chap. 2.

The second step toward coming to appreciate the seriousness of the problem that conflicts present is to realize that it cannot be sidestepped by pointing out that all conceptions of a good life face conflicts. For the strength of the Socratic ideal and of other monistic conceptions is that there is implicit in them a method for resolving conflicts. The method is to choose between the conflicting values on the basis of their importance to the one and only reasonable conception of a good life. But if it is denied that there is such a conception, because there is a plurality of reasonable conceptions, then this method of conflict resolution becomes unavailable. If the plurality of values is taken seriously, then the conflict of values presents a major problem, and it is one from which monistic conceptions are free.

The deep source of the problem of conflict is to be found in the nature of values. Conflicts suggest that the values to which reasonable people may be reasonably committed may not form a harmonious system of compossible values. The values upon whose realization good lives depend may exclude each other. And if this is so, and the values are indeed reasonably prized as components of good lives, then their conflicts stand in the way of living according to them. This is why conflicts may present permanent adversities.

There are, of course, many different kinds of conflicts, so it is important to be clear about the kind that create permanent adversities. The relevant conflict is not between two or more persons, nor between individuals and institutions; it is not a clash between the contrary inclinations to pursue some value or to do instead something else or nothing; nor is it between means and ends, reason and passion, or good and evil. The source of the conflict is not some specific human weakness, vice, or ignorance; and it is not a concatenation of unfavorable circumstances either. The problem of conflict is not the problem of contingency.

The problem of conflict is created by the combination of three factors. First, we, acting as individual moral agents, reasonably commit ourselves to the realization of two values. Our commitment follows from our conception of a good life, and the conception is itself reasonable. Second, the two values to which we are thus committed are incompatible. Third, they are also incommensurable. The last two factors require explanation, the third more than the second.

The incompatibility of values is partly due to qualities intrinsic to the conflicting values. Because of these qualities, some values are so related as to make living according to one totally or proportionally exclude living according to the other. Habitual gourmandizing and asceticism are totally incompatible, while a lifelong commitment to political activism and solitude are proportionally so. The incompatibility of values, therefore, derives at least in part from the nature of the values, rather than from our attitude toward them. For the favorable attitude of some people toward both of the incompatible values does not make them compatible. Their compatibility depends also on whether or not the intrinsic qualities of the values exclude each other. But the intrinsic qualities of some values are only partly responsible for their incompatibility. Another part is contributed by human nature. It is only for beings like us that the intrinsic qualities of some values are incompatible. If gourmandizing did not give us pleasure, it would not be incompatible with asceticism. And if split personalities were normal for us, then we could combine solitude and political activism.

It is worth noting, if only in passing, that the incompatibility of values, created by the conjunction of qualities intrinsic to them and qualities intrinsic to human nature, constitutes a further reason for regarding at least some values as objective. For their incompatibility shows that prizing them is not merely a matter of having a favorable attitude toward them, but that we prize them also because our favorable attitudes are toward qualities intrinsic to the values which exist independently of our attitudes.

The problem of conflict would not be a serious matter if it were merely an indication that we are committed to two incompatible values. For, in that case, the conflict could be resolved by comparing the two values and deciding which is more important to realizing our conception of a good life. The added reason that makes the problem so intractable is that often there is no basis on which the conflicting values could be compared because they are incommensurable.

The basic idea of incommensurability is that there are some things so unlike as to exclude any reasonable comparison among them. Square roots and insults, planets and puns, canasta and the Supreme Court are utterly disparate, and they seem to exclude any common measure by which we could reasonably evaluate their comparative merits or demerits. This is rarely bothersome because there is rarely a need to compare them. It is otherwise, however, with values. It often happens that we are committed to incompatible values, and then it becomes important to compare them so that we could choose between them in a reasonable manner. But if incompatible values are also incommensurable—lacking in common measure—then the reasonable comparison of such values becomes problematic.

A more precise statement of incommensurability is that two or more values are incommensurable if and only if:[12]

   (a) there is not some one type of highest value or combination of values in terms of which all other values can be evaluated by consid-

---

[12] This account is indebted to Bernard Williams, "Conflicts of Values," in his *Moral Luck* (Cambridge: Cambridge University Press, 1981), 77–80, on which it draws, but from which it also departs.

ering how closely they approximate it; thus, there is no summum
bonum; happiness, for instance, is not it; and

(b) there is not some medium in terms of which all the different
types of values can be expressed and ranked without any significant aspects left out; thus, different types of values are not fungi-
ble; not all values can be expressed and ranked, for instance, in
terms of preference-satisfaction; and

(c) there is not some one principle or some principles which can
provide an order of precedence among all values and be acceptable to all reasonable people; thus, there is no canonical scheme
for ranking values; the greatest happiness principle, for instance,
is not adequate to this task.

It is crucial to understand that what incommensurability excludes is the
possibility of comparison which meets two requirements: it must be based
on characteristics intrinsic to the values being compared, and the result of
the comparison would have to be acceptable to all fully informed and reasonable people. Meeting the first requirement without the second would
lead to question-begging comparisons, for it would assume that a certain
ranking of values is the reasonable one, when that is precisely at issue. We
may compare the value of telling a painful truth to a friend with the value
of our friend's happiness by asking which would give more pleasure. But
of course whether pleasure is an appropriate basis of comparison is a matter of reasonable dispute.

Similarly, meeting the second requirement without the first would also
fail to yield what is needed. For even if, unlikely as it is, all reasonable people agreed to a particular ranking of two values, their agreement may
merely betoken a universally held human attitude, which may be independent of the respective intrinsic merits of the values in question. We
may all think that justice is more important than mercy, and we may all be
mistaken. In asserting the incommensurability of some values, therefore,
one is committed to denying that both requirements could be met simultaneously.

What makes this troubling from the moral point of view is that it often
happens that incommensurable values are also incompatible and conflicting. As a result, the values about whose ranking there are reasonable disagreements may also be values that we want to realize but cannot because
they totally or proportionally exclude each other. It is thus the coincidence
of the incommensurability and incompatibility of conflicting values that
creates a permanent adversity for our moral life.

What reasons are there, then, for regarding some values as incompatible
and incommensurable? The first reason derives from the nature of some

conflicts among values. If some values were not incompatible and incommensurable, then all conflicts among values should have a decisive resolution because reasonable people would recognize that the higher of the conflicting values is better and so it should be preferred. But, then, it would be unreasonable to feel a sense of loss or regret on account of having missed out on the lesser value. If, say, we thought that all values derived from their contribution to happiness, then we would simply choose the value that gave more happiness, and we would not regret having foregone lesser happiness, since what we want is greater happiness. Similarly, if there were a medium for comparing all values, such as money, then, by finding ourselves willing to pay more for one than for the other, we should have no qualms about having gotten the one for which we were prepared to pay more. And last, if we really believed in some scheme for ranking values, for instance, that duty comes first, then honor, and then country, then it would be a sign of infirm conviction to regret that honor requires us to tell some painful truth about our country. We may regret that there is a painful truth to tell, but we could not reasonably regret telling it, if we really thought that honor required it.[13]

But this is not how we respond to the conflicts we encounter. We do not believe that by choosing the better of two conflicting values we are somehow compensated for the loss of the other. And the explanation that makes the best sense of this belief of ours, and of the experience of loss and regret even about some of our most eminently reasonable choices, is that some values are incompatible and incommensurable. That is why the choice of one value may go hand in hand with our realistic estimate that it is unfortunate that we had to forego the other.

The second reason has to do with the historical failures of the numerous attempts to establish the compatibility and commensurability of values. These failures would have to be argued for in each case, but there is a general point that counts against all of them: while it may be reasonable to accept some particular ranking of values, it remains unreasonable to suppose that such a ranking could do justice to all the different types of values there are. We may decide to resolve conflicts by accepting the authority of some method of ranking, but such decisions are themselves evaluative because they exclude or demote values that fail to conform to the accepted authority. Rankings of this sort are consequently moral not simply in the sense that they have good lives as their subject matter, but in the further sense that they represent attempts to promote one conception of a good life over others. There need be nothing wrong with this, for it may be reasonable to accept such a ranking.

---

[13] For a discussion of this point, see Williams, "Moral Luck."

But the possibility of there being such a ranking does not show that the values ranked are not incompatible and incommensurable. What the ranking shows is that *either* the ranked values are not incompatible and incommensurable, *or* that, although they are incompatible and incommensurable, we still have to resolve conflicts between them in order to get on with life, even if the resolution involves the moral choice of favoring one conception of a good life over another. Only if the second alternative is eliminated is it reasonable to accept the first.

The weight of evidence, however, favors the second alternative over the first. That evidence is the frequency with which fundamental values conflict, the persistence of disagreements among fully informed and reasonable people about resolving some of these conflicts, and the failure of monistic attempts to defend a summum bonum, or the fungibility of values, or a canonical scheme of conflict resolution.

The type of conflict that creates a permanent adversity may then be identified as occurring for a person who is committed to two incompatible and incommensurable values. The reason why such conflicts constitute permanent adversities is that their occurrence calls into question the efficacy of the motivational force of our conceptions of a good life. If the values upon whose realization the goodness of our lives depends cannot be realized together, then no matter how virtuous we are in our efforts to realize them, we may fail. And the failure is not always attributable to contingency, or to our lack of virtue. The failure may be due to the incompatibility and incommensurability of the values we reasonably want. Conflicts of this kind, therefore, make us doubt the optimistic vision implicit in the Socratic ideal, as well as in many other monistic conceptions of a good life, that the chief obstacles to achieving them are human shortcomings. This vision is optimistic because it assumes the possibility of good lives and because it is able to point in the direction of improvement of our condition. If, however, the very possibility of good lives is open to doubt, and if even our best efforts may be unavailing, then conflicts present for us permanent adversities indeed.

EVIL AND HUMAN WICKEDNESS

The existence and frequency of evil is an unfortunate and central fact of human life.[14] No consideration of the nature and prospects of good lives can avoid, therefore, taking account of evil and offering some explanation of its source. Socrates' explanation is that evil is due to ignorance of the good. This is expressed in one of the Socratic paradoxes: No one

---

[14] The discussion in this section draws on Kekes, *Facing Evil*, chap. 1.

does evil knowingly. The thought behind it is that if we know what the good is, then we will act on our knowledge, since it would be irrational not to do what we can to bring about what we ourselves believe would be a desirable state of affairs.

This explanation was rejected in the previous chapter on the grounds that it overlooks the existence of motives that are either contrary to or contradictory of the motive to do what we know is good. Motives that may be contrary to the good are, for instance, jealousy, the desire for pleasure, resentment, and envy. They may on occasion conflict with the motivational force of our knowledge of the good, and they may be sufficiently powerful to override it. The motive that is contradictory of the motive to do good is to do evil. The two motives may coexist in us. Evil may come to dominate over the good, either habitually or episodically. If it does, we may knowingly and intentionally choose to do evil rather than good. These difficulties show that Socrates' earlier explanation of evil is much too simple.

The later Socrates, however, recognized the tripartite division of the soul, and he could thus account for the existence of motives contrary to the good. He allowed that evil actions need not stem from our ignorance of the good, since they may be motivated by the lower parts of the soul. These low motives may acquire such strength as to prevail over motives prompted by the highest part of the soul, which gives us knowledge of the good. The later Socrates was thus able to go much further than the earlier one in recognizing the complexity of human motivation. He could still insist that knowledge of the good is necessary for good actions, and yet deny his own earlier belief, which created the difficulties noted above, that knowledge of the good is also sufficient for good actions. But this still leaves the difficulty that knowledge of evil may motivate us in a way that is contradictory to and yet parallel to our knowledge of the good.

This is the background against which the importance of Aristotle's explanation of evil emerges. Aristotle distinguishes between three pairs of moral states. The paired states are contrasted with respect to their propensity to result in good or evil actions.[15] These states are superhuman virtue and brutishness, virtue and vice, and moral strength and moral weakness. The first pair may be ignored, since its contrasting states are rarely, if ever, to be found in normal human beings. The remaining four states may be distinguished with the aid of the following illustration:[16]

---

[15] Aristotle, *Nicomachean Ethics*, 1145a15–1145b21.
[16] This is an amended version of an illustration provided by John O. Urmson, *Aristotle's Ethics* (Oxford: Blackwell, 1988), 32.

AGENTS' STATES	MOTIVE	AGENTS' ACTION	AIM
VIRTUE	good	good	good
MORAL STRENGTH	evil	good	good
MORAL WEAKNESS	evil	evil	good
VICE	evil	evil	evil

In a virtuous state, agents have a good motive, which leads them to perform a good action, in order to achieve a good aim. In the state of moral strength, agents have an evil motive, but they overcome it and perform a good action, in order to achieve a good aim. In the state of moral weakness, agents have an evil motive, which they fail to overcome, and it leads them to perform an evil action, although they have a good aim, from which they are diverted. In a vicious state, agents have an evil motive, perform an evil action, in order to achieve an evil aim. By "wickedness" this last possibility is meant: the state of vice. One respect in which Aristotle's account is an improvement over Socrates' is that Aristotle's does, while Socrates' does not, leave room for wickedness. This aspect of Aristotle's thought has not been much remarked upon, so it is necessary to document it.

To begin with, Aristotle thinks that there are some people with "bad natures."[17] Such people are in a state "called wickedness simply," which may be contrasted with "wickedness not simply but with the qualification 'brutish'" (*NE* 1149a16–17). Brutishness is less evil than wickedness or vice because wicked people have a good part, which has been perverted, while brutish people have no good part (*NE* 1150a1–3). This means that brutish people cannot help being moved by evil motives, performing evil actions. and having evil aims because, lacking a better part, they are incapable of being otherwise. But wicked people act "in accordance with choice" (*NE* 1151a6); they are not like a city without laws, but "like a city that uses its laws, but has wicked laws to use" (*NE* 1152a24). For these reasons, "we do not forgive wickedness" (*NE* 1146a2).

Moreover, Aristotle does not think that wickedness is a rare state. He thinks that "most men tend to be bad—slaves to greed, and cowards in danger—it is, as a rule, a terrible thing to be at another man's mercy."[18] Because of their wickedness "men do wrong to others whenever they have the power to do it" (*Rhet.* 1382b9). And this wickedness is not the absence of goodness, but an end in itself (*Rhet.* 1364a31–33). "The wrongs a man does to others will correspond to the bad quality or quali-

[17] Aristotle, *Nicomachean Ethics*, 1148b18–19.
[18] Aristotle, *Rhetoric*, 1382b4–6.

ties that he himself possesses" (*Rhet.* 1368b14–15). Thus "the causes of our choosing harmful or wicked acts . . . are vice and . . . [wickedness]" (*Rhet.* 1368b12–13). And we may choose to do such acts "with knowledge and without constraint . . . [and] all chosen acts are done with knowledge—no one is ignorant of what he chooses" (*Rhet.* 1368b10–12). In this way, Aristotle rejects both the earlier Socratic view that no one does evil knowingly and the later one that knowledge of evil is not a source of motivation in competition with knowledge of the good. In fact, Aristotle goes further than merely acknowledging both good and evil as competing sources of motivation; he thinks that in many people wickedness dominates over goodness.

Against this view, however, there stands the central question, which lends such great force to the Socratic paradox: Why would people knowingly act to hinder what they themselves regard as good and to foster what they see as evil? What explanation could they give to themselves of their own wickedness? As a matter of moral psychology, how can the rejection of the Socratic paradox—no one does evil knowingly—be made plausible, given the obvious facts about how we function?

To these questions, there are two answers. The first applies only to a minority of agents, yet it is important because it establishes a possibility that shows the untenability of the Socratic approach to evil. The second applies to most cases of wickedness, but it assumes considerable complexity in human motivation, and it is unclear whether Socrates would find it acceptable.

The first answer takes at its face value Aristotle's view that in some people there is "wickedness simply." Such people may be identified as "moral monsters." Moral monsters make it a policy for themselves to acquire knowledge of evil, and they systematically choose to act on that knowledge. The psychological source fueling this policy may be violent hatred, passionate resentment, self-loathing projected outward, destructiveness, cynicism, and so forth. And the cause of these manifestations of misanthropy may be real or imagined injustice, profound dissatisfaction with oneself, lifelong brutalization, or extreme selfishness.

Moral monsters, however, are surely rare, probably rarer than moral saints, who follow the same policy, except that the saints' knowledge and choices have the good as their object. Moral monsters are likely to be rarer than moral saints because monsters not only have to have as clear vision, great strength of character, and exceptionally strong sense of purpose as saints do, but they must also hide from others their true nature, since public opinion is generally disposed to favor the good. Being a moral monster is very difficult, and so few people can be supposed to succeed, if that is the word, in becoming monstrous and in continuing in the same state. It would be quite implausible, therefore, to attribute the existence and frequency of the evil we encounter in our daily life to these rare few moral monsters. Many people certainly are wicked, but not simply wicked. Nevertheless, the mere existence of a single moral monster is sufficient to establish what Socrates denies, namely, that evil can stand as a source of motivation that competes with and parallels the good.

The second answer does not take Aristotle's "wickedness simply" at its face value, but endeavors to interpret it by placing it in a wider context. The interpretation proceeds from the considerably more plausible view that human motives are mixed and that we are complex beings. We are moved by the good, but we are also moved by evil. Our virtues coexist and conflict with our vices. The inner life of the overwhelming majority of us is a struggle in which confused motives, lack of self-knowledge, defective judgment, inflated sense of self-importance, fantasy, fear, greed, as well as love, decency, pity, and a sense of justice are the soldiers of the ignorant armies clashing in the dark. The sources of evil are such people: wicked in some ways and in some circumstances, virtuous in others; people like most of us. We are therefore the agents of evil, and of the good, and we act one way or another, depending on our imperfect knowledge, mixed motives, unclear aims, and on the pressures exerted on us by the historical, political, cultural, and other forces to which we are subject.

Unlike moral monsters, however, agents who do evil in this second way do not adopt the pursuit of evil as a conscious and deliberate policy. They certainly do evil, but they disguise its nature from themselves. In a sense, they know what evil is because they can recognize it in others and may be brought retrospectively to recognize it even in themselves. Moreover, they choose their evil actions, since they perform them voluntarily in circumstances where they could act otherwise. But they do not see their actions as evil.

Something intrudes between their general knowledge of evil and their recognition of their own actions as falling under it. Their own cruelty is seen by them as justice, selfishness as claiming their due, hatred as just condemnation, envy as commitment to equality, or fanaticism as being principled. They know that cruelty, selfishness, hatred, envy, and fanaticism are evil, but they do not know that their own actions exemplify these evils. And they do not know it because they foster or allow something in themselves that prevents them from seeing the true nature of their own conduct.

This something may be self-deception, fantasy, egocentrism, a deep sense of inferiority or superiority, or any one of the numerous ruses by which we are led, or lead ourselves, to lose objectivity. Some of us act in this way habitually and predictably, others only episodically. In the former case, the agents are wicked; in the latter, they are merely prone to act wickedly in some circumstances. The fact of the matter is, however, that the vast majority of the evil that besets us is attributable to this source, rather than to rare moral monsters.

The answer to the Socratic question of whether these agents do evil knowingly must be that in one sense they do, but in another they do not. It is idle to speculate whether the sense in which they do would have been acceptable to Socrates, for if he had developed the complex moral psychology that allows for this sense, then we would be putting the question to a philosopher other than the one we celebrate under the name of Socrates. It is worth noting parenthetically that this thought may contribute to understanding the reasons behind Aristotle's ambivalence toward his distinguished predecessor.

From now on in this book, "wickedness" will be understood to be this second kind. The wickedness, that is, of those many agents who knowingly and intentionally perform evil actions, although they do not realize that their actions are evil. They know in general what evil is, but that general knowledge is not brought to bear on the particular case that is constituted of their own conduct.[19] This kind of wickedness is to be distinguished from the kind moral monsters have, who also possess general knowledge of evil, but, in addition to it, they know as well that the particular actions they intentionally perform are evil. Indeed, they perform them because they are evil. Since moral monsters are rare, they will not figure prominently in subsequent arguments.

One vexing question about frequently occurring wickedness has to do with the moral responsibility of their agents for their evil actions. They certainly cause evil, but there is a sense in which they do not know that it is evil they cause. Their moral responsibility, therefore, depends, at least in part, on whether they could or should have had the knowledge they lack. Or, to put the same point in different words, the question is whether their ignorance is culpable.

The knowledge, or its lack, in question is self-knowledge. That is what agents lack who deceive themselves, who confuse their fantasies with reality, who fail to recognize their own egocentrism and feelings of inferiority or superiority, or who mistake the external pressures to which they succumb for their own inclinations. Moral responsibility for wickedness, therefore, depends on the answer to the question of how much self-knowledge could or should a wicked agent have or on how much ignorance of themselves is excusable. To this question, however, there can be no gen-

---

[19] This kind of wickedness is made famous by Hannah Arendt's description of it under the label of "the banality of evil"; she took it to be personified by Eichmann. See Hannah Arendt, *Eichmann in Jerusalem: A Report on the Banality of Evil* (New York: Viking, 1964).

eral answer. The correct answer depends, in each case, on the character, history, and circumstances of the particular agent about whose conduct the question is raised.[20]

This finally leads back to the reason for discussing wickedness in the present context. Evil is a permanent adversity handicapping the pursuit of a good life. A very great deal of evil is due to human wickedness, whose source is lack of self-knowledge. But the amount of self-knowledge we have depends on our character, history, and circumstances, and it is an open question how much control we have over them. Our character is partly shaped by our genetic inheritance, which may or may not enrich us with the intelligence, temperament, motivation, and strength required for the cultivation of self-knowledge. Our personal history is strongly influenced by the conduciveness of our society, family, and upbringing to the development of self-knowledge. And our economic, social, and political circumstances—whether or not we live in peace, prosperity, or revolution, whether or not the powers over us are intrusive, dictatorial, or intolerant, whether or not the educational system aims at indoctrination, whether or not the possibilities of life open to us are numerous or few—may also exert formative pressures on us to foster or hinder our growth in self-knowledge.

The extent of our self-knowledge, therefore, is often beyond our control. And, as a result, so is much of our wickedness and the resulting evil we cause. Evil and wickedness, however, are obstacles to living a good life. The extent to which we lack control over these obstacles is yet another indication that doing the best we can to live a good life is not sufficient for achieving it because, in addition to contingency and conflict, evil is yet another permanent adversity we must face.

CONCLUSION

There are three closely related respects in which the discussion of permanent adversities deepens the understanding of moral wisdom. The first concerns the nature of the knowledge moral wisdom gives. It was argued in Chapter 1 that moral wisdom differs from both philosophical and practical wisdom. The latter two should not be viewed as yielding two different kinds of knowledge; they are, rather, two different ways of arriving at knowledge needed for living a good life. Aristotle thought that philosophical wisdom provides knowledge "about things that cannot be otherwise," while practical wisdom does so "about what can be otherwise."[21]

---

[20] For an excellent discussion of this topic, see Joel Kupperman, *Character* (New York: Oxford University Press, 1991), esp. chap. 3.

[21] Aristotle, *Nicomachean Ethics*, 1140b27.

Philosophical wisdom is knowledge of first principles and causes, while practical wisdom is knowledge of the human good. But our knowledge of permanent adversities cuts across this distinction. For it reveals that our being subject to contingency, conflict, and evil cannot be otherwise, and yet knowing this has the highest importance for the human good. Furthermore, although permanent adversities are among the first principles and causes, what they are first principles and causes of are human good and evil. Our knowledge of permanent adversities, therefore, is part of moral wisdom, and it is a part that brings closer together the philosophical and practical aspects of wisdom that Aristotle kept apart.

The second respect in which the discussion of permanent adversities bears on moral wisdom concerns the reflexivity of moral wisdom. Socrates supposed that moral wisdom's knowledge of the good is self-knowledge, which we reach by elenctic examination. This knowledge enables us to control the shortcomings which hinder our pursuit of good lives. Not even perfect self-knowledge can be sufficient for moral wisdom, however, because the goodness of our lives depends also on conditions external to us, and moral wisdom requires knowledge of them as well. Knowledge of permanent adversities is knowledge of conditions external to us, whose significance is that they hinder our pursuit of good lives. This is part of the reason why Socratic self-knowledge is not an adequate account of the knowledge moral wisdom provides. Permanent adversities are conditions beyond our shortcomings which we need to try to learn about and control.

Yet knowledge of permanent adversities is not entirely distinct from self-knowledge. It is knowledge of conditions external to us, but it is also reflexive because the conditions external to us are also internal to us. Contingency, conflict, and evil are objective features of the world. It is a fact that what happens to us often has nothing to do with our merits, that the values to which we are reasonably committed often exclude each other, and that human wickedness destroys good lives. But it is also a fact that these regrettable facts are often brought about by human agency, and that human agency includes ourselves. Knowledge of permanent adversities shows, therefore, not only that we are subject to these external conditions, but also that we ourselves are often among the agents who produce the conditions which in turn produce the regrettable facts. If we learn through moral wisdom that we are not only potential victims of permanent adversities but also their potential agents, then we shall have understood that increasing our control over them requires us to exert such efforts as we can both internally—reflexively—and externally.

The third respect in which the discussion of permanent adversities connects with moral wisdom is through the motivation and the control we need to live a good life. Knowledge of permanent adversities shows that our control is insufficient to guarantee that we shall achieve a good life if we conduct ourselves virtuously. Moral wisdom helps us face and cope with this truth about our condition. Permanent adversities, however, are not due to shortcomings that could be eliminated from our lives. Contingency, conflict, and evil are unavoidable features of human existence. If we face this fact and endeavor to cope with it, we must realize that moral wisdom must do more than motivate us to live according to our conception of a good life and redouble our efforts to remedy our shortcomings. To be sure, such efforts are unlikely to be wasted, since our shortcomings are numerous. Not even the most virtuous of these efforts, however, can eliminate permanent adversities, since their sources are not our shortcomings. We must look to moral wisdom, therefore, not only for motivation but also for control. Our efforts should not be directed merely at trying to ameliorate permanent adversities, but also at trying to control our reaction to the realization that we are going to remain subject to contingency, conflict, and evil, and that nothing we can do will free us from that subjection. Moral wisdom teaches us that although we need external goods to live a good life, whether we have them is a contingent matter; that good lives require the satisfaction of a plurality of values, but these values conflict and their conflicts often cannot be resolved without serious loss; and that we want to live a good life, but unintentional and nonconscious evil stands in the way.

If we resolve to face this fact in the right way, then we shall want moral wisdom to guide us in two directions: toward strengthening the motivational force of our conception of a good life and toward preventing us from reacting inappropriately to the realization that permanent adversities will unavoidably stand in the way. To succeed in this is to ameliorate permanent adversities by reducing the scope they have in our lives. What we can do to this end is the subject of the rest of the book.

Judgment and Control

$\mathbf{M}$oral wisdom is composed of a conception of a good life and the knowledge, evaluation, and judgment required for living according to it. The knowledge is of good and evil as they affect ourselves and of the conditions, permanent and changing, that form the context within which we must do what we can to live according to our conception of a good life. The objects of our knowledge of good and evil are thus our character, permanent adversities, and the possibilities and limits set by the historical, social, political, and economic realities surrounding us. The evaluation involves viewing particular aspects of our character, the actual contingencies, conflicts, and evil we face, the concrete opportunities we have, and the specific restrictions placed upon us in the light of our conception of a good life.

This kind of evaluation, however, is frequently difficult because it presupposes an accurate description of the yet to be evaluated situations, and many, perhaps most, situations lend themselves to several alternative and apparently reasonable descriptions. Once we have an accurate description, the subsequent evaluation is often a simple matter. But there is no routine, rule-governed method, no formalizable technique, for getting the descriptions right. Nor is there a method or technique for coping with the variety of ways in which contingency renders uncertain the knowledge we have to rely on, conflict makes us question the values to which we are committed, and unconscious and unintentional evil forces us to suspect the motives of both ourselves and others. This is why we need judgment. Through it, we transform complex moral situations into simple ones. Simple moral situations are easily describable; our knowledge of their constituents is adequate; and our evaluations of them readily follow from our conceptions of a good life. As a result, what we ought to do in simple moral situations is obvious. This sense of obviousness is one of the most desirable benefits of moral wisdom. To be morally wise is to find simple the moral situations that others find complex. And while the same can be said of being foolish, there is a deep difference: the morally wise have overcome the complexities, while the foolish are not aware of them.

Most of us are neither morally wise nor foolish. In our middling state, we perhaps wish for the good judgment moral wisdom would provide, but we fall more or less short of it, and the realization that this is so is itself a matter of judgment. The way to moral wisdom is to endeavor to fall less short, by making our judgments better, and that involves increasing our control. The process requires enlarging the area of our lives that we can order so as to conform to our conception of a good life. It is a process of shaping ourselves to become the person our conception requires. And it depends both on the motivation to conform to the ideal embodied in the guiding conception and on controlling to the extent we can the adversities we encounter along the way. The aim of this chapter is to provide a general account of how control is possible. In subsequent chapters, the general account will be made less general and more concrete.

THE PROBLEM OF CONTROL

The extent to which we have control is the extent to which we approximate the Socratic ideal of self-sufficiency. Total control would be to be completely self-sufficient. This is an ideal state, and it is not to be expected that we reach it; our moral growth consists in approximating it. It is a state in which we are masters of our character and circumstances. We know what we desire; we know that it is good; and we live so as to achieve it. Our knowledge, desires, capacities, and values, in a word, our characters, are what we consciously decided they should be. Our lives, therefore, are shaped by self-direction, and not by external influences. And even if we act according to external or internal influences which we have not created, we act according to them because we have evaluated them and assigned to them a place in our conception of a good life.[1]

Part of the significance of permanent adversities is that they appear to demonstrate the futility of this ideal. Contingency, conflict, and evil seem to

---

[1] The aspiration toward this ideal state has been well expressed by Isaiah Berlin: "I wish my life and decisions to depend on myself, not on external forces of whatever kind. I wish to be an instrument of my own, not of other men's acts of will. I wish to be . . . moved by reasons, by conscious purposes, which are my own, not by causes which affect me, as it were, from outside. I wish to be a doer, . . . deciding, not being decided for, self-directed, and not acted upon by external nature." Isaiah Berlin, *Four Essays on Liberty* (Oxford: Oxford University Press, 1969), 131.

be unavoidable obstacles to moral growth conceived in this manner. They stand between virtuous and good lives in the form of hostile external influences, which may render even the most reasonable and morally praiseworthy of our efforts unavailing. They are also responsible for our internal conditions, which make it doubtful that this ideal of control can even be approximated, let alone achieved. The reason for the latter difficulty is that permanent adversities pervade not only the world outside of us, but also our own selves. Contingency affects our character because the knowledge, desires, capacities, and values we have or lack are often due to accidents of heredity and upbringing; conflict is a product of the values to which we ourselves are committed; and evil, at least in its unconscious and unintended form, permeates our own desires, just as much as it does those of other people. Permanent adversities, therefore, are not only external influences, often too powerful for us to overcome, but also internal ones. These internal influences jeopardize the only way we have of increasing control, because they make our efforts to increase control subject to forces beyond our control.

To appreciate exactly how the problem of control arises, it is necessary to be more precise in describing the necessary and sufficient conditions for control. For the sake of simplicity, the description is framed in terms of a single action, performed by a normal mature human being, in ordinary circumstances. Once a description of when such an action is in the control of its agent is available, it can be easily generalized to patterns of controlled actions, and thus to character traits.

The natural state to begin with is a desire. We want something in the belief that, in some sense, it would be good to have it. "Desire" is to be understood in the widest possible sense. Its object may be to have or to do something, or to avoid or to refrain from doing it; it may be pleasure, our own or someone else's, or it may be revenge, justice, a good insect repellent, death, dishonor to an enemy, recognition, a quick lunch, anonymity, wealth, or some combination of these and similar human goals. The desire may be very strong or quite weak, deeply serious or trivial; it may involve a long-term project, requiring planning, stages, and much application, or it may be a fleeting impulse, soon forgotten, whether satisfied or not. Its satisfaction may be a matter of life and death, or it may be a dispensable frivolity.

We may or may not be aware of having the desire. Correspondingly, the belief that its satisfaction would be good may or may not be conscious or articulate. We may hold the belief only in the weak sense that our actual or potential action is or would be such as to make the ascription of the belief to us reasonable. And, although the belief is that the satisfaction of the desire would be good, the good need not be a positive benefit. It could be the lesser of two harms, or, for that matter, the lesser of two benefits. We need not desire the best, not even what we believe is the best. Moreover, we may be mistaken in our belief that the satisfaction of the desire would be good. Such mistakes can occur because what we take to be the benefit or the harm associated with the desire need not be actually beneficial or harmful. Understood in this way, then, "desire" includes wishes, whims, wants, needs, impulses, aspirations, efforts, inclinations, and so forth, provided they conform to the description just provided.

The satisfaction of desires partly depends on our having the capacity to satisfy them. We may range desires along a continuum at one end of which there are largely inborn physiological desires, while at the other are largely acquired desires formed by our individual and cultural circumstances. The evolutionary process can be relied on to supply us with the capacity to satisfy the desires close to the physiological end of the continuum, but there is no similar source to which we can look to endow us with the capacity to satisfy desires formed by our personal idiosyncrasies and cultural context. Yet without the capacity to satisfy it, a desire is doomed to frustration. It may, however, be doomed anyway because it is also necessary that we should have the opportunity to exercise the capacity we possess. We may say, therefore, that control requires having, first, a desire, second, the capacity to satisfy it, and third, the opportunity to do so.

Although these conditions are necessary, they are not sufficient for control. We often have desires we cannot help having, and these desires may be so strong as to be virtually irresistible. In many cases, however, if it were in our power not to have such a desire, we would certainly rid ourselves of it. If we satisfy a very strong and unwanted desire of this kind, the action may still not be in our control, even though the conditions of having a desire and the capacity and the opportunity to satisfy it are met. The most obvious cases in point are desires for drugs to which we are addicted; other examples are desires we regard as evil, obsessive, or shameful.

This consideration points in the direction where an additional condition necessary for control may be found. It is a fact about our ordinary functioning as normal and mature adults that we have a large number of desires during some fixed period of time, such as a day or a week. Of these desires, only a fraction is satisfied, and yet we do not, on that account, exist in a state of frustration. To be sure, we may be frustrated; if we are, however, it is not merely because we have unsatisfied desires, but because we regard it as important that the unsatisfied desires should be satisfied. It is part of our normal functioning that we encourage the satisfaction of some of our desires and discourage the satisfaction of others. This point may be put by saying that we routinely evaluate our desires, and our subsequent actions may or may not reflect these evaluations.

Our evaluations need not involve a deliberate, articulate, quasi-judicial proceeding. It may be nothing more than a quick, intuitive, routine approval or disapproval. No doubt, such unreflective evaluations are made possible by our past experiences, education, including moral education, and the facility with which we have learned to take stock of our circumstances. The evaluations, of course, may also involve a great deal of soul-searching and questioning of our priorities. What matters for our present purposes, however, is that we routinely evaluate very many of our desires; how much thinking goes into these evaluations, and how good that thinking is, is not yet of concern.

The additional condition necessary for control then is that the desire that we act to satisfy should have been favorably evaluated by us. Actions prompted by unevaluated or adversely evaluated desires are, of course, possible, but they are not controlled by us. We perform these actions because the desires are so strong that they override adverse evaluation, or because for any one of a variety of reasons we are ignorant of the desires that prompt them. Such actions are caused by addictive cravings, brainwashing, posthypnotic suggestion, stupidity, self-deception, unwillingness to face the truth about oneself, or various forms of mental illness. By contrast, if we are aware of having a desire, have the capacity and the opportunity to satisfy it, and if we have favorably evaluated it, then, it may be thought, the resulting action intended to satisfy the desire is in our control.

According to this way of thinking, we are in control of our actions insofar as we identify with the desires that prompt them.[2] If the occasion or the need arose, requiring us to be reflective and articulate about our favorable evaluation, we would say that we want to be, or at least that we do not mind being, the sort of person who aims to satisfy that sort of a desire. We may not be consciously engaged in forming our character, nonetheless it is being formed, and we could or would say upon reflection that we approve of the way in which its formation is proceeding.[3]

[2] A number of important and suggestive works have been published recently exploring the implications of this idea. See, for example, Harry G. Frankfurt, "Freedom of the Will and the Concept of a Person," in *The Importance of What We Care About* (Cambridge: Cambridge University Press, 1988); Charles Taylor, "Responsibility for Self," in *The Identities of Persons*, ed. Amélie Rorty (Berkeley: University of California Press, 1976); Gary Watson, "Free Agency," in *Free Will* (Oxford: Oxford University Press, 1982); and Susan Wolf, *Freedom within Reason* (New York: Oxford University Press, 1991). A representative collection is Gary Watson, ed., *Free Will* (Oxford: Oxford University Press, 1982); another useful anthology, with a bibliography, is John M. Fischer, ed., *Moral Responsibility* (Ithaca: Cornell University Press, 1986).

[3] "We are spinning our fates, good and evil, and never to be undone. Every smallest stroke of virtue or of vice leaves its never so little scar. . . . [We] may not count it; but it is being counted none the less. Down among . . . [our] nerve cells and fibres the molecules are counting it, registering and storing it up to be used against . . . [us] when the next temptation comes. Nothing we ever do is . . . wiped out. Of course, this has its good side as well as its bad one. As we become permanent drunkards by so many separate drinks, so we become saints . . . by so many acts." William James, *Psychology: Briefer Course* (New York: Henry Holt, 1922), 150.

This identification or, as the case may be, rejection, proceeding by way of our evaluation of our desires, is, of course, a second-order activity. Its aim is not to satisfy a particular desire, but to decide whether a particular desire should be satisfied. The decision is based on the evaluation of the desire in the light of the standard set by our conception of a good life. We approve or disapprove of the desire, and we act to satisfy or to suppress it, not merely because the desire is what it is, but also because the desire is aiding or hindering our development of the character we wish to have. And we wish it because our conception of a good life calls for it.

Before discussing why this condition is still not sufficient for control, it is worth pointing out that the notion of second-order evaluation, and the consequent identification with or rejection of a desire, is, if not derived from, then readily compatible with the later Socrates' tripartite division of the soul. The desires we evaluate are in the lowest, appetitive, part of the soul, where they clamor for satisfaction. We are in control, according to this model, if we decide which of these desires are to be satisfied, and if that decision is based on the evaluation of the desires by the highest, rational, part of the soul. These evaluations are not always as effective as they should be, because the middle part of the soul, the emotive and imaginative part, may strengthen or weaken the wrong desires, and thus move us against our better judgment. But if feelings and imagination are properly directed by reasonable considerations, then the joint forces of the two higher parts of our soul are sufficient to subdue unruly desires. When we act to satisfy a desire, and our action is supported by the favorable second-order evaluation of the first-order desire, then we can be said to be in control of the action.

The Socratic ideal, however, fails to take into account the seriousness of the extent to which permanent adversities undermine the possibility of control. The attempt to remedy this defect through second-order evaluation cannot succeed because contingency, conflict, and evil permeate second-order evaluations in precisely the same way as they do first-order evaluations. The problem second-order evaluation was supposed to solve is that the desires, capacities, and opportunities we have are often not in our control. The contingencies of our genetic inheritance and individual history, the conflicts that make our values incapable of joint realization, and the evil in us of which we are not aware often shape what desires we regard as important and try to satisfy, what capacities we have and develop, and what opportunities we recognize and seize. It was as a way of overcoming this lack of control that the importance of second-order evaluation was stressed. Through it, we were to eliminate or minimize permanent adversities by making us aware of the contingency, conflict, and evil we face, and through that awareness evaluate our desires, capacities, and opportunities, and thus assume control over them. The guiding thought behind this attempt to assume control is not to deny the prevalence of permanent adversities, but to provide a way of coping with them. And that way depends on rising to a level above them, in order to ask and answer the question of how we can best live in accordance with our conception of a good life, given that contingency, conflict, and evil stand in the way.

The difficulty is that as we rise to the higher level, we cannot leave permanent adversities behind. *We* rise to that level, and permanent adversities are *in us*, as well as outside of us. It is human agency that is permeated by contingency, conflict, and evil; consequently no efforts of ours could succeed in getting rid of them. The endeavor to rise to the level from which second-order evaluations could be made is also dependent, therefore, on our having the desire, capacity, and opportunity to do so, and they are just as much subject to contingency, conflict, and evil as the desires, capacities, and opportunities are on the lower level we are endeavoring to transcend.

It must be concluded, therefore, that the combination of the four necessary conditions discussed so far—having a desire, and the capacity, as well as the opportunity, to satisfy it, and having favorably evaluated the desire—is still not sufficient for the ascription of control. The reason why it falls short is that, due to permanent adversities, we often lack control over the amount of control we have. This creates a very serious difficulty because it is beginning to look as if no additional condition could supply what is needed. For whatever further condition is proposed, it would have to involve us in doing something to achieve control, but whatever that may be will be as subject to permanent adversities as second-order evaluations and as first-order desires, capacities, and opportunities are. The problem of control, therefore, is a problem indeed.[4]

EASING THE PROBLEM OF CONTROL

The problem of control is intimately connected with the problem created by the conflict, or the appearance of a conflict, between free will and determinism. This latter problem is one of the most intractable philosophical problems. The three traditional attempts to solve it—determinism, libertarianism, and compatibilism—keep being restated by each philosophical generation. The arguments and counterarguments are advanced in increasingly sophisticated forms, as the available logical and analytical techniques grow more refined. It would be generally conceded, nevertheless, that we are no closer to a widely accepted solution than we

---

[4] For a parallel argument, see Wolf, *Freedom within Reason*, chap. 2.

were fifty, one hundred, or two hundred years ago. Progress is made only by strengthening weak arguments, but that progress is made by all parties to the debate.

In the light of this, the approach here adopted may perhaps be regarded with some measure of sympathy. It is to sidestep the free will versus determinism issue, and the vocabulary in which it is couched, in order to approach the problem of control from another angle. The discussion, therefore, will proceed without references to scholarly literature.[5] To do otherwise would be to go back to the controversy, the arguments, and the vocabulary we are trying to leave behind. This approach, of course, has the implication that even if it succeeds in saying something of worth about the problem of control, the bearing of that on the free will versus determinism issue will be unclear. On balance, it seems, however, that that is a price worth paying. Armed with these caveats, let us now see what can be done to ease, if not to solve, the problem of control.

It must be said at once that if the problem of control is taken to be the problem of achieving total control, that is, achieving control over the amount of control we have, then the problem is unsolvable. We cannot control all the influences affecting us. Not even the greatest possible control in the present can escape having been subject to uncontrolled influences in the past. The further back we go in the life of any one of us, the more influences will there be over which we have no control. These uncontrolled influences affect the amount of control we have, and they are ineliminable.

The problem of control, however, is not the problem of achieving total control; it is not whether we can gain control over all that influences what we are and do. The problem is whether it is possible to *increase* the control we have. And we can do that even if we acknowledge, as it is reasonable to do, that no one can ever have total control.

What needs to be done to increase our control is neither mysterious, nor, in the normal course of events, beyond human capacity. Suppose that we, acting as normal and mature agents in ordinary circumstances, meet the four necessary conditions of control: we have a desire, we have the capacity and the opportunity to satisfy it, and we favorably evaluate the desire. We arrive at the judgment that the satisfaction of a particular desire is at least consistent with, and perhaps even called for, by our conception of a good life. The reason why the combination of these conditions is insufficient for control is that the judgment may seem acceptable to us only be-

---

[5] There must, however, be one exception. The writings of Stuart Hampshire have fundamentally influenced the present approach, and this is hereby gratefully acknowledged. See in particular Stuart Hampshire, *Thought and Action* (London: Chatto & Windus, 1960) and *Freedom of the Individual* (Princeton: Princeton University Press, 1975).

cause permanent adversities have influenced us in certain ways. If the contingencies of our life were different, if the conflicts among our values could be eliminated, if we were not moved by unconscious and unintended evil desires, then our judgment would be different. This makes obvious what we must do to increase our control. We must, first, become aware of the possibility that our judgment may be influenced by permanent adversities, then, second, endeavor to find out whether it is influenced by them, and then, last, do what we can to free our judgment from their influence.[6]

To take these steps, we need to focus on the psychological processes through which permanent adversities may influence us. Crucial to this is to find ways of identifying and surmounting obstacles that weaken our control, rather than to look for some way in which we could further strengthen our control. We should, therefore, ask: What, if anything, prevents us from focusing on the possibility that a judgment we have arrived at in the appropriate way may not be reasonable? And if we find that something does prevent us, then we should ask: What, if anything, can we do to counteract its influence? Typical obstacles to doing either are inattention, fear, laziness, weakness, fantasy, or strong desires. Improving our judgment and thereby increasing our control depends on trying to overcome these obstacles.

Suppose, then, that we reflect on the possibility that a particular judgment of ours may not be reasonable, and we form the view that it is, or that while it was not, we have corrected it, and now it is. The nature of this kind of reflection (simply "reflection" from now on) is a complicated matter, which will be discussed in detail beginning with the next chapter. But something needs to be said here, at least in general terms, to give some content to the notion of reflection. The aim of reflection is to increase our control by overcoming obstacles in the way of our judgment.[7] These obstacles may be external or internal. Their discussion will begin by focusing

---

[6] "It is through the various degrees of self-consciousness in action, through more and more clear and explicit knowledge of what I am doing, that in the first place I become comparatively free, free in the sense that my achievements either directly correspond to my intentions, or are attributable to my incompetence or powerlessness in execution. . . . A man becomes more and more a free and responsible agent the more he at all times knows what he is doing, in every sense of this phrase, and the more he acts with a definite and formed intention. He is in this sense less free the less his actual achievements . . . correspond to any clearly formed intention of his own." Hampshire, *Thought and Action*, 177.

[7] "Knowledge of the factors that have been influencing my conduct without my knowledge does in itself open up to me new possibilities of action. The mere recognition of a causal correlation between my behaviour and some external conditions is the recognition of the change that would be necessary for the behaviour to be different in the future, even if the change cannot now be achieved by any decision of mine." Hampshire, *Thought and Action*, 190.

on internal obstacles, which prevent us from judging reasonably whether a particular desire of ours should be satisfied, given our conception of a good life. These internal obstacles may be due to the influence of permanent adversities on our character and circumstances. Through reflection, then, we consider the reasonability of our judgments.

Reflection has three modes: moral imagination, self-knowledge, and moral depth. Moral imagination enlarges our field of possibilities. It provides a wider range of values and a better understanding of them than we initially possessed. It makes it thus possible to transcend the obstacles contingency, conflict, and evil present to approximating our conception of a good life. Self-knowledge transforms our character. It brings us to understand the springs of our actions and it motivates us to strengthen or weaken them in the light of our conception of a good life. It enables us to identify and to do what we can to counter the influence of permanent adversities upon our life. Moral depth acquaints us with the limits we must acknowledge and the limits which only appear to curtail us. It helps us face and understand the extent to which we are subject to permanent adversities and the extent to which we can overcome them.

The three modes of reflection, then, have the common aim of improving our judgments. Judgments become more reasonable as they are better able to assess how, given our character and circumstances, we can approximate our conception of a good life. And what makes that possible is the identification and the amelioration of the internal obstacles, the most serious of them being permanent adversities.

In the light of this, a fifth condition necessary for control may be added to the previous four: the judgment we make to satisfy a desire must pass the test of reflection. The test involves determining whether the judgment was made without the interference of the sort of internal obstacles indicated above, or, if some internal obstacles had been present, determining whether they have been sufficiently overcome to free the judgment from them.

These five conditions unite two central features of the proposed approach to the problem of control. The first is to interpret the problem of control as that of increasing control. Part of the significance of this interpretation is that it provides a readily defensible starting point for the present approach, in contrast with those of its competitors'. It begins where we are, in the middle of living our lives. The common human experience is that we want to have more control over how we live. We are constrained by limits, and we strain against them. There is, therefore, a natural and spontaneous impetus for trying to increase our control. The opportunity to do so will appeal to everyone, in normal circumstances. It requires no metaphysical commitments to have a vested interest in the subject.

If the problem of control is interpreted differently, then the alternatives are unavoidably handicapped by a controversial starting point. If that point is an ideal state of control, such as total self-direction, or control over the external forces acting on us, or some part of ourselves that is not subject to natural necessity, then it is not possible even to begin to try to consider how the ideal state could be approximated because it will rightly be suspected of incoherence. Alternatively, the starting point may be the picture of the world science gives us, and then we wonder how we fit into that picture. How could we have any control, if the world is as science tells us it is? The answer must deny either the scientific world view or our capacity for control, but one of these denials is as implausible as the other. In neither case can we actually begin to increase our control because the starting point of the required effort taxes our credulity. But if the starting point is where we are, and if we aspire only to the modest goal of increasing our control in certain particular ways, without aiming at an ideal state or at escaping from nature, then we can be quite realistic about the small steps we need to take to achieve what we want, and we can eschew dubious metaphysical commitments.

There is a suggestive analogy between the effort to increase our control and the effort to reform our society. There are two unpromising approaches to social reform. One is to try to improve the status quo by trying to approximate an ideal state. The other is to try to improve existing arrangements by trying to free us from all organized arrangements. But just as piecemeal reform is a vastly preferable *via media* between the unattractive extremes of Utopianism and anarchism, so increasing our control is a *via media* between libertarianism and determinism.

The second significant feature of the present approach to the problem of control is that it recognizes two different types of conditions as necessary for increasing our control. The first four necessary conditions concern what is reasonable to do, while the fifth concerns what is reasonable not to do. Conforming to the first four conditions answers the question of whether a particular desire of ours that could be satisfied should be satisfied from the point of view of our conception of a good life. Conforming to the fifth condition makes it possible to cope with internal obstacles, many of which are created by permanent adversities. The first four conditions involve judging what we ought to do to bridge the gap between where we are and where we want to be. The fifth condition obliges us to direct our reflection inward in order to correct some defect in ourselves. In the normal course of events, all five are necessary.

Suppose that all of this is acceptable. Can it be concluded then that the five necessary conditions are jointly sufficient to justify the ascription of control to an agent whose action conforms to them? It cannot be, because not all obstacles are internal. Even if all internal obstacles were overcome, there would remain external obstacles to the satisfaction of our desires. Permanent adversities affect us not only internally, but also externally. Contingency, in the form of accidents, conflict, in the form of social instability, and evil, in the form of injustice, may doom us to frustration even if our internally directed control were as good as it needs to be.

Furthermore, even if the external obstacles are ignored and the five conditions are regarded as jointly sufficient for control, it would still have to be concluded that no one could be said to have control because not all internal obstacles can be overcome. Permanent adversities not only create internal obstacles, they also affect the capacities we need to overcome them. The intelligence, emotional balance, strength of will, and so forth required for overcoming internal obstacles through reflection may simply be lacking, or may be present but insufficient.

The conditions needed, however, are not of control, but of increasing control. The considerations just adduced establish that there are formidable, perhaps decisive, obstacles to increasing our control in some ways. Yet we can still increase our control in other ways: internally, rather than externally, and by making use of the capacities we do have, rather than lamenting the ones we lack. So the claim is that the five conditions are jointly sufficient for *increasing* our control. The claim is not that if the five conditions are met, then our control will be increased in all the ways in which it would be desirable to increase it. It is only the much more modest claim that meeting the five conditions will increase our control in some ways.

MORAL INEQUALITY

By way of deepening this account of improving our judgments and thereby increasing control, three apparently troublesome implications need to be considered. Upon examination, however, the problems they raise will turn out to be apparent, not real. They concern moral inequality, to be discussed now, and responsibility and character, which will be discussed in the next two sections.

It is an implication of the present account that we differ not only in the extent to which we have achieved judgment and control, but also in the extent to which we possess the capacities and opportunities required for achieving them. This is so because the achievements, as well as the capacities and opportunities necessary for them, are influenced by the contingencies of our genetic inheritance, upbringing, and present circumstances, by the nature and seriousness of the conflicts among the values available to us, and by the extent to which our unconscious and unintentional evil desires have been nourished by our character and circumstances. Our control over these influences, however, is also varied. It follows, therefore, that the differences among us in respect to the extent to which we possess judgment and control are often produced by conditions over which we do not have control. We are, consequently, unequal in respect to our judgment and control, and our inequality is often not of our own making.

In the case of very many character traits, inequality is generally taken for granted. The fact that its source is not in something we did or could have done is acknowledged as a fact of life. Talents, skills, pleasing physical appearance, aptitudes, temperaments, levels of energy, intelligence, and so forth are unequally distributed in any general population. The capacities for judgment and control, however, are morally relevant character traits. They are essentially connected with living a good life, with the amount of good and evil we cause and experience, and so it is natural to regard judgment and control as virtues. That we differ in the extent to which we possess these virtues will also be generally conceded, since inequality of moral achievement is obvious. The point that may seem to present a difficulty is that there is inequality also in the degree to which the *capacity* for moral achievement is distributed. What sticks in the craw is the implication of the view here defended that moral inequality is not merely a matter of achievement, but also one of potentiality. It is a deep belief of modern sensibility (i.e., contemporary, Western, liberal, influenced by Christianity and/or the Enlightenment) that our moral capacity is the same. Our moral achievements differ, it is supposed, because, and only because, of what we do or what happens to us as we try to act on our capacity.

The belief in equal moral capacity, however, cannot withstand critical examination. It unites a substantive moral commitment with confusion and the refusal to face the relevant facts. The substantive moral commitment is to treat each other on the assumption that we have equal moral capacity. We may think of this as the moral analog of the judicial principle that we are to be treated as if we were innocent until proven guilty. Analogously, we are to treat each other on the assumption that we have the same moral capacity until proven otherwise. The assumption, of course, can be and often is defeated, and then we do have good reasons to treat those in question as guilty or as having unequal moral capacity. If the assumption is undefeated, however, then it is both reasonable and decent not to subscribe to invidious moral gradations among people. It is certainly not the intention, or an unintended consequence, of the view of judgment and control here defended to object to this assumption.

It must be asked, however, what makes this assumption reasonable. It may be the *fact* that human beings possess equal moral capacity, or it may be that the *procedure* of treating all human beings as if they possessed equal moral capacity is the best available to us. It does not require much reflection to realize that it is not as a fact but as a procedure that the assumption is reasonable. This becomes obvious if we raise the same question about the analogous judicial assumption. If the assumption of innocence were based on the fact of innocence, then the assumption would be blatantly unreasonable, since many people are guilty. But if the assumption of innocence were based on the procedure guiding the determination of guilt or innocence, then we could and should embrace it as a reasonable measure more likely to serve the interest of justice than any alternative.

Arguments from analogy, of course, are never more than suggestive, so it needs to be considered why the assumption of equal moral capacity would fail if it was supposed to be based on the allegedly corresponding fact. The reason for this is that our moral capacity depends on many other capacities, such as intelligence, adequate memory and imagination, mental health, hormonal balance, and so forth, and these other capacities are recognized by all parties as being unequally distributed. Insofar as moral capacity depends on these other capacities, it too must be unequally distributed.

If this is acknowledged, as it surely must be, then the question may well arise of why we should follow the procedure of treating each other as if we had equal moral capacity, when in fact we do not. The answer is that the procedure is reasonable because while we know that moral capacity is unequally distributed, we do not know whether particular individuals possess it to a greater or lesser extent. We should not, therefore, attribute to each other greater or lesser moral capacity, unless we have good reason to do so. We should treat each other, in the absence of such reasons, as if we had equal moral capacity, even though we know that we do not. Our knowledge of unequal moral capacity is general; our treatment of individuals as having equal moral capacity is particular. Our treatment of individuals should change only when we find out how the general knowledge applies to them.

If we clearly distinguish between the factual question of whether moral capacity is equally distributed and the procedural question of whether we ought to treat each other as if we had equal moral capacity, then we can consistently answer the first negatively and the second affirmatively. And then we can interpret the substantive moral commitment to be to a procedure and not to an alleged fact. Part of the trouble with the belief in equal moral capacity is that it confuses these two questions. If it did not, then the implication of the present view of judgment and control that people possess unequal capacity for both would not appear to be a difficulty.

There is, therefore, no need, and certainly no justification, for the desperate maneuver of refusing to face the plain fact of moral life that we differ both in our moral capacity and moral achievement. We can consistently acknowledge the fact of moral inequality and reject noxious hierarchies of a priori discrimination. We *are* morally better or worse; there *is* a moral hierarchy; and our position in it *does* depend on differences in our moral capacity. Both our capacity and our standing, however, are to be judged on the basis of the evidence provided by our actions. Knowing the extent of the relevant capacity normally provides evidence for the likelihood of corresponding achievement; similarly, knowing the achievement normally provides evidence for the likelihood of the extent of the corresponding capacity. The evidence is certainly not conclusive, but it is evidence. And it can be strengthened considerably if the achievement is not a unique event but a pattern in the life of a person. There is no good reason for supposing that this general point fails to be true of the moral capacity and the moral achievement connected with judgment and control.

The advantages of acknowledging inequality in respect to our capacity for judgment and control are several. First, doing so does justice to the facts of moral life. Those of us who habitually act morally wisely in a wide variety of circumstances are likely to be morally wise. What makes it normally possible for us to act morally wisely is our capacity for judgment and control. We possess that capacity unequally and that is one main reason why we differ in respect to our morally wise (or foolish) actions. Second, the importance of judgment and control is that they enhance the chances of living a good life. The lives of most us fall more or less short of being good. Recognizing that we are unequal in our capacity for and in our achievement of judgment and control provides one explanation of why so many lives are not good. Third, such capacity as we have for judgment and control is often due to conditions over which we have little control. Improving our chances of living a good life depends, therefore, on increasing such control as we have over our capacity for judgment.

DEGREES OF RESPONSIBILITY

Suppose that we perform an action that meets the five severally necessary and jointly sufficient conditions for increasing control. We are then responsible for the action. And that means that it is reasonable to praise or blame us for having acted the way we did. There is a difficulty, however, with this apparently obvious point. It concerns the question of how it could be reasonable to hold us responsible for actions within our control, if our capacity for control is not within our control. It has been argued that the further back we go in the lives of normal and mature human beings, the more the ratio between controlled and uncontrolled actions shifts in favor of the latter. It follows, then, that such control as we have must arise out of conditions, both external and internal, over which we have no control. We *can* increase our control, but by how much, over what actions, on what occasions, at the cost of overcoming obstacles of what difficulty are not things that we can control. If responsibility attaches to control, and if we have no control over how much control we have, then how could it be reasonable to praise or blame us for performing actions that happened to be within our control? It is beginning to look as if the present account of increasing control leaves no room for responsibility.

But this appearance rests on the failure to recognize that both control and responsibility are matters of degree. It will help to appreciate the significance of this point if causal and moral responsibility are distinguished.[8] Suppose that there is no doubt about the attribution of particular actions to us, acting as agents. There is, then, a sense in which we are responsible for our actions. This sense, however, is purely causal. Being responsible means that we are the pivotal links in the causal chain leading to our actions. We can ascribe responsibility in this sense and simultaneously withhold praise or blame on the ground that we could not evaluate or reflect on our actions. This will be referred to as "causal responsibility."

In the case of moral responsibility, unlike that of causal responsibility, it is appropriate to praise or blame us for performing our actions because we have control over our actions. Control connects us to our actions not just causally but also morally. We do not merely perform the actions, we do so in the light of our evaluation and judgment. The praise or blame properly attributed to us is thus at least partly due to our capacity for evaluation and judgment. But according to the present account of control, we may have no control over these capacities. We may, therefore, be merely causal, not moral, agents of our actions. The difficulty with the present account of increasing control thus may be that it fails to maintain the crucial distinction between causal and moral responsibility.

This only appears to be a difficulty, however, because of the mistaken assumption that the ascription of moral responsibility should proceed on an all-or-none basis. We are supposed either to meet the conditions for increasing our control, or not. If we do, we are morally responsible; if we do not, we are causally responsible. But this is not how we actually ascribe moral responsibility, nor would it be reasonable to change our practice to conform to the exclusive disjunction built into this assumption.

To bring out what is wrong with this assumption, let us recall that one crucial question upon whose answer the ascription of moral responsibility depends is whether the action we performed was a characteristic one for us. I did pick up the baseball bat and assault my victim; you did tell the

---

[8] For discussion of a similar distinction, see Wolf, *Freedom within Reason*, 40–45.

hard truth, even though it was risky. But how we think of the praise or blameworthiness of these actions partly depends on whether I am a violent man who has a history of assaults, or a peaceful and kind one who has never done anything remotely like it; or on whether you are an honest woman who would not tell a lie, or a self-righteous one who enjoys inflicting pain if she can find a moral justification for it.

If the action is in character, if it is but the latest instance conforming to a pattern, we feel much more confident about holding the agent morally responsible for it than if it is an exceptional episode in the life of a person whom no one would have expected to act in that way. If the action is in character, we readily assign praise or blame for both the action and the character the action reflects. If the action is uncharacteristic, we reserve judgment until we find out what made the agent act that way. And then we seek to explain the action not by reference to the agent's character but to some unusual concatenation of events, which led the agent to act out of character. The degree of moral responsibility we are ready to ascribe to the agent is, then, less than it would be if the action were a characteristic one.

There seems to be no doubt that this is how we normally proceed. We recognize that moral responsibility is often a matter of degree, and not necessarily a yes-or-no question. We ascribe moral responsibility not merely on the basis of individual actions, but also on the basis of character, which characteristic actions reveal. We also recognize a wide variety of cases having to do with the formation of character. These cases may be thought of as ranging on a continuum beginning with characters formed by genetic defects, such as Down syndrome; neurological disorders, such as dyslexia; mental illness, such as autism; going on to the formative influence of severely traumatic events in early life, such as prolonged malnutrition, a long and painful illness, being orphaned, years of humiliation, extreme poverty, discrimination; then shading into the effect upon character of being thought ugly or stupid, being unpopular, living in a cruel family or community, being discouraged from developing talents, being made ashamed of our family, origin, or some physical characteristic, not having the right accent, the right clothes, good manners, and so on to the other end of the continuum where we find characters formed consciously and deliberately. There are, of course, many other kinds of adverse influences, and there are, fortunately, also just as many and as various benign ones. The significance of these cases on the continuum is that while they are all character-forming influences, they range from influences over which we have no control to influences which are within our control. In between the two extremes fall the vast majority of cases in which our control is neither totally present nor totally absent, but mixed.

What actually follows from this account of increasing control is that the ascription of moral responsibility, and of praise or blame, ought to be proportional to the degree of control we have over the relevant aspect of our character. There is no precise point at which causal responsibility turns into moral responsibility, for the two shade into each other. But from the existence of difficult cases of mixed responsibility, it does not follow that there are not also clear cases of both causal and moral responsibility. If we recognize that we are morally responsible to different degrees, and that the extent of our moral responsibility depends on the extent of our control, then the apparent difficulty in the present account that it cannot distinguish between causal and moral responsibility will disappear.

A doubt may still linger nonetheless about the appropriateness of praise or blame for actions within our control if our control is not within our control.[9] This doubt, however, overlooks the crucial significance of the fact that we can increase our control because we can evaluate, judge, and reflect on our conduct. We are, therefore, often capable of controlling our conduct to some extent. But this will not quiet the doubt because it will again be said that whether we can increase our control is not in our control. The proper response to this is to grant the point but deny its force. There is nothing that could provide the desired control over increasing control. If control over increasing control depended on the possession of some further state or capacity, then control over that further state or capacity would also have to be controlled. And so on for all subsequent levels of control. The reasonable question to ask is not whether we have control over increasing our control, but whether we can increase our control sufficiently for the ascription of moral responsibility. The demand for increasing control over control is a demand for the impossible. On the other hand, the question of whether we can increase our control sufficiently for moral responsibility has already been answered in terms of the distinction between causal and moral responsibility, of the notion of there being many degrees between the two, and of the account of the conditions upon which the ascription of increased control and the corresponding degree of moral responsibility depend. Nothing further is either possible or necessary.

But why is the impossible demanded? Because of the worry about being subject to permanent adversities. That worry, however, ought to be as-

---

[9] "When we hold a person deeply responsible . . . we understand her to be accountable . . . in a different way from that in which other objects can be accountable. It is only in the context of this distinctive kind of accountability that the question of whether an individual *deserves* praise and blame . . . make sense." And "the inclination to regard the victim of deprived childhood as an individual who is not responsible for her behavior arises from the thought that . . . she is not in control of who she ultimately is, and thus . . . her actions are the mere unfolding of the inevitable role she is fated to play in the blind ceaseless flow of the world's events." Wolf, *Freedom within Reason*, 43 and 44.

suaged, to the extent to which it is possible to assuage it, by the fact that it is possible to increase our control. It has to be recognized, however, that not everyone can do that because not everyone has the capacity and the opportunity to do it. Moral responsibility and praise or blame are proportional to the extent to which those who can do so succeed in increasing their control. To want more than this is not to want a better account, but to want the human condition to be other than it is.

CHARACTER AND CONTROL

Suppose that it is granted that we are morally responsible for what is within our control. But are we morally responsible *only* for what is within our control? If not, the account of moral responsibility in terms of control cannot be adequate. And it seems that moral responsibility ranges beyond control because it may be reasonable to hold us morally responsible for actions not within our control on the ground that we ought to have control over them. The coward who cannot control his fear and predictably gives in to it once again may be reasonably blamed for having failed to control his fear. How could this be reasonable, if moral responsibility depends on control?

The answer is that moral responsibility depends on increasing control, not merely on actual control. To see why this is so it is necessary to get clearer about the connection between character and control. Until a more detailed account is given in Chapter 6, our character may be said to be constituted of the enduring patterns of desires, capacities, opportunities, and values which ordinarily motivate our conduct.[10] When an action is said to be a characteristic one for us, what is meant is that it is readily assimilable to one of our enduring patterns of action. Given our character, the characteristic actions we perform is just what would be expected of us in that sort of situation.

The class of actions within our control may or may not be a subclass of our characteristic actions. Whether or not it is depends on how far we have succeeded in increasing our control. If it becomes characteristic for us to control our actions, then we have advanced quite considerably toward transforming our character from what it was to what our conception of a good life prescribes that it should be. The usual condition, however, is that some of our characteristic actions are within our control, while some are not. There may be, and there usually are, enduring patterns of desire and action, which constitute important parts of our character, but over which we have no control.

[10] For an excellent analysis of the nature of character, see Joel Kupperman, *Character* (New York: Oxford University Press, 1991).

The reasons for our lack of control are many and various. It may be that we need no control over some of our characteristic actions because they naturally fit in with our conception of a good life. Or they need to be controlled because they are contrary to our conception of a good life, but they are too powerful or our capacity for control is too weak. Another possibility is that we are struggling to increase our control, and we sometimes succeed, sometimes fail. Then, we may be at such an early stage of trying to increase our control that we have not yet become aware of several of our characteristic but uncontrolled patterns of conduct, consequently we cannot control them because we do not know that they exist. Or, while we do know in some sense that they exist, we may mis-describe them due to fantasy, fear, self-deception, laziness, and so on, and mistakenly conclude that control is unnecessary.

To return now to the question posed above: Can we be held morally responsible, can we be reasonably blamed, for our uncontrolled actions, on the ground that we ought to have control over them? It will be apparent that the answer depends on answers to two further questions: Do we have the capacity to increase our control? and What is the nature of the blame to which we may be reasonably subjected?

The practical difficulties in the way of ascertaining the possession of this capacity are formidable because of the inaccessibility of the relevant facts. This difficulty, however, is mitigated by its rarely being the case that our capacity for increasing control is absent or unexercised. Usually, the capacity exists, we exercise it to some extent, and the question is whether we could have exercised it to a greater extent. We can try to decide that, on the one hand, by considering what we did or did not do in numerous other situations that called for control. And, on the other hand, by considering what others normally do in that sort of situation, whether we deviated from the norm, and if so, why. But the practical difficulties, great as they are, do not create a theoretical difficulty, provided the following points are recognized. Moral responsibility does not depend merely on actual control, but also on the capacity for increasing control. Both moral responsibility and the exercise of that capacity are matters of degree. The degree of moral responsibility depends on the degree to which the capacity for increasing control is exercised.

This raises the question of the nature of the blame that may be reasonably assigned to us for our uncontrolled actions. The claim that we are blameworthy for not having increased our capacity for control is ambiguous. It may mean that we are blameworthy for not *exercising* our capacity for increasing control, or that we are blameworthy for not *having* the capacity for increasing control. Corresponding to these two senses, there are two senses of blame (and of course also of praise): "weak" and "strong."

Weak blame connects up with causal responsibility, while strong blame is naturally allied to moral responsibility.[11]

It is reasonable to blame us strongly if we have the capacity for increasing our control but fail to exercise it. It is reasonable to blame us weakly if we lack the capacity for increasing control or, while we have the capacity, unavoidable obstacles, such as permanent adversities, prevent us from exercising it. Both weak and strong blame indicate, provided that they are reasonably ascribed, that we performed some morally blameworthy action. The difference between them is how the condemnation of the action reflects on us, their agents. Strong blame attaches to us if we are moral agents, because we have and could exercise our capacity for increased control, but failed to do so. Weak blame attaches to us if we are merely causal agents, because we lack or cannot exercise our capacity to increase control over the relevant actions. Since both the capacity for increasing control and its exercise are matters of degree, there will be very many intermediate cases of blame which fall between being clearly weak or clearly strong. Just as cases of responsibility range from causal to moral, so cases of blame range from weak to strong. Given both the desirability of increasing control and the serious obstacles to it created by permanent adversities, most cases of responsibility and blame will be mixed. And they will be mixed because our capacity for increasing control is itself a matter of degree.

So the answer to the question of whether we can be held morally responsible and be liable to strong blame for our uncontrolled actions on the ground that we ought to have control over them is in the affirmative. If we could have increased control, but did not, and that is why we performed the blameworthy actions, then we are morally responsible and we are to be strongly blamed. The number of cases, however, in which we can give this answer confidently will be small. For the typical cases will be those in which we could have increased control to some degree, but permanent adversities prevented us from increasing it sufficiently. The reasonable verdict, therefore, will hold us morally responsible and blame us to some extent, and it will eschew simpleminded extremes. This makes matters complicated. The reasonable answer, however, sometimes is complicated.

But is this answer consistent with the present view of the connection between responsibility, blame, and control? If moral responsibility and strong blame may be ascribed appropriately for uncontrolled actions, then how can they depend on control? They do not depend on control; they depend on the capacity for increasing control. The greater that capacity is and the more it is exercised, the greater our moral responsibility is and the stronger the blame to which we are liable. Contrariwise, the smaller the ca-

---

[11] This is Wolf's distinction. See *Freedom within Reason*, 40–45.

pacity is and the less it is exercised, the weaker our moral responsibility is and the blame to which we are liable.

CONCLUSION

The central argument of this chapter has been that growth in moral wisdom depends on increasing control. The reason for this is that moral wisdom consists in living in accordance with our conception of a good life, and that, in turn, consists in using our knowledge, evaluation, and judgment to transform the complex moral situations we encounter into simple ones. The capacities we have, the situations we face, and the judgments we make are, however, subject to the influences of permanent adversities. The appropriate exercise of our capacities, facing the situations in the right way, and making reasonable judgments requires coping with contingency, conflict, and evil, and that is possible, if at all, only by increasing our control.

CHAPTER FIVE

Moral Imagination:
The First Mode of Reflection

If the moral situations we encountered were all simple, what we should do would be obvious, because the nature of the good life we desired to live would be clear, the description of the situation in which we had to decide how to act would be unambiguous, and the obstacles would be manageable. The actual moral situations in which we find ourselves, however, are often complex, not simple. The ends are unclear; the situations are ambiguous; the obstacles are formidable; and, as a result, the course of action we should follow is uncertain. We need judgment to make the right decision in a state of uncertainty. Moral wisdom may be understood, therefore, as the character trait that enables us, to the extent to which we have been able to develop it, to transform complex moral situations into simple ones.

This intended transformation, however, is rendered problematic by the permanent adversities that stand in its way. Contingency, conflict, and evil affect our character, and they often jeopardize our capacity to make the efforts required to overcome them. They also affect the circumstances in which we have to reach decisions and act according to them, and they often create obstacles that reason and decency cannot overcome. Permanent adversities, therefore, weaken the control we have over transforming complex moral situations into simple ones. A deeper understanding of moral wisdom thus leads to seeing it as the capacity for increasing control.

Different people possess that capacity to different degrees, and even those who possess it to a sufficiently high degree differ in the opportunities they have to develop and exercise it. The reason for this is that one of the fundamental ways in which we differ from one another is the extent to which our characters and circumstances have been affected by permanent adversities. Two highly significant consequences of permanent adversities are, therefore, the fact that our chances of living a good life are not proportional to our reasonable and morally praiseworthy endeavors, and the fact that moral inequality, affecting both moral capacity and moral achievement, must be recognized as an ineliminable feature of moral life.

In the light of these facts, the central problem for growth in moral wisdom becomes that of increasing our control. How can we do that, if permanent adversities are indeed as formidable obstacles as they have been depicted as being? The answer is that we can only try, and that unless we try and succeed at least to some extent, we cannot live a good life. It is true that we differ in the capacities and circumstances upon which trying and succeeding depend, but the possibility that success may reward our efforts exists. Increasing control is concerned with realizing that possibility, and that, in turn, depends on meeting five conditions: having a desire, having the capacity and the opportunity to satisfy it, having favorably evaluated the desire, and the judgment to satisfy the desire having passed the test of reflection.

The argument in the preceding chapter was aimed at establishing the mere possibility of increasing control. It is necessary to concentrate now on what specifically is required for realizing that possibility. And that leads to the last condition of increasing control: reflection. The aim of reflection is to cope with obstacles in the way of reaching a reasonable decision about the satisfaction of a favorably evaluated desire. These obstacles may be internal or external to us, as we try to reach reasonable decisions. Internally directed reflection has three modes: moral imagination, self-knowledge, and moral depth. The first will be discussed now, the second in the next two chapters, and the third in the one after that. After these, reflection directed outward, toward external obstacles will be considered.

POSSIBILITIES AND IMPOSSIBILITIES

Consider a chess game played by a master against an advanced chess computer, such as Deep Thought.[1] Suppose that Deep Thought wins. It is, then, conclusively established that Deep Thought could defeat its human opponent. But it is not similarly certain that the master could

---

[1] Deep Thought was designed at Carnegie-Mellon University. It played against world-class human chess players. The world champion, Gary Kasparov, beat it, but not with ease. Against various international masters, Deep Thought often won. It is constantly improving, and it appears to be one of the best-performing chess computers in the world at the time of this writing (1994).

not defeat Deep Thought. Experts analyzing the game may conclude that the master did not play with his usual strength. His game was lackluster, he made more mistakes than it is usual for him, and his preparation was less thorough than it might have been. The experts conclude that although Deep Thought won, the master could have won, if he had played as well as he was capable of doing. The master, upon being interviewed, agrees with the experts. He explains that he was not going all out because he was conserving his energies for a coming major tournament.

Suppose, however, that the master wins. In what sense could it be said then that Deep Thought could have won? Deep Thought does not have off days, does not, indeed cannot, hold itself back. Deep Thought always plays to the limits of its capacity. After all, that is just what it was designed to do. If it lost, then it could have won only in the sense that it could be possible to improve its capacity beyond what it now is. If there is a sense in which Deep Thought can be said to have desires, then, in that sense, it is an essential characteristic of Deep Thought that its capacities and its desires completely overlap. They cannot diverge because Deep Thought cannot desire to play less well than it is capable of playing. Deep Thought is the perfect embodiment of the Nietzschean will to power. The master's capacities and desires, however, can diverge. On the hypothesis that the master lost, although he could have won, he lost because his capacities and desires did diverge. He did not desire to play up to his capacity, and that is why he lost.

The point of the contrast between Deep Thought and the master is not that chess computers could not play better chess than human beings; nor is it that machines could not replicate human activities; the point is to call attention to the essential human characteristic that our capacities and desires can diverge. Increasing control depends on this characteristic because it consists in shaping our desires to do or not to do what we have the capacity to do.[2]

The logical and psychological space within which the possibility of increasing control could exist is indicated by the ambiguity of the true description of normal human agents that they can or cannot do something. They can or cannot do it either because they do or do not have the capacity to do it, or because, although they have the capacity, they do or do not desire to exercise it. The possibility of increasing control depends on the possibility of shaping our desires, and thus influencing what we can or cannot do.

---

[2] It would not affect the argument if it turned out that machines could be constructed whose capacities and desires diverged. We would have to say in that case that machines can also increase their control.

Consider now a case in which a person cannot act in a certain way, although he has the capacity. He might also have the desire, but his desires have been shaped so that he now passionately desires not to act in that way, and he is utterly averse to acting in that way. He cannot, therefore, now act in that way. It is the nature of this "cannot" that is important. The case in point is Ajax in Sophocles' tragedy of that title.[3]

The setting of the play is the Greek army besieging Troy. Ajax is generally recognized as the second greatest Greek warrior, coming immediately after Achilles, whose preeminence is due to his divine origin. Achilles, however, dies, and there comes the ceremonial distribution of his arms. What is at stake, both symbolically and actually, is the inheritance of his mantle. Ajax's claim to it is excellent, but it is not honored. Agamemnon, Menelaus, and Odysseus, the leaders of the Greeks, combine forces and appropriate Achilles' arms. Ajax is thus deprived of the honor that is due to him.

We first encounter Ajax in a bizarre situation. He is in his tent whipping cattle tied to his tent post. He is surrounded by the bleeding corpses of eviscerated cattle he has just slaughtered. Ajax is mad. He believes that the slaughtered cattle are Greeks and the one he is whipping is Odysseus. He believes himself to be taking revenge on those who dishonored him. He later comes to his senses, sees what he has done, and realizes that he has made himself ridiculous in the eyes of his enemies and pitiful to his friends and subjects. He sees himself dishonored by not having gotten what he deserved, by not having taken revenge over it, and by being the object of ridicule and pity. His sense of honor is irrevocably injured. He cannot live without it, he resolves to kill himself, and he does. To understand why Ajax could not have done otherwise, we need to understand better his sense of honor.

Ajax is a hero, and he himself expresses his creed: "Let a man nobly live or nobly die / If he *is* a nobleman" (479–480), and the chorus says: "Ajax, no one could ever call those words / Spurious or alien to you. They are your heart's speech" (481–482). The hero is a high ideal among the Homeric Greeks, and in *Ajax* we find one of Sophocles' treatments of it. As Knox says in a perceptive study: "The hero chooses death. This is . . . the logical end of his refusal to compromise. . . . He cannot compromise and still respect himself. Surrender would be spiritual self-destruction. . . . [T]he hero is forced to choose between defiance and loss of identity. And . . . [his] sense of identity, of independent, individual existence, is terribly strong. . . . [Heroes] have a profound sense of their worth as individuals, and this exacerbates the anger they feel at the world's denial of respect. In the crisis of their lives . . .

---

[3] Sophocles, *Ajax*. References are to the lines of the play.

they have nothing to fall back upon for support but this belief in themselves, their conception of their own unique character and destiny."[4]

But this is an incomplete characterization, unless we understand that the crisis in the heroes' lives would not have occurred in other lives. It occurs because the heroes pit themselves against human limits. They refuse to accept what others regard as impossible, and they go down in defeat as they struggle against it. The greatness of the heroes does not come from succeeding at the impossible, but from their attempt to defy it. They will be defeated, but their defeat is a victory for the human spirit. "The hero offered the ancient Greeks the assurance that in some chosen vessels humanity is capable of superhuman greatness, that there are some human beings who can imperiously deny the imperatives which others obey in order to live. . . . [H]e is a reminder that a human being may at times magnificently defy the limits imposed on our will."[5]

This is the mold from which Ajax was cast. As he was leaving home for Troy, his father said to him: " 'Child,' he said, / 'Resolve to win, but always with God's help' " (764–765).

> But Ajax answered with a senseless boast:
> "Father, with God's help even a worthless man
> Could triumph. I propose, without help,
> To win my prize of fame." In such a spirit
> He boasted. And when once Athena stood
> Beside him in the fight, urging him on
> To strike the enemy with his deadly hand,
> He answered then, that second time, with words
> To shudder at, not speak: "Goddess," he said,
> "Go stand beside the other Greeks; help them.
> For where I bide, no enemy will break through."
>   (766–777)

Ajax was a hero and he suffered defeat for the same reason: he "kept no human measure" (778). His leitmotif is: "I am going where my way must go" (690). Athena punished Ajax for his hubris by sending the humiliating madness on him. It was meant to teach him his place, to shame him, to punish him for his presumptuous self-confidence and for spurning the goddess. But that was not a lesson he was willing to learn. "Let a man nobly

---

[4] Bernard M. W. Knox, *The Heroic Temper* (Berkeley: University of California Press, 1964), 36. See also Cedric H. Whitman, *Sophocles: A Study of Heroic Humanism* (Cambridge: Harvard University Press, 1951).

[5] Knox, *The Heroic Temper*, 57.

live or nobly die / If he *is* a nobleman" (479–480), and so he dies nobly. He cannot do otherwise.

Ajax lacks not the capacity but the desire to live. He explicitly entertains and rejects the possibility of continuing to live. He could adopt the rule: "Give way / To Heaven, and bow before the sons of Atreus [viz., Agamemnon and Menelaus]. / They are our rulers, they must be obeyed" (667–668). He asks himself, "Shall not I / Learn place and wisdom?" (674–675), and he answers, as heroes must, not by argument but by action. He refuses to obey, disdains to learn his place, and spurns wisdom. What stops him, however, is not lack of capacity, but an overpowering aversion to employing his capacities to what he regards as a dishonorable end, and a similarly strong desire to die since he cannot live on his own terms.

The source of his aversion and desire is the heroic conception of a good life to which he is unquestioningly committed. His desire to live that way and his aversion to living in any other make it impossible for him to do anything but kill himself. He is acting under a necessity, but the necessity is one that he imposes on himself. His commitment to the heroic ideal is so strong and it informs his understanding of the situations he encounters so thoroughly as to make even the most complex situations appear simple to him. Yet, Ajax is foolish, not wise. His transformation of complex situations into simple ones is accomplished by ignoring the complexities. By understanding what has gone wrong, it becomes possible to understand better how desires should be shaped so as to increase control.

What should alert us to something having gone wrong is reflection on the great evil Ajax has caused. He destroyed himself. But, given his society and his position in it, his self-destruction was not an isolated act: he thereby betrayed his responsibility and caused undeserved harm to numerous people whose welfare depended on him. He doomed his wife and son to an uncertain future; the troops who loyally followed him to Troy and fought under his command were left stranded on foreign soil, far from home, in the midst of Trojan enemies and hostile fellow Greeks whom Ajax has alienated; he betrayed the Greek cause to which he was bound by oath; and he left his city without a successor to his aged father. And he did not do all this in a fit of passion.

Sophocles shows how Ajax hears and rejects the pleadings of his wife and troops, the common sense represented by the chorus, and the voice of his own doubts. He knowingly and intentionally embarks on a course of action that will cause great evil to those he cares most about. But he does not see that. What he sees is the stain on his honor. The complex situation into which he is thrust appears simple to him because he is unaware of possible ways of viewing it other than the one that holds him in its grip. He lacks a sufficient degree of moral imagination to acquaint him with alternative possibilities.

THE NATURE OF MORAL IMAGINATION

Imagination is responsible for a wide variety of human activities, among which four are particularly important.[6] The first is the formation of images, such as the face of an absent friend; the second is resourceful problem-solving, exemplified, for instance, by nonlinear thinking; the third is the falsification of some aspect of reality, as we do when we fantasize that the facts are other than they are; and the fourth is the mental exploration of what it would be like to realize particular possibilities, such as being very rich.[7] Moral imagination belongs to the fourth kind of imaginative activity. It is moral because one central concern of it is with evaluating the possibilities from the perspective of a conception of a good life.

It is an obvious observation that we are endlessly involved in trying to understand each others' conduct. If we could not do this successfully with much of the conduct of other people as it affects us, our civilized interaction would break down. Social order presupposes some degree of predictability, and in most cases involving social life we can reliably predict only what we at least to some extent understand. The same point holds, although for different reasons, with respect to understanding our own conduct. If we did not know what we desired, and if we could not reasonably predict that some of our desires will and others will not persist for some time, we could not plan for the future, and since such planning is necessary for living a good life, we would be doomed to frustration.

The first step toward achieving this understanding of ourselves and others involves gathering knowledge of what the agents actually have been doing. It is possible to reconstruct the lives of individuals by compiling a list of their more important publicly observable actions. But this cannot be more than a first step, for unless we understand something about the context in which they lived, the reasons for their actions, and what made some of their actions important, we could not be said to understand the actions. We might, then, know what they did, but not the significance of their deeds.

---

[6] The literature on imagination is vast. It is a central concept in Hume, Kant, romantic thought, and aesthetics. Eva Brann, *The World of Imagination* (Chicago: University of Chicago Press, 1986), and Mary Warnock, *Imagination* (London: Faber and Faber, 1976), are excellent overall guides to the subject. Specifically on moral imagination, see Mark Johnson, *Moral Imagination: Implications of Cognitive Science for Ethics* (Chicago: University of Chicago Press, 1993); Sabina Lovibond, *Realism and Imagination in Ethics* (Minneapolis: University of Minnesota Press, 1983); and David Novitz, *Knowledge, Fiction, and Imagination* (Philadelphia: Temple University Press, 1987).

[7] This kind of imagination is a central theme of Stuart Hampshire's *Thought and Action* (London: Chatto & Windus, 1960), and *Innocence and Experience* (Cambridge: Harvard University Press, 1989). Both works have deeply influenced the present argument.

Understanding the context, the reasons behind, and the importance of actions matters because it reveals what the agents' possibilities were and what led them to realize one among them. It is the nature of this type of understanding that it should attempt to illuminate the significance of what happened by considering what might have happened. The assumption behind it is that the significance of a particular action emerges only by viewing it against the background of competing possibilities and by identifying the agents' reasons for attempting to realize one of these possibilities.[8]

Moral imagination is an essential element of this understanding because it is the activity by which we attempt to re-create the possibilities particular agents faced. But this attempted re-creation is a complicated matter. It must involve ascertaining both the possibilities that were available to the agents and the possibilities that the agents believed themselves to have. Both are needed for understanding the significance of particular actions, but it is necessary to keep them separate; otherwise we could not evaluate the reasons agents give for realizing a particular one among their possibilities.

It is a further complication that not even for thoroughly reasonable agents do these two sets of possibilities coincide, since even they may lack all sorts of information that is generally available in their context. If they had the information, their beliefs about their possibilities would change accordingly, but they are not blameworthy for not having it, for they did not choose their ignorance. Of course, few agents, if any, are thoroughly reasonable. The beliefs they form about their possibilities may be mistaken, and often these mistakes could and should have been avoided by them. It is, therefore, essential to evaluating the reasons agents give for their actions to form some conception of what beliefs about their possibilities were reasonable for them to have, given the available possibilities. Understanding the significance of particular actions consequently requires the imaginative re-creation of possibilities that were generally available in the agents' context, possibilities that the agents could reasonably have been expected to believe themselves to have, and possibilities that the agents actually believed themselves to have.

This threefold imaginative re-creation of possibilities goes beyond the bare knowledge *that* they exist. To know that much does not require imagination. In order to understand the significance of particular actions, we

---

[8] "A person . . . explains himself to himself by his history . . . as accompanied by unrealized possibilities. . . . His individual nature, and the quality of his life . . . emerge in the possibilities that were real possibilities for him, which he considered and rejected for some reason or other. From the moral point of view, it is even a significant fact about him . . . that a certain possibility, which might have occurred to him as a possibility, never actually did occur to him. In self-examination one may press these inquiries into possibilities very far, and this pressure upon possibility belongs to the essence of moral reflection." Hampshire, *Innocence and Experience*, 101.

must appreciate the attractions, risks, novelty, general regard, emotive connotations, prestige, and so on, associated with the possibilities, and we must appreciate them as they appear to the agents. The understanding of significance cannot, therefore, be merely cognitive, it must also have a large affective component capable of conveying the appeal the relevant possibilities had for the agent. What is needed, therefore, is a cognitively and affectively informed imagination to re-create the richness of the possibilities whose significance we want to understand. Only against that background does it begin to become understandable why agents desire to realize a particular one among their possibilities.

The imaginative re-creation of the background, however, is still insufficient for understanding the significance of actions. For there is also the question of the evaluation of the reasons agents give for what they do. In the simplest situation, the possibilities the agents actually believe themselves to have coincide with the possibilities reasonable agents would have in that context, and the agents give as their reason that the possibility they realized was more desirable than its competitors. In such a case, having re-created the agents' possibilities, we come to appreciate how one of them could have been found to be more desirable by that agent than alternatives to it. And then we could rightly claim to have understood the significance of the particular action.

But what if we encounter what is so often the case, namely, that some of the beliefs the agents have about their possibilities are in some way unreasonable? It may be that their possibilities are more or less numerous than they believe, or that they find possibilities desirable or undesirable because they ignore readily available features whose acknowledgment would incline them in another direction, or it may be that they are deceiving themselves, or that their beliefs are misled by anger, fear, fantasy, spite, or envy. In such cases, knowing the reasons the agents give is not enough for understanding the significance of their actions. The search for understanding, then, must go beyond these reasons and explore the question of why there is a discrepancy between what the agents believe about their possibilities and what is reasonable for them to believe. By understanding why the agents are unreasonable, we may come to understand the significance of their actions, even though it is hidden from the agents themselves.[9]

---

[9] Marxists, Freudians, deconstructionists, sociologists such as Erving Goffman in *The Presentation of Self in Everyday Life* (New York: Doubleday, 1959), and anthropologists such as Clifford Geertz in *The Interpretation of Cultures* (New York: Basic Books, 1973) and *Local Knowledge* (New York: Basic Books, 1983), suppose this to be the typical condition of humanity, a condition from which only exceptional individuals, like themselves, succeeding at exceptional efforts, can free themselves. The position defended here is not committed to such far-fetched and mistaken views.

Although this sketch of the workings of moral imagination may make it seem dauntingly difficult, this appearance is deceptive. The kind of understanding described above is routinely achieved by ethnographers in describing conduct in other cultures; by historians in describing past contexts of action; by literary critics who, unswayed by current destructive practices, still aim to enhance readers' appreciation of the predicaments confronting fictional characters; by all of us in trying to enter sympathetically into someone else's frame of mind so as to understand the significance of his or her conduct; and by all of us again in the course of the necessary task of trying to make concrete to ourselves what it would be like to realize our own possibilities and live according to them, so that we may shape our future in as informed a manner as we can achieve.

The systematic cultivation, practice, and achievement of moral imagination is one traditional task of the humanities. Its interest is not in the causes of human conduct, but in its significance. Its aim is not to form lawlike generalizations, but to concentrate on the reciprocal interaction between particular persons and their cultural contexts. The explanation it yields is not of how anyone would act in that particular context, but of why particular individuals have acted as they did in that context. Its task is partly descriptive, yet what it describes are not the objective possibilities open to everyone, but the evaluations by individuals of what they take to be the possibilities that confront them as different ways of shaping their own future. It aims to explain what happened not by identifying the causes that made it happen, but by identifying the reasons the agents rightly or wrongly believed themselves to have for doing what they did rather than the numerous other things they might have done.[10] Moral imagination is, of course, not restricted to the humanities; travel, films, or television may also provide it. But the humanities seek it, as it were, ex officio.

Locating the systematic pursuit of moral imagination in the humanities and stressing its differences from scientific understanding is not meant to suggest that there is anything ontologically odd about it. Everything we do has causes; the causes also have causes; and there is no reason why a scientific account of all these causes should not be possible. The understanding moral imagination yields is not in competition with scientific understanding. They are different modes of understanding, each having its legitimate sphere and importance. One aspires to understand human conduct from the outside, from the point of view of observers, objectively, *sub specie aeter-*

---

[10] Following Hampshire's "Subjunctive Conditionals," in *Freedom of Mind* (Oxford: Clarendon Press, 1972), the point may be put by saying that the imaginative understanding central to the humanities is characterized by singular subjunctive conditionals, in contrast with scientific understanding, which requires general counterfactual conditionals.

nitatis; the other aims to understand the same thing from the inside, from the point of view of the agents, anthropocentrically, *sub specie humanitatis.*[11]

When imaginative understanding takes on a moral emphasis and concentrates on evaluating relevant possibilities in moral terms, the resulting moral evaluation is not abstract but refers to the specific agents living in the specific circumstances whose possibilities are being considered. Given this unavoidable individuation, there are still two importantly different ways the evaluation can be interpreted: the agents may be evaluating themselves and their own possibilities, or others and their possibilities. There is a deep connection between these two ways. We frequently begin to learn about our possibilities by imitating others as they are realizing their possibilities; but understanding their possibilities requires an imaginative effort that at least at the time when we learn to make it involves envisaging their possibilities as if they were ours. Moral education develops the learners' moral point of view by teaching them about the moral points of view of others. What matters in the present context, however, is not the education of moral imagination, but its exercise by full-fledged moral agents. And its self-directed exercise matters more than the other-directed one, since the second presupposes that agents direct themselves to exercise their moral imagination in a particular way. What, then, is involved in the kind of imaginative understanding through which agents are trying to envisage and evaluate their own possibilities by asking whether it would be good to live and act according to them?

Our usual situation is that we are born into a tradition, and as we try more or less consciously, with greater or lesser control, to make our lives good, we find our aspirations and opportunities defined by the conventional possibilities our tradition provides. We have a vague sense of what we desire and we attempt to realize it by seeking some non-Procrustean fit between what we take to be desirable and the possibilities we are aware of having. Moral imagination acquaints us with these conventional possibilities.

This process is not that of initiating individuals standing outside of the tradition into its ways. We do not begin with a self-generated initial conception of a good life and then develop it along conventionally accredited ways. Our first rudimentary view is already couched in terms we have learned from our tradition, since the identification and conceptualization of what we desire already presuppose an evaluative vocabulary that we possess, if at all, only if we have learned it from our tradition. Initiation into the tradition, therefore, consists in becoming articulate about ourselves and

---

[11] This roughly coincides with the objective and subjective views discussed by Thomas Nagel, especially in *The View from Nowhere* (New York: Oxford University Press, 1986). In a splendid collection of essays, Santayana shows the workings of this kind of imagination; see *Interpretations of Poetry and Religion* (New York: Harper, 1957).

our surroundings by learning to view both through the available conventional possibilities. Finding a fit between how we think it would be good to live and how we can live is, therefore, a matter of identifying, among those conventionally provided, the possibilities we find desirable because we think that they allow the development and perhaps the realization of what we regard as good potentialities in ourselves. It would be a mistake to suppose, however, that we cannot free ourselves from the consequences of this unavoidable cultural conditioning. Moral imagination enables us to carry the exploration of our possibilities beyond the confines of our tradition.[12]

The scope of our moral imagination enlarges as we become acquainted with possibilities other than those in our tradition. Through the development of a historical perspective, an understanding of other cultures, and immersion in literature, especially in novels, plays, and biographies, we come to appreciate that the conventional possibilities do not exhaust the possibilities of life, but merely form that small subset to which the contingencies of our upbringing have given us access. As we acquire imaginative understanding of new possibilities, so we grow in breadth. And breadth enriches our own possibilities in two ways.

The first is simply by increasing the number of possibilities we have. History, ethnography, and literature show us ways of living and acting, which we can adapt to our circumstances, and thereby enlarge our possibilities. But it often happens that the new possibilities we learn about are so remote from our circumstances as to make it impractical even to attempt to adopt them as our own. Yet they can still enrich us in a second way. The increasing breadth of moral imagination helps us appreciate our own possibilities by providing a point of view from which we can reflect on them better. Breadth allows us to step outside of our tradition and view it from an external vantage point, not by committing us to it, but by providing a basis for contrast and comparison. On that basis, we can see better the dangers, pitfalls, and losses that we confront by committing ourselves to some among our own possibilities.

We may, then, come to see, for instance, that from the point of view of an aristocratic tradition, which we have no wish to revive, our commitment to equality incurs the heavy cost of discouraging personal excellence, or that from the point of view of a puritanical tradition, which we are happy to consign to history, the sexual revolution tends to undermine the inti-

---

[12] See the exchange among Clifford Geertz, " 'From the Native's Point of View': On the Nature of Anthropological Understanding," in *Local Knowledge* (New York: Basic Books, 1983), Lionel Trilling, "Why We Read Jane Austen," in *The Last Decade* (New York: Harcourt, Brace, 1979), Clifford Geertz, "Found in Translation: On the Social History of Moral Imagination," in *Local Knowledge*, and Giles Gunn, *The Culture of Criticism and the Criticism of Culture* (New York: Oxford University Press, 1987), chap. 5.

macy of exclusive sexual partners. These costs of equality and sexual liberation are not easily seen by those who are immersed in their commitments to them because they have nothing to compare them with. The point, of course, is not that if we appreciate the costs, we shall weaken our commitment to realizing some possibilities; rather, by appreciating the costs we shall be able to work for the realization of the possibilities in a more reasonable way.

Moral imagination thus contributes to our growth in breadth; breadth enlarges the field of possibilities our tradition initially provides; and the new possibilities, derived from exposure to other traditions, usually through history, ethnography, and literature, enable us to view critically the possibilities with which we start by acting as a basis for contrast and comparison.

THE ENLARGEMENT OF POSSIBILITIES

Returning now to Ajax, it becomes apparent that he was severely deficient in moral imagination; he lacked breadth, and, as a result, he could not cast a reflective eye on the possibility of life to which he was so utterly committed. The trouble was not that he was unaware of alternative possibilities. Sophocles shows us, more or less explicitly, that Ajax's father, wife, and troops presented alternatives to the heroic ideal, and so did the sinuous Odysseus, Calchas the prophet, and the goddess Athena. We are shown Ajax toying with some of these possibilities, but they are not, what William James called, live options for him.[13] Intellectually, he perhaps recognizes them as possible ways of life, but they are not possibilities for him because, to use James's expression again, his passional nature is absolutely opposed to them. What he desires in life and what he most wants to avoid are inseparably connected with the heroic ideal he has made his own. The fundamental reason, then, that Ajax could not but enact the tragic role into which he cast himself is not that he lacked the capacity to act otherwise, but that his desires were ill-formed.

Desires may be deficient in many ways: they may be inconsistent, vicious, misdirected, incapable of satisfaction, misunderstood, trivial, perverse, and so forth. But Ajax's dominant desires were faulty in a special way: they did not meet the fifth condition for increasing control: they did not pass the test of reflection. The fault was not that he failed to reflect on his desires. He did reflect on them in the light of his heroic conception of a good life. The fault was rather that his reflection was defective. Ajax violated the Aristotelian requirement about desires and aversions that we

---

[13] William James, "The Will to Believe," in *The Will to Believe* (New York: Dover, 1956).

should "feel them at the right times, with reference to the right objects, to-wards the right people, with the right aim, and in the right way."[14] What then is it that Ajax, and others who fail the test of reflection, should do or have done?

Following scholastic usage, Kant famously distinguished between perfect and imperfect duties.[15] A perfect duty obliges us to perform a specific act, such as to keep a promise or pay a debt. An imperfect duty obliges us to act in a particular manner, benevolently or loyally for instance, but it leaves it to our discretion when, toward whom, how frequently, and at what cost to ourselves we should act in that manner. Imperfect duties, therefore, allow considerable latitude as to how we meet the obligations they create.[16]

Taking this once again (see also the Introduction) as a clue from Kant, it suggests a distinction between perfect and imperfect desires, or, more id-iomatically, between specific and general desires. A physically exhausted person's desire for rest is specific; an ambitious person's desire for success is general. Specific desires call for a specific type of action, as exhaustion calls for rest. General desires also call for action, but not for a specific type, since the desire may be satisfied in many different ways. The success that would satisfy an ambitious person may be some particular accomplish-ment, such as winning the Nobel Prize, or the possession of power or wealth, or being honored, respected, or loved, or having written *the* book on the field, climbed the greasiest pole, or learned self-control.

In the case of specific desires, the judgments we have to make are re-stricted to whether or not we should perform the specific type of action which would satisfy the desire. The judgments involved in satisfying gen-eral desires, however, are considerably more complex. In their cases, we must first come to see a specific type of action as being a possible way of satisfying the general desire. These judgments, therefore, presuppose that we have transformed an abstract possibility into one that is a possibility for us. It is thereby changed from being just one among countless logical and empirical possibilities into one that we have reason to take seriously. It be-comes *our* possibility; we come to see it as a live option.

This kind of judgment is not a decision to realize the possibility; it pro-vides only one of the options about which we have to decide. The judg-ment mediates between the general desire and the corresponding action by allowing us to see various possibilities as potential satisfactions of the general desire. Part of what makes some moral situations complex is that

[14] Aristotle, *Nicomachean Ethics*, 1106b21–24.
[15] Immanuel Kant, *Groundwork of the Metaphysics of Morals*, trans. H. J. Paton (New York: Harper, 1964), 89 and 91 (or Prussian Academy numbering 421 and 424).
[16] See H. J. Paton, *The Categorical Imperative* (Philadelphia: University of Pennsylvania Press, 1971), 150.

there are several possibilities thus interpreted and we have to decide which, if any, we should act on. This is one context in which we need judgment. We use it well, if we decide by reflecting on the available possibilities in the light of our conception of a good life.

Another reason for the complexity of some moral situations is that by coming to see a possibility in a certain way, we give specific form to our general desire. The desire becomes a desire for that specific possibility. Success becomes identified with winning that competition, prevailing over that adversity, accomplishing that task. Our general desire, dictated by our conception of a good life, thus becomes a specific desire for a specific possibility. The general desire and the specific possibility we decide to realize thus mutually shape and form each other. The general desire becomes more specific and the specific possibility becomes more desirable. The object of our judgment, then, is to reflect on and to decide whether we should desire that possibility. And that also depends on whether and how the satisfaction of that desire by realizing that possibility fits into our conception of a good life.

Such judgments may be adequate or inadequate, depending on their assessment of the available possibilities. It needs now to be considered what may be responsible for their inadequacy. It was argued earlier in this chapter that imaginative understanding requires the re-creation of possibilities generally available in the agents' context, the ones agents would believe themselves to have, if they were thoroughly reasonable, and the ones agents actually believe themselves to have. One function of moral imagination is to overcome the gap between the last two. This is a necessary task due to our natural propensity to err in judging our possibilities. The sources of this type of misjudgment are numerous. For the present purposes, it will be sufficient merely to indicate some of the more obvious ones.

The tacit assumption in the argument has so far been that the exercise of moral imagination is good because it improves our view of our possibilities. But observation of the way we actually conduct ourselves belies this assumption. Keeping our possibilities in the focus of our attention is burdensome. Life, after all, cannot be a permanent revolution. Adventurousness of spirit is fine and good, but life largely consists in performing everyday, routine, unadventurous tasks. Even creative artists, explorers, and other free spirits must shop for groceries, have their cars serviced, balance their bank accounts, pay their bills, have their hair cut, and negotiate with countless people on whom they rely for various services. After the embarrassing stage of adolescent rebelliousness is over, we cannot help conforming to the prevailing conventions, if we want to get on with our lives. And getting on with them means, for the vast majority of us, that we live according to some small subset of conventional possibilities. We settle into them—we settle for them—and it is nothing but unwelcome irritation to have to form some attitudes toward possibilities that people other than ourselves may conceivably entertain.

Step by innocuous step we are thus led down the path to narrow-mindedness. We learn to live by exclusion, by saying "no" to the examination of possibilities that may make our lives better. We suppress our dissatisfactions with the life we have settled for, and we call this suppression a sign of maturity. And so we place ourselves in a situation where we cannot increase our control because we deprive ourselves of the possibilities whose realization would improve our lives. This understandable propensity toward laziness of spirit and willingness to stay with the familiar is one source of the misjudgments we tend to make of our possibilities: we exclude many of those we could make our own, and the exclusion is motivated by our desire for comfort and by our aversion to expanding our horizons.

Another common source of the misjudgment of our possibilities is the confusion between two forms of imagination: one is fantasizing about our possibilities and the other is exploring them through moral imagination. The confusion is understandable since both fantasy and moral imagination concentrate on presently unrealized possibilities. Furthermore, both are emotionally charged, since the envisaged possibilities are colored by our desires and aversions. They are envisaged as possibilities for us, about how our lives may go, and it is natural to have strong feelings on that subject.

Envisaging some possibilities may degenerate from moral imagination into fantasy when our feelings become disproportionately strong. They do not merely color the way in which we see the relevant possibilities, but come to alter our beliefs about their nature. Our desires and aversions may become so assertive as to force our attention only on those aspects of the possibilities which reinforce the feelings we already have. They lead us to ignore, overlook, or forget other equally salient aspects. In this way, desire for love may lead us to ignore signs of infidelity in our partner, or the desire for success may cause us to miss the seamy underside of the glamorous life upon which we embarked with great ambition. Similarly, aversion to risk may make us see possibilities as threats; it may make us overestimate negligible dangers inherent in them; or it may cause us to deny our abilities in order to avoid the prospect of failure. The damaging effect of fantasy is to motivate us to explore unsuitable possibilities or to undermine our motivation to explore suitable ones. Fantasy can have this effect because it derives its force from desires and aversions whose strength is disproportionate to what elicits them. Moral imagination is free from this defect, then, if our desires and aversions are realistic reactions to the possibilities we envisage.

The misjudgments of fantasy, then, have a more subtle source than those of narrow-mindedness. Both involve the exclusion of possibilities, but while the first just ignores them, the second recognizes them and then excludes them on the basis of pretended reasons. Narrow-mindedness does not involve even pretended reflection on the reasonability of the excluded possibilities, while fantasy involves the pretense of reflection, but it is nothing but a sham; it is rationalizing, not reasoning.

An additional source of misjudgment is a particular form of self- deception. The fundamental reason for concentrating on our possibilities is to increase control over our lives. We can do so by attempting to realize possibilities which, we believe, would improve our lot. This, of course, requires the possession of a conception of a good life with reference to which we select the possibilities whose realization we desire. But this conception must also be regarded as desirable; otherwise it could not motivate us with sufficient force to overcome the contrary desires we also have, but whose satisfaction would be inconsistent with it. From this conception, there follows a desire whose object is to make us satisfy only those desires that conform to the conception. We have desires to realize some possibilities, and we have desires about the satisfaction of our desires. We may call the first "substantive" and the second "regulative" desires.

These two kinds of desires routinely conflict because the satisfaction of our regulative desires leads to the frustration of many of our substantive desires. This conflict is bound to occur, because deciding to satisfy a particular desire normally dooms some other desires to frustration. We have more desires than we can attempt to satisfy, and the scarcity of resources, prevailing conventions, unavoidable spatial and temporal restrictions, limited energy, and so forth curtail which of our desires we can reasonably seek to satisfy.

Self-deception occurs in the context of this conflict. It is a device by which we disguise from ourselves the reasons against realizing some of the substantive desires that conflict with the regulative desires. Its mechanism is to underplay the significance of violating the conception of the good life from which the regulative desires follow by convincing ourselves of the harmlessness of satisfying the substantive desire that is incompatible with the regulative one. We say that a few lucrative acts of betrayal will not make us faithless to the cause dear to our heart, that occasional ruthlessness toward our competitors will not destroy the benevolence we feel we ought to maintain, or that making some exceptions for people we favor will not compromise our commitment to justice. And we believe what we say because in the forefront of our attention is the satisfaction derived from the aberrant substantive desire, and not the satisfaction of the regulative desire, which the realization of the possibility prompted by our conception of a good life would produce. We contrive thus to go against what we ourselves believe are the possibilities we should aim to realize.

In this way, self-deception leads to an even subtler misjudgment than what is involved in fantasy. In fantasizing, we may pretend to reason, when we are in fact rationalizing. In self-deception, we really do reason, but the force of our substantive desires makes us reason badly. Our reflection is led astray because we do not prevent the strength of our feelings from clouding our judgment.

Narrow-mindedness, fantasy, and self-deception all lead to the misjudgment of our possibilities by excluding them. Moral imagination is the form of reflection that aims to avoid such misjudgments, and thus to remove obstacles to the satisfaction of those substantive desires that would make our lives better. And the way in which moral imagination attempts to achieve its aim is to cultivate in those receptive to it an aliveness to such possibilities as are available to them in their context. These possibilities will inform desires by transforming them from barely articulated, quite general, poorly directed velleities into clear, focused, articulate preferences for living according to a particular conception of a good life. The larger the field from which our possibilities are adopted, the more informed are our decisions to give them scope in our lives. By enlarging the field, moral imagination makes our options richer and more various, and thus increases the control we have over our lives.

How good moral imagination may become depends, of course, on our capacities, personal circumstances, and on the general features of the context in which we live. The cultivation of moral imagination is thus as subject to permanent adversities as all our capacities and the personal and impersonal conditions are that create our context. Nothing that has been said about moral imagination is intended to suggest that it can overcome permanent adversities. The argument has been that within the limits set by them, we can still make our lives better or worse, and that one way of making them better is by the cultivation and exercise of such moral imagination as we are capable of having, given our character and circumstances.

CONCLUSION

In closing, the case of Ajax should be reconsidered—not so much to understand *him* better, but rather to appreciate the significance his failure has for all of us. Did Ajax misjudge his possibilities, and if he did, to what was his misjudgment due? That he misjudged them is clear. The heroic ideal to which he was committed was only one among the possibilities in the Homeric world. Clear textual evidence shows that Sophocles intends us to see that Ajax was aware of at least some of them; otherwise he could not have rejected them. Given his total commitment to the heroic ideal, it was, of course, impossible for him not to reject them.

The impossibility, however, was of his own making; it was not created by permanent or other adversities. The question is why he created it. He did so because his desire for honor dominated his life and rendered other, conflicting desires insignificant. To understand Ajax's failure it is crucial to see that what he is properly faulted for is neither his overpowering desire to live in a particular way nor his willingness to die if he could not do so. Indeed, the strength of his commitment is perhaps Ajax's most admirable quality. What has gone wrong is that the overpowering desire was ill-formed. He put all his eggs in one basket, but it was the wrong basket. The significance of what Sophocles shows is that the heroic ideal and the total devotion to honor, understood in the heroic way, have tragic consequences. A life in which the highest ideal is to pit oneself against unavoidable limits cannot be a good one. There may be something awesome and even sublime about such lives, but they are not reasonable possibilities for human beings.

This becomes particularly clear if Ajax's case is contrasted with Socrates' death. Socrates had as strong a desire to live in a particular way and as strong an aversion to live otherwise as Ajax had. Yet Socrates' death comes down to us as an ideal and Ajax's as a warning. Each had a conception of a good life; each was totally committed to it. Each had desires and aversions formed by his conception. Each had a chance to go on living in violation of his conception, and each opted for death instead. What, then, is the difference? What makes Socrates a moral exemplar and Ajax a tragic figure?

The difference is that Socrates' judgment passes the test of reflection, while Ajax's does not. As a result, Socrates had control over his possibilities, but Ajax did not. Both acted under a moral necessity. They could not but decide to die once they encountered the particular destructive manifestations of the permanent adversities in their different contexts. Any other decision would have been a betrayal of their values. But the moral necessity under which Socrates acted was a product of his reflectively judged desires, while the moral necessity that compelled Ajax was produced by ill-judged desires. Socrates had considerable control over his life because he learned to control his desires. Ajax's control over his life was negligible because he was overpowered by a desire he had not reflected on. Socrates had breadth; Ajax lacked it. Ajax could have increased his control over his life by exercising his moral imagination better, acquiring greater breadth, and correcting the misjudgments that so severely limited his possibilities. But he did not do so. Socrates' decision to die was thus a sign of moral wisdom, while Ajax's decision was a consequence of his foolishness in creating a situation in which he had to take that decision.

CHAPTER SIX

Self-Knowledge: The Second
Mode of Reflection

One theme that connects moral imagination, self-knowledge, and moral depth is that moral wisdom involves improving our judgment and increasing our control through reflection; growth in one is growth in the other. Control requires evaluating our desires, capacities, and opportunities in the light of our conception of a good life. But this is not sufficient for its achievement because both the evaluation and its objects are subject to permanent adversities. Contingencies affect our character and circumstances; conflicts permeate the values embodied in our conception of a good life; unconscious and unintentional evil tendencies motivate us, and they may render our thoughtful and sincere evaluations unreliable. The aim of the kind of reflection that is involved in control is to counteract the influence of permanent adversities and to bring our evaluations increasingly under the influence of our conception of a good life.

Control changes the internal conditions of our evaluations, and it does so through the three modes of reflection. The preceding chapter has shown how moral imagination broadens our possibilities by endeavoring to overcome the narrowness that contingency, conflict, and evil foster through erecting internal obstacles to increased control. The topic of this chapter and the next is how self-knowledge can increase control. The central thought that will be developed is that self-knowledge is a mode of reflection which aims at the transformation of our character by understanding the significance of our past actions, evaluating our desires, capacities, and opportunities, and values, and motivating us to act according to favorably evaluated desires. The achievement of self-knowledge does not free us from permanent adversities, but it reduces the extent to which they create internal obstacles to living according to our conception of a good life.

Socrates identified moral wisdom with self-knowledge, and in doing so he got something deeply right and something deeply wrong. What is right is that Socrates saw that we grow in moral wisdom as we come to a better understanding of our character. Many of the obstacles that prevent us from living a good life are defects in our character, and through self-knowledge we may become aware of them. What is wrong is that Socrates supposed that this awareness would result in overcoming these obstacles, and that once they are overcome, we would be assured a good life. But this is impossible partly because some obstacles to living a good life are permanent adversities and partly because the obstacles we need to overcome are not only internal but also external and so unavailable to self-knowledge. The present discussion will follow Socrates' lead in recognizing the great importance of self-knowledge to moral wisdom, but it will not follow it all the way because there is more to moral wisdom than self-knowledge.

CHARACTER AND SELF-KNOWLEDGE

The object of self-knowledge is the knower's character. As a first approximation, it may be said that character is composed of enduring patterns of motivation and action.[1] To act characteristically is to do what we would normally and predictably do in a given situation. What makes our action normal and predictable is that we are regularly motivated by certain desires, possess certain capacities, and are guided by certain values. If we find ourselves in a situation where we have the opportunity to satisfy our desires by exercising our capacities according to our values, then we naturally perform the appropriate action. If this happens time and time again, so that the pattern formed of particular desires, capacities, opportunities, values, and actions is a recurrent feature of our lives, then we may identify it as one component of our character.

Not all enduring patterns, however, can be properly identified as part of character. Routine conventional behavior (such as wearing whatever counts as appropriate clothing to work), trivial habits (such as brushing one's teeth before rather than after a shower), and physiologically connected action-patterns (such as taking a daily decongestant pill during the hay fever season) may be enduring patterns in a life, but they are not of sufficient significance to include them in our character. Our biography would not be incomplete if it omitted mention of them. This suggests two further features that an enduring pattern should have in order to be considered a component of our character.

---

[1] This account of character is indebted to Joel Kupperman, *Character* (New York: Oxford University Press, 1991), chap. 1.

The first is that it should have some significance in our life. It is impossible to say in advance which particular enduring patterns will or will not have this feature. What has significance depends on our desires, capacities, opportunities, values, and actions, and there are, of course, enormous variations among us in these respects. But we can identify one very general value that is always significant and always lends significance to the desires, capacities, opportunities, and actions which facilitate its achievement: living according to our conception of a good life. This leaves its inevitable mark on our character, and it provides the most important criterion by which we can decide whether or not some enduring pattern should be counted as part of our character. If it seriously aids or hinders our endeavor to live a good life, then it should be so counted, while if it plays no such role, then there is good reason for regarding it as irrelevant to our character. This reason is not decisive, however, because values other than living a good life may be significant, but a case needs to be made to explain what makes them significant, if it is not their contribution to a good life.

The second feature imposes a further restriction on enduring patterns that should be regarded as part of our character. It concerns the effort we need to make in order to maintain the enduring pattern. An enduring pattern qualifies as part of the agent's character only if it is maintained in the face of some internal or external obstacle. Speaking one's mother tongue, remembering names and faces, and using one's limbs are enduring patterns significant in living a good life, but ordinarily they can be taken for granted and do not merit mention as components of our character. If, however, we are handicapped or obstructed in some way, but manage nevertheless to prevail, then this normally taken-for-granted pattern is backed by the effort that then qualifies it for inclusion in our character. Just how strenuous the effort needs to be is difficult to say. The guiding thought in reaching a decision is that "character" is not merely a descriptive term. It also denotes a low-level achievement that is within the reach of all normal human beings, but it requires more than coming to maturity under normal conditions. Its status is comparable to that of being literate, or a licensed driver, or a taxpayer, at each of which, of course, we can be exceptional, average, or poor, just as our character can be noble, middling, or base.

"Character" will be understood, then, as the collection of enduring patterns formed of desires, capacities, opportunities, values, and corresponding actions which are significant given our conception of a good life, and which require us to make some effort to maintain. There are some, but surely very few, normal adults who do not have a character in this sense. Their motives and actions are so fickle as to form no or only very few enduring patterns; they lack a conception of a good life, or they are not motivated to live according to it; or they are so beset by adversity or ruled by such sloth as to be incapable or unwilling to make even the minimum effort to maintain some enduring pattern beyond those created by the most elementary physiological and psychological drives. But these are exceptional cases. Most of us can be supposed to have a character.

The extent to which we form our character, however, is quite varied. At one extreme, we are largely passive possessors of the important enduring patterns that rule our lives. The patterns, in such cases, are formed by influences to which we are subject and over which we have little control. The meager efforts we make consist in continuing to conduct ourselves in our habitual manner. Our character, then, is not of our own making, but the product of genetic inheritance and postnatal conditioning. Such characters will be called "fortuitous." At the opposite extreme, we actively participate in the formation of our character. The enduring patterns then are shaped not merely by the forces that have influenced us but also by our reflection and resulting judgment about them. These efforts are much more extensive than what is required by fortuitous character, for they require that we habitually oppose or encourage patterns we find in ourselves. Characters formed by our active, reflective judgments will be called "deliberate." Characters then can be arranged on a continuum ranging from fortuitous to deliberate. The more deliberate is our character, the greater is our control over the desires, capacities, opportunities, values, and actions which constitute the substantive content of these patterns.

Increasing control may be understood, therefore, as the transformation of our fortuitous character into a deliberate one. Or, since both the transformation and the extent to which characters are fortuitous and deliberate are matters of degree, increasing control is the process of making our character less fortuitous and more deliberate. The reason we should want to effect this transformation is to decrease the extent to which we are victims of permanent adversities and to increase the extent to which the enduring patterns of our character aid rather than hinder living according to our conception of a good life.

The central importance of self-knowledge is that it is one of the ways through which the deliberate formation of our character occurs. The description of self-knowledge, therefore, involves describing the process whereby fortuitous character is made more deliberate. To begin with, self-knowledge is a *conscious* process. It is not just something that goes on inside us, like the processes that enable us to use language, but a process of which we are conscious as it is going on. Its occurrence and our awareness of it are contemporaneous. This is true of many forms of knowledge, but self-knowledge is distinguished from them by being *reflexive*. In its case, the knowing subject and the known object are intimately connected because self-knowledge is knowledge of part of the self of the knower. Self-knowledge, therefore, is not merely a conscious, but a *self-conscious*, process. It is knowledge directed inward by the knower.

Self-knowledge has both a *descriptive*, truth-directed aspect and a *motivational*, action-guiding one. In its descriptive employment, we know facts about ourselves. If we know ourselves well in this way, we can construct an accurate psychological self-portrait. We then know our desires, capacities, opportunities, and values. This kind of knowledge is objective. It is connected with truth, verification, and falsification. Knowing ourselves in this manner is the same kind of knowledge as we have of others. But since in self-knowledge the knower is far more likely to possess the relevant information, interest, and motivation than in knowledge of other selves, self-knowledge tends to be more reliable.

A further difference between them emerges in considering the motivational aspect of self-knowledge. Self-knowledge is connected with action in a way in which knowledge of other selves is not. Being motivational is a constitutive feature of self-knowledge, while it is merely a contingent feature of knowledge of others. To know something about ourselves is to have a motive to employ the knowledge. There may be reasons why we should not act as the motive prompts us, but in the absence of countervailing reasons, self-knowledge leads to action. If we know that we need privacy, we tend to seek it. But if we know something similar about another person, there is no analogous motive for doing anything at all. We may lack the opportunity, be indifferent, or not want to meddle. In our own case, however, we cannot meddle; indifference is exceptional; and the opportunity to employ our knowledge normally exists.

Through descriptive self-knowledge we know facts about ourselves. But there are facts and facts. Some are simple, like being surprised at getting a Great Dane puppy as a birthday present. Others are complicated, involving patterns formed of simple facts, such as the connection between particular desires, capacities, opportunities, values, and actions. Between simple and complex facts, there are many and various intermediate possibilities. Knowledge of simple facts, at one extreme, tends to be descriptive; knowledge of complex facts, at the other extreme, tends to involve a particular kind of *interpretation*.[2] In intermediate cases, the descriptive and interpretive features of self-knowledge shade into each other.

What calls for interpretation, however, is not the complexity of some facts, but their significance. The complex facts we know about ourselves are usually more significant than simple ones, and that is why knowledge

---

[2] For a suggestive discussion of this aspect of self-knowledge, see Richard Wollheim, *The Thread of Life* (Cambridge: Harvard University Press, 1984), especially chap. 6.

of the former is more likely to be involved in interpretation than knowledge of the latter. In any case, this kind of interpretation is connected with distinguishing between what is significant and insignificant. It is through this feature of self-knowledge that we distinguish between momentous and trivial events in our lives, between formative and banal experiences, or between everyday occurrences and the exciting, unexpected, dangerous, or shameful signs that we are not what we supposed ourselves to be.

The simple facts we come to know about ourselves through descriptive self-knowledge are, as it were, the data out of which we construct knowledge of our character. These data need to be organized; connections among them need to be discerned; and coherence and intelligibility must be imposed on them—these are the aims of the interpretation involved in self-knowledge. It is often unclear where description ends and interpretation starts, and perhaps no datum is purely descriptive. What is clear, however, is that both features are necessary for self-knowledge, since description without interpretation has no significance and interpretation without description lacks content.

Interpretation, of course, plays a central role not just in self-knowledge, but also in history, literary criticism, biography, and jurisprudence, to mention some examples. Interpretation in these other contexts, however, need not involve evaluation of the pattern imposed on the relevant facts. A historian may believe that the worldliness of the clergy was an important factor in the rise of the Reformation, but this belief need not carry an evaluation of the priesthood. Accuracy, not morality, is what matters to the historian's judgment.

Contrast this with John Stuart Mill's claim that Harriet Taylor has exercised a profound influence on his philosophical development. This is an interpretation that is essentially connected with Mill's self-knowledge, and as such, inescapably evaluative. Opinion on Harriet Taylor is divided. Some thought of her as a ghastly woman, infused with great fervor about half-baked ideas, fueled by unrealistic ambitions and petty resentments. Others regarded her as a fine human being whose sterling intellectual and moral qualities made her prevail over Victorian stupidity about women. We need not take a side on this issue, but the point is that Mill could not avoid doing so. He could not say: "Harriet Taylor has a profound influence on my thoughts and feelings, but I am indifferent to whether she is a termagant or a moral hero." Mill could not remain neutral because his view of Taylor was essentially connected with his conception of a good life, a connection that was established through his hard-earned self-knowledge, as we learn from his *Autobiography*.[3] It is this complicated connection that

---

[3] John Stuart Mill, *Autobiography* (Indianapolis: Bobbs-Merrill, 1957).

needs to be understood in order to see why the interpretation involved in self-knowledge is inescapably *evaluative*.

The task of interpretation, the determination of significance, requires a standard. It is with reference to it that we interpret the relative significance of the facts. And, as Mill's case suggests, that standard, in the case of self-knowledge, is our conception of a good life. Interpretation of the significance of various facts about our character is thus evaluative because it derives from our conception of a good life and contributes to living according to it. Historical, literary, and other interpretations are not usually connected with this sort of evaluative perspective and standard.

This initial account of the interpretive aspect of self-knowledge must be revised, however, because it misleadingly suggests that self-knowledge is connected with what may be called "self-ratification."[4] Through interpretation we decide that some facts about our character are significant because they have a formative influence on living according to our conception of a good life. But this influence does not merely make some facts more and others less significant when we interpret them from the point of view created by our conception of a good life. Some facts that we know about ourselves may be actively inconsistent with that conception, and among such facts permanent adversities occupy a prominent position. Through interpretation we judge, therefore, not merely that some facts about us are significant or insignificant, but also that they are significant and shameful, just as others may be significant and admirable. The interpretation involved in self-knowledge should be seen therefore as yielding both favorable and unfavorable evaluations.

These evaluations, however, are action-guiding. We do not merely take cognizance through them of the truth that some facts about our character aid and others hinder our desire to live a good life. Favorable evaluations reinforce the enduring patterns that constitute our character, while unfavorable ones weaken them. And both commit us to appropriate action. In this way the interpretive aspect of self-knowledge incorporates its descriptive, evaluative, and motivational aspects. If we understand that this kind of interpretation appeals to our conception of a good life as a standard, then we shall understand also that it must contain the other aspects of self-knowledge. We may therefore characterize self-knowledge as interpretation of our character whose aim is to make our character less fortuitous and more deliberate. And the reason for wanting to engage in this kind of

---

[4] The term is from Joel Kupperman, "Character and Self-Knowledge," *Aristotelian Society Proceedings* 85 (1984/85): 219–238. Kupperman ties self-knowledge to self-ratification, although he holds, inconsistently it seems, that self-ratification may involve both self-loathing and the resolve *not* to change one's character.

interpretation is to overcome the obstacles in us—including permanent adversities—which stand in the way of making our lives better.[5]

Self-knowledge is both backward-looking and forward-looking. It derives its content from the past and its significance from the future. The known facts of our character—our desires, capacities, opportunities, actions, and our evaluations of them based on our conception of a good life—have all occurred in the past. In endeavoring to develop knowledge of them, we have to look backward. But we do not look backward because we have a disinterested curiosity about our past. We look because we want to increase control over our actions, and the way to do that is to increase control over our character, from which our actions usually follow and which they usually reflect. Our past interests us because it is a key to our future. What we shall do is deeply influenced by what we have done. The means by which this influence is exerted is our character. It stretches from the past to the future because the enduring patterns that constitute it are at once constructions of the past and action-guiding tendencies for the future. Increasing control is the endeavor to remove obstacles from the way of our future actions. This presupposes knowledge of the obstacles that, in the case of self-knowledge, are aspects of our character as it has been formed in the past. Since self-knowledge is the effort to transform our character by making it less fortuitous and more deliberate, it must be equally attentive to its undesirable fortuitous past features and to its desirable deliberate future ones. As Kierkegaard memorably remarked: "It is perfectly true, as philosophers say, that life must be understood backwards. But they forget the other proposition, that it must be lived forwards." And, as Richard Wollheim no less memorably added: "What Kierkegaard . . . overlooked is that, for a person, not only is understanding the life he leads intrinsic to leading it, but for much of the time, leading the life is, or is mostly, understanding it.[6]

Essential to giving an account of what is involved in the backward- and forward-looking aspect of self-knowledge, an account that is intended to provide the understanding of which Kierkegaard and Wollheim speak, is the distinction drawn earlier between the significant and insignificant facts of our life. The significant facts are complex events whose features may be characterized either as occupying the foreground or as being relegated to the background. The foreground is occupied by features that are sup-

---

[5] This account of self-knowledge is indebted to David W. Hamlyn, "Self-Knowledge," in *Perception, Learning, and the Self* (London: Routledge, 1983).

[6] Wollheim, *The Thread of Life*, 1 and 283.

posed to account for the significance of the fact, while the background contains the countless features essential to making the fact what it is, but which are regarded as routine and obvious. Self-knowledge, then, reveals that some fact is significant or insignificant, and it is supported by the features of the fact in the foreground, while those in the background are taken for granted.

Consider as an illustration an episode in the life of Neoptolemus, as portrayed by Sophocles in *Philoctetes*.[7] Neoptolemus is a young man, the son of Achilles, aspiring to his dead father's stature. He has recently joined the Greek troops besieging Troy. He is decent, intelligent, well brought-up, ambitious, and he faces a predicament that is as familiar to us as it was to the ancients. He can become a pivotal figure in a strategically necessary plot to deprive the already unfortunate Philoctetes of the weapon he needs for survival and the Greeks need for victory. He can thus add grievous harm to the already great and unjust suffering of Philoctetes, or he can ruin his career, betray his allies, listen to his decent instincts, and refuse. If he opts for expediency, he will "be called a wise man and a good" (119), but at the cost of "casting aside all shame" (120). He has "a natural antipathy / to get my ends by tricks and stratagems" (87–88), but he is told by Odysseus, one of the leaders of the Greeks, his elder, and his superior: "For one brief shameless portion of a day / give me yourself, and then for all the rest / you may be called the most scrupulous of men" (83–85). Neoptolemus replies, "I recognize that I was sent with you / to follow your instructions. I am loath to have you call me traitor" (93–95). Still he wonders, "Do you not find it vile yourself, this lying?" (108), and he is told, "Not if the lying brings our rescue with it" (109). And then he is reminded to "look to your standing . . . look to your plans for the future" (832–834). So he is forced to reflect on the question, "What must I do?" (908), while knowing that he "must decide" (965).

Neoptolemus knows that the result of his reflection will matter not just politically but also personally. He has to reflect on how he should live his life. He is at a critical juncture, and the significance of the episode is that whatever judgment he ends up making, he will embark on a policy of reinforcing one part of himself and weakening another. He knows this much about himself, but he does not know enough to make the judgment easy. Being young and not brought up to this kind of reflection, he naturally and understandably hesitates. In the foreground is the conflict between political expediency, respect for his elders, and personal advancement, on the one hand, and his decency, shame of lying, and compassion for the intended victim, on the other.

---

[7] Sophocles, *Philoctetes*. References in the text are to the lines of the play.

Concentrating on the background for a moment, it is helpful to distinguish between three types of features that form it, not only in the present example, but in all typical instances of self-knowledge: the metaphysical, the social, and the personal. The epistemological status of these features is that as agents seeking self-knowledge we believe them to be true, but they need not be. Their truth is presupposed in our reflection, in the sense that if we did not believe them, our resulting judgments could not be reasonable.

The metaphysical features are our most general beliefs about the nature of reality: that events have causes, that material objects, human beings, God or gods exist, that people can communicate with each other by using language, that things change, that human lives come to an end, that people are capable of benefiting and harming one another, and so on. These features are believed to be generally true, transcending the context in which they happen to be held. The social features are the customary practices of our society governed by religious, political, moral, culinary, sexual, aesthetic, educational, and other similar conventions. They are acknowledged to differ from context to context, but they set standards of appropriate conduct in our own context. The personal features concern our own individual circumstances, our beliefs about our own past, the events that happened to us, and a large variety of autobiographical facts that we have no reason to hold in the focus of our attention.

There is a perfectly good sense in which we all take ourselves to know about such facts as these and about their bearing on our life. It is just that we keep them in the background, take them for granted, and pay no attention to them. They will not normally figure in our self-knowledge. There are so many of them, and they are so various, that they could not occupy the foreground, for reasons Sterne makes so charmingly obvious in *Tristram Shandy*. We shall think of them as forming the necessary background without which there could not be a foreground, but they may also be thought of as the tacit component of our knowledge,[8] or as implicit meanings,[9] or as absolute and relative presuppositions,[10] or as the given part of our form of life that has to be accepted so that we can go on with the rest.[11]

Whatever way we think of them, however, they must be recognized as logically necessary conditions for any judgment's making sense. But they should not be thought of merely as passive components of the background, much as common people living ordinary lives are thought of as

---

[8] Karl Polanyi, *Personal Knowledge* (New York: Harper, 1958).
[9] Mary Douglas, *Implicit Meanings* (London: Routledge, 1975).
[10] Robin G. Collingwood, *An Essay on Metaphysics* (Oxford: Clarendon Press, 1940), part 1.
[11] Ludwig Wittgenstein, *Philosophical Investigations* (Oxford: Blackwell, 1968), 226.

the extras in the drama of history. The distinction between background and foreground, between what is significant and insignificant has a shifting frontier because the background contains highly volatile elements, as well as obvious and boring ones. Where the distinction is drawn is a central part of the interpretive aspect of self- knowledge, but our interpretations are revised, discarded, strengthened, or weakened partly because what seemed significant before has become insignificant, or vice versa.

The most volatile elements in the background are to be found among the personal features. They are most open to and inviting of revision because they are not inert, merely awaiting interpretation to confer significance on them. They are desires felt, capacities exercised, opportunities seized, values pursued, and actions performed. They are infused with pride, shame, guilt, satisfaction, frustration, self-esteem, and self-loathing; they provoke our hopes, fears, fantasies, dreams, and nightmares; they surprise us by being different in actual experience from what we imagined them before; they give us joy, delight, pleasure, sadness, misery, and pain; they are living, pulsating human experiences—our experiences, and they form part of the substance of our inner life.

Interpretation of them involves not merely the imposition of some plausible hierarchy of significance on passive material because the material itself has a voice in deciding the significance it has. And since the interpretation is involved in *self*-knowledge, the material expresses itself through the thoughts and feelings of the agents themselves, who are interpreting, among other things, the significance of those very thoughts and feelings, just as Neoptolemus has to interpret the significance he attaches to shame and glory, ambition and decency, compassion and achievement, when each of these conflicting voices is his own and each finds a responsive echo in himself.

Suppose, then, that we have arrived at knowledge of not just a single fact about ourselves, but at overall knowledge of the enduring patterns these single facts form. The knowledge is backward-looking because it offers a coherent view of the significant facts in our past, and it is forward-looking because the evaluations embodied in it guide our future actions as well. The understanding of what such overall self-knowledge involves will gain depth when we consider the differences between this account and an influential contemporary attempt to provide a similar account.

Alasdair MacIntyre in *After Virtue* discusses "a concept of a self whose unity resides in the unity of a narrative which links birth to life to death as narrative beginning to middle to end."[12] His claim is that in understand-

---

[12] Alasdair MacIntyre, *After Virtue* (Notre Dame, Ind.: University of Notre Dame Press, 1981), 191. Another attempt along similar lines is Martha C. Nussbaum's *Love's Knowledge* (New York: Oxford University Press, 1990), especially chap. 12, "Narrative Emotions."

ing what we are doing "we always move toward placing a particular episode in the context of a set of narrative histories. . . . It is because we all live out narratives in our lives and because we understand our lives in terms of the narratives that we live out that the form of narrative is appropriate for understanding."[13] And he goes on: "In what does the unity of an individual life consist? The answer is that its unity is the unity of a narrative embodied in a single life. . . . The unity of a human life is the unity of a narrative quest. Quests sometimes fail, are frustrated, abandoned or dissipated into distractions; and human lives may in all these ways also fail. But the only criteria for success or failure in a human life as a whole are the criteria of success or failure in a narrated or to-be-narrated quest."[14] MacIntyre's suggestion is, therefore, that self-knowledge has the form of a narrative. His "central thesis" is that "man is in his actions and practice . . . essentially a story-telling animal . . . a teller of stories that aspire to truth. . . . I can only answer the question 'What am I to do?' if I can answer the prior question 'Of what story . . . do I find myself a part?' "[15]

MacIntyre's conception of a narrative from which the facts of our life derive their significance is likely to appeal to contemporary sensibility. It explains the widespread influence of Oriental and homegrown self-improvement cults, each supplying rules, vocabulary, and plot for constructing some narrative to make sense of one's life; it explains as well the like influence of psychoanalysis and the genres of *Bildungsroman*, biography, and autobiography. It speaks to that aspect of our sensibility which finds it natural to look inward, to concentrate on our mental states and experiences, to try to derive significance from within rather than to seek it in religious faith or political commitment. But the very appeal of thinking of self-knowledge as a narrative of our life carries with it the grounds for doubting it.

Self-knowledge, after all, is not the invention of contemporary sensibility. Socrates, Plato, Aristotle, Augustine, Aquinas, Descartes, Spinoza, and Hume, to mention only a few historical figures, were just as keenly interested in it as we are. But they did not suppose it to take a narrative form. It may be that many literary-minded Western intellectuals in the twentieth century try to achieve self-knowledge by attempting to tell true stories to themselves about themselves. There is no good reason, however, for projecting this tendency onto other sensibilities. And, as it will become apparent, there are good reasons for doubting that self-knowledge can be properly characterized as a narrative even by those who share the sensibility to which MacIntyre's view appeals.

[13] MacIntyre, *After Virtue*, 197.
[14] Ibid., 203.
[15] Ibid., 201.

Narratives tell a story by relating facts. The facts may be real or imag-. inary: those of the travels of Marco Polo or those of Gulliver, for example. In some narratives, the narrator makes up the facts as the narration proceeds; in others, real and imaginary facts are mixed. The facts related in a narrative, therefore, may or may not actually exist. But it is a logical point about each fact in a narrative that it is either real or imaginary, and the point holds even if we cannot tell about a narrated fact which it is.

MacIntyre clearly intends us to understand narratives as relating real facts: we proceed by "placing a particular episode in the context of a . . . narrative."[16] So there is, on the one hand, the fact, and, on the other, the narrative in which the fact plays the role the narrator assigns to it. In a narrative of self-knowledge, the fact may be something that we did or something that happened to us or something that we merely think we did or happened to us, although it did not. In both cases, however, the fact is real, not imaginary. In the first case, it is an actual event; in the second, it is an actual thought of an imaginary event. Neither is made up by the narrator; the narrative account of both is about something that has or had existence outside of and independently of the narrative.

One aim of self-knowledge, according to both MacIntyre's and the present view, is to arrive at an interpretation of the significance of actual facts in our life. The reason against identifying narratives with self-knowledge is that self-knowledge demands more than narratives, as they are ordinarily understood, supply.

Consider first what is involved in the backward-looking aspect of self-knowledge in the light of Ermanno Bencivenga's suggestive observation. "When the first caper was tried by the first dancer, that person was not yet a dancer, and that movement was not yet a caper; it was a spontaneous way of releasing energy, of expressing joy, perhaps. But then one caper succeeded another, and on the way they *became* capers, as people started focusing on them, identifying them, and using them deliberately to express or to *communicate* joy."[17] We interpret the significance of facts and so we transform them, as dancers transform movements into capers. We form our deliberate character by interpreting the spontaneous manifestations of our fortuitous character, and through the interpretation we confer significance on them in the patterns that constitute our character. Backward-looking self-knowledge, therefore, involves more than taking a fact and assigning to it some significance in our life.

[16] Ibid., 197.
[17] Ermanno Bencivenga, *The Discipline of Subjectivity* (Princeton: Princeton University Press, 1990), 34.

Self-knowledge proceeds on two levels: on the level of the description of the facts, and on the level of the evaluation of the significance of the facts. Self-knowledge suggests how facts should be seen *as*: joyful physical movements of a certain sort, for instance, *as* capers; and it also suggests how the significance of the facts should be seen *as*, for instance, *as* the dancer having been inspired to new heights of expressiveness by newly found happiness. Narratives, by contrast, usually proceed on one level: they take facts as given, and they provide their significance.

We could, of course, decide to call self-knowledge a form of "narrative." What we can reasonably decide, however, is not entirely optional. Narratives are intended to be accounts of real or imaginary facts; they construct a story about their significance. Self-knowledge, however, is a more complicated process. Seeing something *as* certainly requires that there be something to be seen, but it is part of self-knowledge that what is there is itself open to interpretation. It is a fact that Neoptolemus lied in order to take possession of the weapons without which Philoctetes could not survive. But whether this fact is to be taken as shameful and cruel or wise and good is not settled by the fact. It is doubtful that the word "narrative" is sufficiently capacious to include all this content. What is really important, however, lies elsewhere. It is that self-knowledge must move on two levels.

Self-knowledge, however, is richer still than its backward-looking aspect suggests: it is also forward-looking. It commits us to a particular judgment of our character, including a particular standard for evaluating our desires, capacities, opportunities, and past and future actions. This judgment and the evaluations it suggests necessarily motivate us. We cannot form a view of what is significant to us, have the capacity and the opportunity to do something about it, and then be unmotivated to act. But in their usual sense, narratives need not motivate us. They may, but it does not require a special explanation if they do not. For narratives to do what self-knowledge does, they would have to intend to tell a true story; the story would have to be about the narrator; it would have to be about something significant in the narrator's life; and its significance would have to be such as to motivate the narrator's future actions. To call such a thing a "narrative" would obscure what it is and impute connotations that the word does not possess in accepted usage.

THE NEED FOR SELF-KNOWLEDGE

By way of summarizing the emerging account of self-knowledge, it should be noted that it is a mode of reflection, involving judgment, whose aim is to make our character less fortuitous and more deliberate. This is the same process as that of increasing control, for what moves our character in the desired direction is that we control it so as to approximate more closely than before our conception of a good life. This desirable transformation proceeds through the evaluation of our desires, capacities, opportunities, values, and actions with a view of forming out of them such enduring patterns as we regard conducive to living a good life.

Neoptolemus had insufficient self-knowledge, and, as a result, he did not know what to do. Being young, inexperienced, and unformed, he had only his fortuitous character to guide him. This character was serviceable enough for simple moral situations, but it did not have sufficient resources to cope with complex moral situations. If his situation had been simple, Neoptolemus would not have been morally obliged "to be clever in mischief against his nature and will" (1014), he would not have felt that he ought to go against his "natural bent . . . to contrive such mischief" (79–80), and he would not have had to overcome his "natural antipathy / to get my ends by tricks and stratagems" (87–88).

Neoptolemus discovered, however, that in the midst of the complexities he encountered, what came to him naturally, the promptings of his fortuitous character and simple decency, were insufficient. And so he did not know what to do. He appealed to the heavens, "Zeus, what must I do?" (908), and he wrung his hands, "I would I had never left / Scyrus [i.e., home], so hateful is what I face now" (969–970). Circumstances, however, forced him to act, and then he acted inconsistently. He first went against the promptings of his fortuitous character and lied. Then he wanted to have it both ways and told the truth, while keeping the weapon gained by lying. Then he changed his mind again, and gave the weapon back. And at the end he reverted to the clichés of his upbringing, "The fortunes that the Gods give to us men / we must bear under necessity" (1317–1318), while trying to persuade Philoctetes to do voluntarily what he was told at the beginning that it was out of the question that Philoctetes would do.

Neoptolemus's irresolution shows that he is out of his depth, but that is natural and understandable for all those whose character is only fortuitous. At a certain point in our moral development, we all find ourselves unprepared in complex moral situations. This unpreparedness, however, may be a productive event in our moral growth. It may lead us to the realization that we must move beyond our conventional upbringing and the fortuitous character it has produced. We may realize, as we reflect on newly encountered complexities, that our desires, capacities, opportunities, and values, which hitherto motivated our actions, are incoherent. And yet the only resource we have for deciding what we ought to do in the complex moral situation we face is to listen to the incoherent promptings of the incoherent patterns that make up our incoherently formed character.

Our irresolution, or forced resolution resulting in inconsistent action, is a natural consequence of our insufficient self-knowledge. The significance of such complex situations as Neoptolemus's is that they suggest to us that we are morally adrift. The trouble is not that we lack desires, capacities, opportunities, and values that would motivate us to act; it is rather that these elements of our character are incoherent. They incline us in different and incompatible directions, and we lack a way of overcoming their incoherence. We need better self-knowledge to improve our description and evaluation of these elements and to achieve better direction of their motivational force.

The need for self-knowledge, therefore, is not an externally imposed requirement, but one that arises naturally and spontaneously from finding ourselves irresolute in complex moral situations. There are and always will be moral situations rendered intrinsically complex by permanent adversities. But the complexity of very many other moral situations is due to the insufficient resources we bring to coping with them. We see these situations *as* complex because they force us to face the incoherence of the patterns of desires, capacities, opportunities, values, and actions which have formed our character in the past and which provide poor guidance for the future. Part of the aim of self-knowledge is to remove this incoherence to the extent to which the permanent adversities operating within us permit it. If we are reasonable, therefore, we shall seek to improve such self-knowledge as we have.

The place at which we must start are the facts that make up our more or less fortuitous character. Self-knowledge, then, proceeds in three steps, which may be separated in analysis but not in real life: description, evaluation, and motivation. Through description we become conscious of and endeavor to characterize the relevant facts; through evaluation we weigh their significance to our living according to our conception of a good life; and through motivation we are moved to appropriate action. Self-knowledge is both backward- and forward-looking because it is concerned both with the strengthening or weakening of the enduring patterns that constitute the deliberate character we are in the process of forming and with removing the incoherences of the patterns that have formed our fortuitous character.

FROM FORTUITOUS TO DELIBERATE CHARACTER

The irresolution of Neoptolemus helps us see why the possession of a fortuitous character is not enough, not even if it predisposes us to act virtuously. A fortuitous character is utterly conventional, and the natural consequence of it is moral drift and alienation. In simple moral situations—where there is a clear moral principle and an equally clear case that unambiguously falls under the principle so that what we ought to do is obvious—a fortuitous character formed by the prevailing conventional morality is sufficient. But as soon as we encounter a complex moral situation—where clarity is lacking about what principle is relevant, how the case before us is to be seen, and thus what we ought to do—we need more than the conventional resources of a fortuitous character.

We need to know how to resolve the complexities created by the ambiguity that permeates both the principles and the cases. For this, we need judgment. Judgment, however, requires having gone beyond our fortuitous character formed by conventional morality and having reflected on the assumptions on which it rests. This may lead us to endorse all or some of them, or to repudiate them completely or partially. Whatever its outcome is, however, self-knowledge initiates the transformation of a conventional fortuitous character to a more deliberate, more reflectively formed one.

The motivation for acquiring self-knowledge and for transforming our character is provided by the intrinsically undesirable conditions of moral drift and alienation. Moral drift occurs when our moral resources are wholly derived from conventional morality and we find those resources inadequate. We have, then, nowhere to turn for guidance. We know only that whatever we do in that situation is going to be wrong by conventional standards, and so we do not know what to do. We are morally adrift, and the symptom of it is the kind of irresolution shown by Neoptolemus.

Alienation occurs because the fit between our conventional morality and fortuitous character is inevitably imperfect. We are bound to have some desires, capacities, opportunities, and values, and to have performed some actions that are adversely evaluated by the standards of conventional morality. But since these condemned elements of our character are our own, and they motivate us, we feel reluctant to doom them, and thus ourselves, to frustration. Conventional morality demands sacrifices from us, and it is natural to ask why we should make them. There may be good reasons available as answers, but often the answer is cant, moral blackmail, or dogmatic appeal to authority. Good reasons may or may not be accepted as such, and obfuscation is sooner or later seen through. But however we treat the answers we get, the mere fact of needing them is a sure sign that we are at least somewhat alienated from conventional morality. This is no trivial matter because if our character is a conventionally formed fortuitous one, then, as before, and to the extent of our alienation, we are left without coherent guidance about what we ought to do even in simple moral situations.

We want to escape these conditions of moral drift and alienation, and so we are forced to seek self-knowledge. The more we come to know our-

selves, however, the more our character changes from fortuitous to deliberate because the result of self-knowledge is to transform the patterns
formed of desires, capacities, opportunities, values, and actions, which
constitute our character, from what they happened to have been to what
we decide they ought to be.

There is an additional reason for seeking self-knowledge and the transformation of our character, although this one is unlikely to occur to us if
we are in Neoptolemus's position and have only conventional morality and
our fortuitous character to guide us. To feel its force requires us to have already a fair degree of self-knowledge, for the reason stems from the realization that our fortuitous character embodies permanent adversities and
thus it is not sufficiently within our control. Such a character is formed by
the contingency created by our genetic inheritance, the accidents of our
upbringing, and the moment at which we happened to be educated in the
constantly shifting conventions of the society into which we were born. It
is riddled with conflicts among the values of the conventional morality we
have internalized, as well as with conflicts among our own desires, capacities, and opportunities. It is subject to the unintentional and unconscious
evil that may motivate us, since we have not yet acquired enough knowledge of our motives. The greater the role that contingency, conflict, and
evil play in our character, the smaller is the extent to which we control the
patterns that constitute our character. And since living according to our
conception of a good life requires a great deal of control, we have good
reason to want to increase our control by making our character less fortuitous and more deliberate.

If we succeed in this, Plato's description will apply to us: "He is a master
of himself, puts things in order, is his own friend, harmonizes the . . . parts
[of the soul]. . . . He binds them all together, and himself from a plurality
to a unity. . . . [H]e thinks the just and beautiful action . . . to be that which
preserves the inner harmony and indeed helps achieve it, wisdom to be
the knowledge which oversees this, . . . an unjust action be that which destroys it, and ignorance . . . which oversees that."[18] Self-knowledge, then,
may be seen as that part of moral wisdom through which we bring about
the harmony of the soul, or, to put it less poetically, that part of moral wisdom through which we impose coherence on the various elements that
constitute our character.

The imposition of coherence is the result of increased control. It has a
positive aspect, which motivates us to evaluate our desires, capacities, opportunities, and actions by the values that form our conception of a good
life. It also has a negative aspect, which motivates us to overcome obstacles

[18] Plato, *Republic*, 443d–e.

to living according to that conception by subjecting our evaluations to the test of reflection. In the case of self-knowledge, that test involves the endeavor to free our descriptions, evaluations, and motivation from the obstacles created by permanent adversities and by our individual short-comings. Self-knowledge may be understood therefore as the imposition of coherence on our character by constructing an interpretation that pre-scribes how we should see the elements we are trying to make coherent. This view is "the coherence theory of self-knowledge."

The question now is whether the coherence theory of self-knowledge gives an adequate account of this centrally important component of moral wisdom. MacIntyre's view is that the coherence theory is adequate. As he says: "The unity of a human life is the unity of a narrative quest. Quests sometimes fail, are frustrated, abandoned or dissipated into distractions; and human lives may in all these ways also fail. But the only criteria for suc-cess or failure in a human life as a whole are the criteria of success or fail-ure in a narrated or to-be-narrated quest."[19]

It has already been argued that MacIntyre's view is faulty because it iden-tifies the relevant aspect of self-knowledge with the construction of a nar-rative. The coherence theory of self-knowledge, however, need not be committed to this identification; indeed, it need not mention narratives at all. What is essential to it is the supposition that the criteria by which we judge the coherence of a life are internal to the conception of a good life that is intended to provide the coherence. MacIntyre is far from being alone in making this supposition, for the supposition is nothing but rela-tivism applied to the case of self-knowledge, and it is a widely held view.[20] The thought behind it is that just as cultures, *Weltanschauungen*, forms of life, and the like can be judged without begging the question only by cri-teria internal to them, because there is no criterion outside of some per-spective or another, so also must we do in the case of the conception of a good life involved in self- knowledge. Although there is much to be said for—and against—this view, in the case of self-knowledge at least, it is un-tenable.

Showing that it is so requires first appreciating its strength. Self-knowl-edge involves not merely the distinction between significant and insignifi-

[19] MacIntyre, *After Virtue*, 203.

[20] There is a large body of literature on relativism. For useful surveys and bibliographies, see Martin Hollis and Steven Lukes, eds., *Rationality and Relativism* (Oxford: Blackwell, 1982), Michael Krausz and Jack W. Meiland, eds., *Relativism: Cognitive and Moral* (Notre Dame, Ind.: University of Notre Dame Press, 1982), Michael Krausz, *Relativism: Interpretation and Confrontation* (Notre Dame, Ind.: University of Notre Dame Press, 1989), as well as the book-length treatments by David R. Hiley, *Philosophy in Question* (Chicago: University of Chicago Press, 1988), and Joseph Margolis, *The Truth about Relativism* (Oxford: Blackwell, 1991).

cant facts, placing the former in the foreground and the latter in the background, but also the very description of the facts. It is true that the desires, capacities, opportunities, values, and actions that comprise the facts exist independently of our description of them, yet the way we describe them carries with it evaluative and motivational implications. Few self-descriptions are without evaluative and motivational implications, and if some are, then that already suggests the judgment that they are without significance. It seems, therefore, that self-knowledge shapes the facts which are its objects.

It adds to the complexity of self-knowledge, however, that the relevant facts bear on what we prize in life, and so they are unlikely to be passive, awaiting our interpretation of their significance. The facts do not lend themselves to all the interpretations which we may wish to impose on them. They have a life of their own because they give us pleasure and pain, they fill us with pride, regret, shame, guilt, sorrow, and joy, and they soothe and bother us. Many of these feelings precede our interpretations of the facts, rather than being reactions to them because the feelings themselves figure among the to-be-interpreted facts. We may try to control these buzzing and booming components of our character by means of deeper self-knowledge, providing better interpretations, but it is unlikely that we can always succeed, or indeed that success is always desirable. Having a strong feeling about something is usually good evidence that it is significant. To try to impose an interpretation on it that would deny its significance and relegate it to the background is often useless and may be worse than that. If the fact is significant, it will not stay there. It seems, therefore, that self-knowledge is shaped by the facts which are its objects.

These last two features of self-knowledge obviously coexist in a state of tension. Self-knowledge shapes facts and facts shape self-knowledge. But which is prior and which has authority over the other? If self-knowledge shapes facts, then how do we know that the facts are facts of our life, rather than products of the interpretations we impose on them? If facts shape self- knowledge, then how can self-knowledge be used to increase our control over the very facts that shape them?[21]

Self-knowledge must begin with a description of the relevant facts, but they can be described in various way. How they—our desires, capacities, opportunities, values, and actions, which are the elements of our character—are described has evaluative and motivational implications. Their description is not a straightforward matter of seeing what is there and then

---

[21] This, of course, is the hermeneutic circle, as it occurs in interpretation involved in self-knowledge. Much has been written on this topic, although not in connection with self-knowledge. See Hans-Georg Gadamer, *Truth and Method*, trans. G. Barden and J. Cumming (New York: Seabury Press, 1975), second part, II, and, for a clear explanation, Georgia Warnke, *Gadamer* (Stanford: Stanford University Press, 1987), chapter 3.

expressing it; it is rather seeing what is there *as* something significant or insignificant, desirable or repugnant, exciting or banal, and so forth. The description thus results in an interpretation and the interpretation involves seeing the relevant facts as they are evaluated by our conception of a good life. In this description, however, facts and self-knowledge are inextricably mixed, neither has priority over the other.

Part of the strength of the coherence theory of self-knowledge is that this is precisely what one would expect, if that theory were an accurate account of our knowledge of the facts of our character. The theory repudiates the view that self-knowledge consists in a description of the relevant facts which represents them as accurately as possible. If this were possible, then criteria of success would not be internal to the conception of a good life from which the facts are viewed. The criteria would then be the measure of how closely putative self-knowledge corresponds to the relevant facts, and thus the criteria would be external to such conceptions. But this cannot be so, according to the coherence theory, because there are no facts independent of our description of them; what creates the facts is the manner in which we characterize them. There is thus no external way of judging whether the coherent conception we impose, through self-knowledge, on our character is successful or not. The judgment is internal to that conception because there can be no external criterion to which the judgment could appeal.

It adds to the strength of the coherence theory if we appreciate what a considerable improvement it is to have self-knowledge, so conceived, over the states of moral drift and alienation. Through self-knowledge, we leave behind the incoherence of our fortuitous character and embark on the process of forming a deliberate one. Where there has been irresolution, there is now beginning to emerge a reflectively formed conception of a good life. It makes it possible to increase our control because we can describe and evaluate elements of our character and motivate our conduct by the standards that conception sets. It may be asked by defenders of the coherence theory: What more is it reasonable to demand either from self-knowledge or from a theory accounting for it?

That it is reasonable to demand more will become apparent if it is realized that the theory does not exclude any coherent conception that could be imposed on the relevant facts. To be sure, having a coherent conception is better than not having one, but are we to accept the implication that there is no reasonable way of choosing between alternative equally coherent conceptions? Say that we acknowledge that the elements of our character must be viewed from some conception of a good life or another, does that mean that all conceptions are equally reasonable?

Consider the consequences if this were so. Suppose that we are roughly in Neoptolemus's position. We are trying to be reasonable and decent, and we have received a proper moral education. But we find ourselves both morally adrift—because the incoherent elements of our character motivate us in a variety of different and incompatible ways—and alienated—because the resources of our conventional morality are insufficient to guide us in the complex moral situations we face. We are thus frustrated about ourselves and contemptuous of the unhelpful conventions of our society. Yet, reason and decency do not permit us to become cynical, amoral, or indifferent. This is a familiar stage in the moral development of many people, and it is readily recognizable in many of us—especially the young—living in our society. The great danger of it is that we become prey to the first coherent conception of a good life that comes our way.

Is it really true, and does anyone really believe, that the conceptions of a good life offered by the Reverend Moon of the Unification Church, the Hare Krishna sect, television missionaries of Protestant fundamentalism, orthodox Catholics, Shiite ayatollahs, Zen Buddhists, Aristotle, John Stuart Mill, Kant, the Lubavitscher Rabbi, the American Founders, Freudian psychoanalysts, Montaigne, Spinoza, contemporary economic theorists, radical feminists, Alcoholics Anonymous, the Marquis de Sade, the Nuer of Evans-Pritchard, the Dinka of Lienhardt, and Geertz's theater state of nineteenth-century Bali are all equally reasonable and that there is no reasonable way of justifying or criticizing them from the outside? Is it really the best advice we can give to young men or women that they should commit themselves to some coherent conception of a good life and endeavor to live up to the criteria internal to whatever commitment they have happened to make? Is that what parents hope for their children? Does it not make a difference *what* the coherent conception is to which they commit themselves? Does it not make a difference to older people who survey their own lives retrospectively that they were inspired by one conception of a good life rather than another? Is it really true that what matters is being inspired and that it is immaterial what it is that inspires?

These are, of course, intended to be rhetorical questions, raised to bring out the unacceptable consequences of the relativistic coherence theory of self-knowledge. It may be said, however, that the reason that the questions are rhetorical and the consequences unacceptable is not that one conception of a good life can be shown to be better than another on the basis of some reasonable external criteria. The reason is rather that the questions are entertained and the consequences are rejected by us, who have already made a commitment to a particular conception of a good life. We view the questions and consequences from that perspective, and so of course we give the expected response. If we *are* committed, then we will not find alternative commitments to have the same merit as our own; if we did, we would not *be* committed.

The coherence theory of self-knowledge, therefore, can account for the fact that no one really believes that one coherent conception of a good life is as reasonable as any other. The question is about the basis of this belief. Is it based on the strength of our arbitrary commitments or on reasonable considerations that could be defended without appealing to criteria internal to our conception of a good life? The argument for the second alternative will be the subject of the next chapter.

CONCLUSION

The description of self-knowledge so far has yielded the following conclusions. The object of self-knowledge is the knower's character, and it is a self-conscious and reflexive process. Its aim is to arrive at a reasonable interpretation of the significant facts of our character. Such an interpretation is unavoidably evaluative because it views the to-be-interpreted facts from the perspective of our conception of a good life. Moreover, the evaluation is bound to be motivational because whether we find aspects of our character conducive or detrimental to living what we regard as a good life will have an effect on our conduct. It follows from this that self-knowledge must have both a backward- and a forward-looking aspect. It looks to our past for its facts, and it looks to our hoped-for future to determine what we ought to do about the facts in order to live a good life. Self-knowledge involves, therefore, not only taking stock of the significant features of our character but also the transformation of it from being the fortuitous effect of pre- and postnatal causes to being deliberately formed by ourselves so as to aid our pursuit of a good life.

The process of acquiring self-knowledge is thus a mode of reflection directed toward the transformation of our character. This requires forming a coherent view in which the significant facts about our character are brought as much as possible into harmony with each other and with our conception of a good life. The formation of such a view takes more than the construction of what is normally meant by a narrative, for narratives, unlike self-knowledge, are not required to tell a true story about the narrator that will guide the narrator's future actions. If it is recognized, however, that a coherent account need not be limited to offering what is commonly understood to be a narrative, the question still remains whether a reasonable and coherent account is sufficient for self-knowledge. It will be argued in the next chapter that it is not. By seeing why it is not, it will become possible to go beyond coherence to give a full account of what is required for self-knowledge.

CHAPTER SEVEN

Self-Knowledge: The Second
Mode of Reflection (continued)

BEYOND COHERENCE: PRIMARY VALUES

A great part of the plausibility of the coherence theory of self-knowledge derives from the tension created by the influence on each other of self-knowledge and the facts that are its objects. Facts are shaped by self-knowledge, and self-knowledge is shaped by facts. This leads the coherence theory to deny that there are independent facts to which self-knowledge could correspond. This is the basic reason for the supposition that the correctness of self-knowledge can be a matter of conforming only to internal, rather than to external, criteria. The error of the coherence theory is that it ignores one half of the tension that has led to its formulation in the first place. The theory concentrates on how self-knowledge shapes facts, and it overlooks the equally important consideration that facts shape self-knowledge. How could that happen if facts were dependent on self-knowledge? And if all facts were so dependent, then how could self-knowledge even begin? What would be its object? Do the relevant facts—our desires, capacities, opportunities, values, and actions—begin to exist as a direct result of our beginning to know them? Do people with little self-knowledge, like Neoptolemus, as a matter of necessity, have fewer desires, capacities, and so forth than people with a great deal of self-knowledge?

The absurd consequences to which these questions point compel the recognition both that self-knowledge shapes facts and that facts shape self-knowledge. And it must also be recognized that this reciprocal influence is possible only if self-knowledge and the facts that are its objects are in some sense independent of each other.[1] The coherence theory, therefore, cannot be an acceptable account of self-knowledge. But to have such an account, the sense in which facts and self-knowledge are independent of each other must be made clear.

This requires granting a point essential to the coherence theory, while denying its supposed implications. The point is that self-knowledge, which involves describing, evaluating, and being motivated by the relevant facts, must proceed from some point of view or another. But this should not be taken to imply that the point of view is arbitrary. In actual fact, the relevant point of view is not optional; it is not a matter of choice, commitment, or of the circumstances of our upbringing. It is the human point of view, and, as such, it is necessarily shared by all normal and mature human beings. It is a point of view that is imposed on us by our nature, and so it is universally human, historically constant, and culturally invariant. Its details have been described in Chapter 2, but, as a reminder, a brief restatement of them may be in order.

The point of view is established by human nature, and it is formed by the most elementary facts about us. These facts are physiological, such as our capacity to perceive the world in certain sense modalities, our need for consumption, elimination, and rest. Further facts are psychological, such as wanting to have pleasure and avoid pain; having and exercising capacities to use language, learn from the past, and plan for the future; needing human companionship; and preferring respect to ridicule. There are also social facts: for instance, the occurrence of inevitable conflicts among us; our need for order, predictability, rules, and authority; our having various roles in social life; and, as a result, having various possibilities, as well as there being limits within which we must conduct our lives.

These facts create benefits and harms in respect to which human beings are alike. And these universally human benefits and harms create, in turn, a set of values that have been called primary. There values are simple goods, such as adequate nutrition, security, and companionship, as opposed to simple evils, such as starvation, terror, and ostracism. In addition to primary values and simple goods and evils, there are, of course, also secondary values and complex goods and evils. Secondary values have no claim to universality; what constitutes complex goods and evils varies with conventional moralities and conceptions of a good life.

---

[1] "Whether we choose life for the sake of pleasure or pleasure for the sake of life . . . seem to be bound together and not to admit of separation." Aristotle, *Nicomachean Ethics*, 1175a18–20. "Surely it can be true both that we desire *x* because we think *x* good, and that *x* is good because we desire *x*." David Wiggins, "Truth, Invention, and the Meaning of Life," in *Needs, Values, Truth* (Oxford: Blackwell, 1987), 106.

The significance of primary values for the criticism of the coherence theory of self-knowledge is that they constitute a set of facts with two noteworthy characteristics. First, they are facts which we come to know from a particular point of view, namely, the human. In this respect, the coherence theory is right. Second, the point of view from which we know them is not one that normal and mature human beings could fail to share. And in this respect, the coherence theory is wrong because it supposes that all points of view vary with the context in which they are held.

By way of making the alternative to the coherence theory concrete, it should be noted that the desire to alleviate our hunger, escape illness, and plan for the future, the capacity to locomote, use language, and perceive the world, the opportunity to make choices, better one's lot, and be free from exploitation, the value that is attributed to satisfying these desires, exercising these capacities, and making use of these opportunities, and the performance of the appropriate actions are universally human, universally valued, and universally constitutive of any reasonable conception of a good life. This is not to deny, of course, that there is a plurality of reasonable and irreducibly different conceptions of a good life. It is to deny, however, that if a conception is of a good *human* life, then it could be both reasonable and fail to incorporate primary values.

This being so, the possession of self-knowledge requires knowledge of a set of facts which we must describe, evaluate, and be motivated by in the same basic way, regardless of what conception of a good life we have. The description, evaluation, and motivation of more complex facts will vary on higher levels, but their variations presuppose the point of view established by the requirement of human nature for the enjoyment of simple goods and the avoidance of simple evils. One reason, therefore, why facts shape self-knowledge is that the self known is human, and some of the facts relevant to it must be appropriately acknowledged by whatever conception of a good life is reflected by our self-knowledge.

BEYOND COHERENCE: ANOMALIES

The second reason for holding that facts shape self-knowledge, just as self-knowledge shapes facts, derives from the recognition that a conception of a good life has a dual aspect. It motivates us to live and act according to it, and it controls our conduct by prohibiting us from satisfying some desires, exercising some capacities, seizing some opportunities, holding some values, and performing some actions on the grounds that doing so would be contrary to it. It is in the context of the latter, controlling aspect, that the force of the second reason against the coherence theory of self-knowledge becomes apparent.

Control is needed because conceptions of a good life have the purpose of transforming our present more or less fortuitous character into a future more deliberate one. It must be the case, therefore, for all conceptions of a good life, that there are patterns formed of desires, capacities, opportunities, values, and actions which our character embodies and which are inconsistent with its intended transformation. If there were no such anomalous facts in our character, then we would not need to transform it because it would already be as our conception of a good life prescribes. Few people, if any, achieve this ideal, but, in any case, the road to it is through increasing our control by attempting to eliminate anomalous facts from our character.

The trouble with the coherence theory is that it cannot account for these unavoidably anomalous facts. If facts were shaped by self-knowledge, and if self-knowledge were not also shaped by facts, then how could there be anomalous facts? How could there be facts then that were incompatible with the conception of a good life whose point of view self-knowledge reflects? According to the coherence theory, self-knowledge leads us to describe, evaluate, and be motivated by the relevant facts in a certain way. It leads us, that is, to see the facts *as* our conception of a good life prescribes. But anomalous facts violate this prescription, so the very facts with which the coherence theory begins present counterexamples to the theory.

It may be asked, however, why it should be supposed that the results of our knowledge of some facts pertaining to our character are bound to be favorable. Why could self-knowledge not lead us to describe, evaluate, and be motivated by some facts about ourselves to condemn them, want to alter them, or to be ashamed on account of them? The answer is that of course this could happen and does happen, and if it did not, then we could not increase our control by transforming our character. The point is that if we are to believe—as we should—that it does happen, then we cannot also believe that what the facts are depends entirely on our knowledge of them, which reflects the point of view of some one conception of a good life.

We could not believe it because the adverse judgment of some elements of our character is forced on us by facts contrary to what we take to be our knowledge of them. These facts are painful and disturbing; they diminish our self-esteem; they cause us to feel guilt, shame, remorse, regret; they force us to open a Pandora's Box of negative reactions to ourselves. It is psychologically incredible to suppose that we would bring all this on our own head if we could help it. But if these negative reactions were produced merely by our self-knowledge, and if our self-knowledge merely reflected our conception of a good life, then we could help it by changing the description, evaluation, and motivation that our self-knowledge suggests. If self-knowledge created the facts, there would be nothing to keep us from creating pleasing rather than painful facts. In reality, it is often the recalcitrance, the hardness of some facts of our character, their unavoidable facticity that forces our knowledge of them to take a certain shape.

The influence of anomalous facts on self-knowledge can be resisted. Ignorance about our character can become a carefully protected state. We can deceive ourselves. We can live in bad faith or with false consciousness. We can misrepresent the facts to ourselves by allowing fantasy, sentimentalism, self-pity, fear, shame, or guilt to falsify for ourselves how we really are. But all the familiar ruses by which we obscure the facts from ourselves presuppose that there are facts to be obscured. And although such strategies can be successful, and their success may even last a lifetime, they may also fail, work only imperfectly, and the self-erected veil of falsification may be penetrated in moments of honesty and lucidity. None of this would be possible if facts did not shape our self-knowledge.

Suppose that this is acknowledged by defenders of the coherence theory, while it is denied that we must, as a consequence, acknowledge the independence of facts from self-knowledge. They may argue that the facts of which self-knowledge prompted by our present conception of a good life must take account are the products of self-knowledge prompted by the conception which preceded the present one. And it must be admitted that this is often so. It cannot, however, always be so; it cannot be that all facts are always the products of self-knowledge because the predecessor conception also had to contend with anomalous facts. In proceeding backward, we are bound to reach the stage in our history when we began to acquire self-knowledge, and at that stage, there had to be pre-existing facts, adverse, pleasing, or neutral, with which our lifelong effort of acquiring self-knowledge had to start. This then, is the second reason for rejecting the coherence theory of self-knowledge.

BEYOND COHERENCE: SURPRISES

A third reason against the coherence theory emerges through concentration on a particular feature of the experiences of people whose character is fortuitous, whose negative control weak, and whose self-knowledge rudimentary. One recognizable type among the many encumbered by this defect are young people who are active, self-confident, ambitious, successful, and have optimistic expectations for their future. Something happens then that causes them to doubt themselves, something assails their rude innocence, and they have the experience relevant in the present context: they surprise themselves. As Neoptolemus does when, as he says, "A kind of compassion, / a terrible compassion, has come upon me" (967–68), when it dawns on him that "I practiced craft and treachery with success" (1228), or when he realizes that what he did "was sin, / a shameful sin" (1249). The first unreflective response to such surprising discoveries is to say, as Neoptolemus does: "All is disgust when one leaves his own nature / and does things that misfit it" (902–3). But a moment of reflection shows the untenability of this response, because the compassion, treachery, and sin that so surprise him are also products of his nature. What is disgusting then is not the departure from one's nature, but that nature itself.

Aristotle called the experience in question "discovery," or "recognition" (*anagnorisis*), and placed it at the center of tragedy.[2] "A discovery is . . . a change from ignorance to knowledge . . . in the personages marked for good or evil fortune."[3] There are many kinds of discovery, but the one that Aristotle has in mind and that is relevant here is the discovery we make about ourselves that brings us from ignorance to knowledge about some element of our character. What we discover is an inconsistency between our view of ourselves and how we really are. We recognize that we took appearances for reality, and since our intentions were formed by appearances, the actions based on such malformed intentions do not have their intended effects. But what is fundamentally disturbing about such a discovery, the reason why it surprises us, and why the surprise is usually nasty, is that the intentions were malformed and the actions miscarried because something in our character made them so. What surprises us, therefore, is not merely that we learn something about ourselves of which we were previously ignorant, but that what we learn is contrary to our conception of a good life.

The causes of our surprises may be trivial matters, or they may be highly significant. Tragedy focuses on significant matters, and so, with Aristotle, will the present discussion. What is significant then in what surprises us is that some part of our character presents obstacles to living according to our conceptions of a good life and that we mistook its nature. It appeared to us to be in one way, when in fact it was in another. The ignorance, therefore, does not consist in our failing to know that something which is there is there. It consists rather in our failing to recognize its significance. If we combine this kind of ignorance with the discovery that the significance of the obstructive element in our character is that it may be beyond our control because it is a manifestation of permanent adversities, then we can appreciate just how nasty is the surprise they cause us.

What surprises us, then, is an incoherence in our character. It jeopardizes our efforts to live according to our conception of a good life, and that is why it is a significant matter. The incoherence strikes us at the beginning

---

[2] Aristotle, *Poetics*, 1450a32–34.
[3] Aristotle, *Poetics*, 1452a30–32.

as if we ourselves, unknown to ourselves, created the obstacles to living the way we think we should. The discovery, therefore, seems to reveal a destructive perversity in our character. Further reflection, however, may show, if we persevere in the search for self-knowledge, that the incoherence is not of our making. It would make matters much simpler if it were, because then we could have control over it. If we made it, we could perhaps unmake it. What self-knowledge often teaches us, however, is that the incoherence is not due to bad habits, self-indulgence, or insufficient thought—defects that through strenuous effort we may correct—but to formative influences upon our character, influences whose effect is not due to, although it may be exacerbated by, our shortcomings. If we proceed even deeper, we may come to the realization that these formative influences are not attributable to personal misfortune, which has accidentally befallen us, but that everyone is vulnerable to them because they are permanent adversities implicit in the human condition.

If this line of thought is pursued philosophically, it becomes apparent that it is necessary to go beyond self-knowledge and reflect on the scheme of things external to us. And it will become apparent as well why our reflection must also focus not merely on the good, but also on evil. For the permanent adversities are, from the human point of view, evil, since they are obstacles to living a good life. And we shall see also that Greek tragedies, especially Sophocles', are texts of great moral importance, since they focus on experience at the moment when tragic heroes discover permanent adversities at the core of their character. The nature of this discovery, when scaled down from the heroic to the mundane, varies with the form of the permanent adversity that befalls us. It always surprises us, and the surprise is usually bad, but it varies with whether its cause is the discovery of contingency or conflict or evil in our character.

Take a case illustrative of the discovery of permanent adversities, beginning with contingency. Suppose I represent it to myself that one of the enduring patterns of my character is that I have a clear conception of a good life, which is to live a political life. I have the desire, capacity, and opportunity to live according to it, and I habitually perform the appropriate actions. Then comes the surprise: I discover that in the course of my political pursuits, I have systematically and seriously injured people I love most, my family, because I have been attending to my success in politics and neglected their welfare. Since I really do love them, the discovery is a nasty surprise. It makes it clear to me that I have to redescribe myself to myself, I have to reevaluate what I have been doing, and I have to redirect my motivation.

As I am struggling to do so, it naturally occurs to me to ask how the enduring pattern I now find objectionable in myself came to be created. Suppose that the answer is that I was born and raised in poverty, and the only way out of it was to make myself ruthlessly ambitious. I did what was necessary, and the required pattern has established itself as an enduring feature of my character. My present objectionable conduct is merely a continuation of that pattern. That I was born in poverty, that the only way out of it required ruthlessness, that I had the capacity and the opportunity to rise above my misfortune, that patterns of action tend to become habitual are simply contingencies of life, which happen to have been instantiated in my character. I have acted according to the enduring pattern in my character, but it was really contingency acting through me. I come to the surprising discovery that at least one aspect of my character has been fortuitous, even though I believed it was otherwise, and so I can set about making it less fortuitous and more deliberate. This is what moves me toward the necessary redescription, reevaluation, and redirection of motivation, toward trying to reduce the extent to which I am ruled by contingency and increase the extent to which I am in control.

Consider next how the discovery of conflict may occur. Suppose, then, that I have made the discovery that it was my life in politics that has led me to neglect my family. I now know, as I did not before, that it was ruthlessness that fundamentally motivated me, and that I became ruthless not out of choice, but because of the contingencies of my genetic inheritance and the influences upon me during childhood and youth. I have taken the first step toward self-knowledge: I now have a realistic description of one aspect of my character. I know that I should see myself as having been ruthless. The next step is to evaluate this fact about myself.

The very description, of course, suggests the obvious evaluation. Ruthlessness is a vice, and so it is bad. Reasonable and decent people, among whom I want to count myself, are not like that. I have a straightforward and powerful impetus, therefore, to change my character from the fortuitous one that contingencies made it to one formed more deliberately by self-knowledge. If I take the process of evaluation seriously, however, then I will think further, and I will have second thoughts. It is clearly bad to neglect the people I love, but that is not the full description of what I have been doing. I neglected them in the course of my engagement in politics, and that engagement was intended to benefit others, as well as to pursue my career to which I am wholeheartedly devoted. Given the nature of politics and limited human resources, I could not do well in politics if I did not devote sufficient time and energy to it. If I did that, however, I would be continuing what I have been doing, and that is to neglect my family. So I discover the second permanent adversity lodged in and acting through my character: conflict.

Love of family and political life are conflicting values in my conception of a good life. It is not the fault of my conception, and certainly not of my family or society, that this is so. The conflict is simply implicit in the social scheme of things surrounding me, and I must face this obstacle to living as I think I should. Ruthlessness is the burden I have to carry if I continue to neglect my family, but if I reform and pay the loving attention to them which they deserve, then I shall neglect my political duties and acquire the onus of irresponsibility. My conflict, therefore, is not a simple one between obligation and inclination. It is a conflict between two goods, love of family and political life, or between two evils, ruthlessness and political irresponsibility. What should I do in this complex moral situation?

The reasonable course of action is to strike a balance between these competing claims on me. And that will involve me, on the one hand, in gauging as realistically as I can the actual demands they make on my time and energy, and, on the other hand, the respective position these two conflicting goods and evils have in my conception of a good life. What I ought to do will be determined by the outcome of that process of reflection. The mode of reflection, however, will be self-knowledge, and it will oblige me to seek greater clarity about what my conception of a good life really is.

Say that I decide that when the chips are down, politics is more important to me than my family, but that I can be much more efficient in managing my affairs, and I can devote more attention to my family than I have been doing. I thus make a decision. I temper it by seeking a compromise, and I can hope that contingencies will not make the conflict so sharp as to exclude the balance I have established.

This may take care of the immediate practical aspect of the situation, but the decision will leave a residue. I may be forced by it, especially if my hope is disappointed and the compromise fails, to seek further self-knowledge in a hitherto insufficiently explored direction. In discovering the conflict and in attempting to cope with it, I took the ruthlessness in my character as simply one of the facts with which I had to contend. And it is certainly a fact, but it is by no means a neutral one. What has actually happened is that I have discovered that among the elements of my character that motivate me, one is evil. The discovery brings me to the third permanent adversity whose vehicle I found myself being: evil.

If I allow or force myself to face this fact about my character, my reaction must be negative, ranging anywhere from dismay to horror. The fact is that when I act spontaneously and naturally in accordance with my conception of a good life, I act in a way I myself find morally unacceptable. That there is a conflict between my pursuit of political life and my love of my family is not then a consequence of the prevailing conventional morality, but of my character being what it is. If I were not as ruthless as I am, then the conflict would not have occurred, or if it had occurred, it would have been of much less significance, and thus it would have been open to a much more easily achieved compromise. If, that is, my character had been formed differently, I would not have injured those I love most. Self-knowledge pursued to this length, thus leads to self-condemnation.

Further self-knowledge, however, will mitigate this self-condemnation, at least to some extent. For it will bring me to the realization that although my character is defective, it was not I who made it so. If I had not been born with my desires and capacities, if my childhood and youth had not been poverty-ridden, if my opportunities had not been few and the competition fierce, then my character would have developed in a different direction. Recalling the distinction from Chapter 4, it would have to be said about me that although I am causally responsible for my ruthless actions, I am not morally responsible for them. Evil acted through me, but I was not a conscious, intentional agent of it. The fact remains, however, that it is I whose character is the carrier of evil, and that there are plenty of other people whose characters are free from it, or at least from this particular manifestation of it. I am ruthless, in contradistinction to others, who are not. This is not a morally neutral fact. Morally speaking, I have dirty hands, while others' are clean.[4]

The great significance of self-knowledge is that once we have achieved it, and its descriptive aspect allows us to see the significance contingency plays in our lives, its evaluative aspect reveals the conflicts among our values, and its motivational aspect makes us face the evil in our character, we cannot leave things as they are. The interpretation we construct of our fortuitous character carries with it the impetus to change it, and thereby make it more deliberate. For what we learn from the interpretation is that our fortuitous character is to a considerable extent captive to the control exercised over it by contingency, conflict, and evil, and we want to increase our control, while diminishing the influence of permanent adversities. The reason for wanting to do so is that these permanent adversities are obstacles to our living according to our conception of a good life.

It remains to point out that the surprises caused by our discovery of permanent adversities acting through our character provide yet a further reason for going beyond the coherence theory of self-knowledge. These surprises disrupt the coherence of the interpretation we have hitherto imposed on our character. They show us the inadequacy of what we took to be our self-knowledge by revealing that what we thought was under our control was actually due to permanent adversities acting through our character. If self-knowledge shaped the facts that were its objects, this could not happen. That it happens shows that there are facts with a crucial bearing

---

[4] See John Kekes, *Facing Evil* (Princeton: Princeton University Press, 1990), for an exploration of this topic.

on our character, and that self-knowledge cannot be adequate if it does not take account of them. The conclusion follows, therefore, that facts also shape self-knowledge, and so the coherence theory cannot be right.

THE ADEQUACY OF SELF-KNOWLEDGE

Its deficiencies notwithstanding, the coherence theory is right on two fundamental points: self-knowledge has to do with the imposition of a coherent interpretation on the facts of our character and this interpretation must reflect some point of view or another. But on each of these points, it goes beyond what the supporting argument warrants, and therein lies its error. It does not follow from the facts of our character needing a coherent interpretation that there are no such facts independent of our interpretation of them. Primary values, anomalies, and surprises show not only that there are, but also that there must be such facts, given the very assumptions of the coherence theory itself. Similarly, although it is true that all interpretations presuppose some point of view, it is not true that the presupposed points of view are always optional, variable, or context-dependent. All interpretations having to do with living a good life must presuppose the human point of view, whatever else may be presupposed by them. That point of view, however, provides a set of facts that any interpretation involved in self-knowledge must take into account and establishes an external standard to which all adequate interpretations must conform. The coherence theory may be summed up by saying that it succeeds in identifying two necessary conditions of self-knowledge, but fails in its attempt to identify further necessary conditions, which, in conjunction with the first two, would provide the sufficient condition for self-knowledge.

It may be said in defense of the coherence theory that its supposed failure is incompatible with common human experience, so there must be something wrong with this criticism of it. Our experience is that if we are morally adrift or alienated, we often yearn for a coherent interpretation of the facts of our life. And when such an interpretation is found through religious conversion, ideological commitment, or participation in a cult promising some form of salvation, then we pronounce ourselves to have found what we were hoping for. We are then provided with an interpretation of our life, of what is wrong with it, and of how we could make it good. How could the enthusiastic, indeed often pervfervid, acceptance of such an interpretation be called into question? We previously lacked a conception of a good life that inspired us; now we have one; we are wholeheartedly committed to it; we are no longer morally adrift or alienated; so what more could be reasonably demanded? Critics of the coherence theory need to account for this experience before their objection to mere coherence can be regarded as telling.

It is clearly true that having a coherent conception of a good life in terms of which we can make sense of the facts of our life is often felt to be a great improvement over the moral drift and alienation that existed before it. In the grip of this feeling, we may correctly report ourselves to be in possession of something necessary for living a good life, something which we previously lacked. Having found it, however, we have not yet found what is sufficient for living a good life. A coherent interpretation is better than no interpretation, but a coherent interpretation that is correct is better still. And what makes an interpretation correct is that it accounts for all the relevant facts and it reflects the appropriate point of view.

There are two crucial differences between a coherent interpretation and one that is not only coherent but also correct. First, the former supplies a ready-made account of the relevant facts, while the latter develops its account on the basis of the reciprocal influence of the facts and tentatively proposed interpretations of them. Second, the interpretation of the former reflects a point of view that has been constructed independently of our individuality, and its intention is to transform our character to fit the requirements of some religion, ideology, or cult, while the interpretation of the latter is constructed from our own point of view, stressing, rather than glossing over, our individuality.

In the former case, the interpretation is there, and the task of self-knowledge is to redescribe, reevaluate, and redirect the motivation exerted by the relevant facts of our character to fit the interpretation. In the latter case, the facts are there, and the task of self-knowledge is to construct an interpretation that would do justice to them. In the former case, the anomalies and surprises we have discussed will be regarded as signs that we have not advanced sufficiently toward the conception of a good life represented by the interpretation. In the latter case, the anomalies and surprises will be taken to indicate that the interpretation fails to do justice to the relevant facts. In the former case, anomalies and surprises are counted as aberrations attesting to our failings. In the latter case, they are regarded as counterexamples which call the interpretation into question.

Both kinds of interpretation reflect a point of view, which must do justice to the universally human, the conventionally variable social, and the individual. Conceptions of a good life must be constructed out of these elements, and one difference among conceptions depends on the element to which they attribute primacy. Controversies about particular conceptions of a good life concern such questions as whether human nature dictates one conception of a good life for all human beings, whether conceptions of a good life merely reflect the conventions of the social context in which they are formulated, or whether the importance of human and social elements derives solely from their contribution to the development of our individuality. These are difficult questions, but there is fortunately no need to contend with them here[5] because the topic is self-knowledge, and there can be no doubt that *it* is concerned with the individuality of the person who is both its subject and object.

The trouble with aiming only at coherence is that it is bound to result in the subordination of our individuality to the religious, ideological, or cult-inspired interpretation that is being imposed on the facts of our character. This cannot be avoided because the interpretation is constructed to fit any individual. There are specific sins we must avoid, specific desires we must overcome, specific possessions we must give up, specific exercises we have to do, specific stages in life's way we have to go through, and so forth. But this specificity applies across the board to everyone in the same way who seeks salvation, enlightenment, grace, or whatnot. Even if one of these conceptions of a good life were proved to be *the* reasonable conception—and reasons against believing this possibility were given in Chapter 3—it would not alter the fact that self-knowledge must assign primacy to our individuality because its object is our character. It must concentrate on the enduring patterns formed of our desires, capacities, opportunities, values, and actions, and in respect to them at least we differ from one another. A correct interpretation goes beyond a merely coherent one by taking our individuality seriously, while acknowledging the universally human and conventionally social aspects of our character.

A coherent interpretation that reflects the point of view of some religion, ideology, or cult necessarily shortchanges our individuality because it had to be constructed as one that would apply to countless individuals. It will be vulnerable therefore to falsification by precisely those anomalies and surprises that have been previously emphasized. A coherent interpretation that is also correct, on the other hand, is constructed by trial and error, involving the constant redescription and reevaluation of the relevant facts of our character, the redirection of our motivation by them, and the revision of the interpretation so that it would fit the facts better. This trial and error process, the correction of the interpretation by how we see the facts and the correction of how we see the facts by the interpretation is a growing body of gradually improving self-knowledge, essentially connected with our individuality, with increasing our control, and with transforming our fortuitous character into a more deliberate one.

---

[5] See John Kekes, *Moral Tradition and Individuality* (Princeton: Princeton University Press, 1989), for an attempt to do so.

The favorable effect created by having a merely coherent interpretation is a placebo-effect. It is created by *having* a coherent interpretation, as opposed to not having one. The content of the interpretation makes no difference to the effect it makes. That is why converts who lose their faith often seek and find something else to which to convert. The favorable effect of a correct coherent interpretation, however, derives from decreasing the gap between appearance and reality, insofar as our knowledge of the facts of our character is concerned.

There is, of course, great scope for self-deception here. Just as we may delude ourselves into thinking that the way we appear to ourselves is the way we are, so the self-imposed delusion may continue after we have discovered the gap and endeavored to close it. That the correction has been made is just as liable to self-deception as the existence of the to-be-corrected gap. What we have, therefore, may just be the appearance of self-knowledge, and not the real thing. The test is the coherence of our interpretation of the relevant facts. This coherence, however, is not the internal one sought by the coherence theory, but one that is open to criticism by appealing to criteria external to it. These external criteria may be formulated both positively and negatively.

The positive formulation focuses on our identification with our character. The condition we aim at is a description of the relevant facts, an evaluation of their significance, and a motivating force that moves us to act in response to the description and evaluation. The condition is that of having surveyed ourselves and having arrived at the correct view of how we are. The condition in which each of us can say to ourselves about ourselves: Yes, that is me, that is how I am. In this condition, we do not feel alienated from ourselves on account of forces or influences that act through us but over which we have no control, nor are we morally adrift due to confusion about our values or lack of inspiration by them. The aspiration to achieve this condition is well expressed by Isaiah Berlin: "I wish my life and decisions to depend on myself, not on external forces of whatever kind. I wish to be the instrument of my own, not of other men's acts of will. I wish to be . . . moved by reasons, by conscious purposes, which are my own, not by causes which affect me, as it were, from outside. I wish to be . . . self-directed."[6]

It is important to see that while the achievement of this identification with our character confers a moral identity on us, it need not carry with it moral approval. We may know ourselves, and not like what we know. The evaluation implicit in self-knowledge may be adverse, and the motivation implicit in it may drive us toward changing ourselves, perhaps even in

---

[6] Isaiah Berlin, *Four Essays on Liberty* (Oxford: Oxford University Press, 1969), 131.

basic ways. As it has been argued in the preceding chapter, self-knowledge need not involve self-ratification, although it must involve either approval or disapproval of its object.[7]

The negative formulation focuses on anomalies and surprises. They are obstacles to coherence. We discover their existence when our tentative interpretations do not fit the facts of our character. This failure may be due to there being facts of which a tentative interpretation has taken no account, or to there being facts whose significance is either greater or smaller than the tentative interpretation has attributed to them. In any case, the discrepancy between the facts and our interpretation of them is forced on our attention by way of the surprises and anomalies that disappoint the expectations we have of ourselves.

We discover that we are not what we supposed we were. In the process of describing, evaluating, and motivating ourselves, something has gone wrong. We encounter some situation, and it provokes in us unanticipated reactions, like Neoptolemus's compassion; or we find that our values provide insufficient guidance to how we ought to respond because the situation is more complex or our values more confused than we are able to accommodate, like Neoptolemus's conflict between, on the one hand, decency, loyalty, compassion, and, on the other, ambition; or we are called upon to act and our incoherent description and evaluation of the situation do not provide clear guidance, so we do not know what to do, like Neoptolemus's being irresolute and inconsistent. The result is that we cannot identify with our character because we are unclear about what it is. The complex situation we have encountered led us to the discovery that we are in some respect wanting. This is the discovery that produces alienation and moral drift, and it is the incompatibility of our supposed moral identity with them that motivates us to seek better self-knowledge than we had before.

If we act according to this motive, we shall aim to formulate an interpretation that fits the facts of our character better than its predecessor did. The improvement will be shown in two connected ways. We shall have fewer surprises and anomalies to contend with than before. And we shall be able to explain why the surprises and anomalies that revealed the inadequacy of the previous interpretation have occurred. The improved interpretation will make it possible to identify the obstacles in our character that prevented us before from recognizing the surprising and anomalous facts of our character; facts that were forced on our attention by the complexity of the situation we have encountered. Self-knowledge grows, there-

---

[7] See David W. Hamlyn, "Self-Knowledge," in *Perception, Learning, and the Self* (London: Routledge, 1983), especially 252–255.

fore, by making our interpretations more inclusive. An improved interpretation will incorporate its corrected predecessor and an explanation of what it was in us that made it defective. This is why an improved interpretation will have to contend with fewer surprises and anomalies.

There is a kind of merciless objectivity in the conjunction of the positive and the negative tests of coherence. We have a conception of a good life and we have a character that we want to transform so as to better approximate the ideal implicit in the conception. This gives us our moral identity. But we are bound to find this moral identity more or less wanting, when we judge it by the standard of our conception of a good life, since if it were not wanting, we would have to regard the conception as having been realized, and few people, if any, can reasonably claim to have done that. We have, therefore, frequent, painful, and firsthand evidence of our own failings. The symptoms of our failings are the surprises and the anomalies we encounter. They are unmistakable signs that we have not achieved coherence, that our moral identity falls short of our moral ideal, that our character still incorporates too many fortuitous and not enough deliberately formed elements.

We can, of course, disguise these failings from ourselves, and we often do so through self-deception and other stratagems for not facing unpleasant facts. But we must now see that resorting to these devices is bound to be unreasonable because they prevent us from trying to overcome the obstacles that stand in the way of living according our conception of a good life.

Suppose, however, that we face facts and we are motivated by the discovery of our failings to overcome them. We will, then, seek to increase our control by transforming our incoherent character into a coherent one. This requires describing the incoherence so that we shall see it as an obstacle, evaluating it adversely in the light of our conception of a good life, suppressing its motivational influence on our actions, and fostering such motives contrary to it as would be consistent with that conception.

THE FORECLOSURE OF POSSIBILITIES

The strategy followed in describing self-knowledge has so far been to establish the necessity of giving a coherent account of the significant facts affecting our character and then to show that such an account is not sufficient for self-knowledge. The basic reason for this is that the significance of some facts—primary values, anomalies, and surprises—does not derive from the account given of them. These facts are intrinsically significant, and an account of them must not only be coherent, but it must also do justice to the pre-existing significance of the relevant facts. Once we have succeeded in giving an account that is both coherent and correct, it will make us conscious of our moral identity, motivate us to remove the surprises and anomalies from our character, and thus bring us closer to living as we think we should. The question that needs to be considered now is about the limits that must be recognized and the possibilities that are opened up by self-knowledge thus understood.

Consider the following initially plausible but nevertheless flawed line of thought. Moral imagination and self-knowledge increase our control by enlarging the field of possibilities available to us. Moral imagination expands the range of our possibilities, while self-knowledge overcomes internal obstacles to the realization of the possibilities we have. Moral imagination increases our control by looking outward, self-knowledge by looking inward. Both are liberating forces: the first by broadening our vision, the second by making us better able to live according to it.[8]

Proceeding in this manner, Stuart Hampshire says: "A man becomes more and more a free and responsible agent the more he at all times knows what he is doing, in every sense of this phrase, and the more he acts with a definite and clearly formed intention. He is in this sense less free the less his actual achievements, that which he directly brings into existence and changes by his activity, correspond to any clearly formed intentions of his own."[9] And he goes on: being a free agent "entails that he is not at the mercy of forces that he does not himself recognize and that are outside his control."[10] Nevertheless, "It is not true that as soon as I understand why I behave in a certain way, where the 'why' connects my behaviour with some regular and general causal pattern, I immediately become, by virtue of this knowledge alone, an exception to the causal law."[11] Knowledge of causal regularity is not sufficient for exempting oneself from it, but it is a necessary condition of it. "Knowledge of the facts that have been influencing my conduct without my knowledge does in itself open to me new possibilities of action. The mere recognition of a causal correlation between my behaviour and some external conditions is the recognition of the change that would be necessary for the behaviour to be different in the future. . . . Now I can think of the causal factors explaining my past behaviour as something that I may at least try in some way to circumvent."[12] The way to take advan-

---

[8] The most searching and suggestive exploration of this way of thinking is Stuart Hampshire's. See his *Thought and Action* (London: Chatto & Windus, 1960), *Freedom of the Individual*, exp. ed. (Princeton: Princeton University Press, 1975), *Morality and Conflict* (Cambridge: Harvard University Press, 1983), and *Innocence and Experience* (Cambridge: Harvard University Press, 1989). The present account is deeply indebted to Hampshire's.

[9] Hampshire, *Thought and Action*, 177.

[10] Ibid., 177–178.

[11] Ibid., 190.

[12] Ibid.

tage of these new possibilities is by "finding the means of evading its [i.e., the causal uniformity's] effects by trying to alter the initial conditions, or the boundary conditions, upon which its operation depends."[13] Although this is most congenial to the account of self-knowledge defended here, it is nevertheless necessary to dissociate it from Hampshire's.

The fundamental reason for this is that an account that concentrates only on the possibilities self-knowledge opens up is one-sided. Hampshire is insufficiently attentive to the limits self-knowledge reveals. As Iris Murdoch says: "Moral change and moral achievement are slow; we are not free in the sense of being able suddenly to alter ourselves since we cannot suddenly alter what we can see and ergo what we desire and are compelled by. In a way, explicit choice seems now less important. . . . If I attend properly I will have no choices and this is the ultimate condition to be aimed at. . . . The ideal situation . . . is . . . a kind of necessity."[14] And she goes on: "This is in a way the reverse of Hampshire's picture, where our efforts are supposed to be directed to increasing our freedom by conceptualizing as many different possibilities of action as possible."[15]

Surely, however, there is no need to choose between Hampshire's account of self-knowledge, which sees it as freeing us to explore a rich variety of moral possibilities, and Murdoch's account, which represents it as removing obstacles from the way of our recognition of moral necessity. It is possible to have a balanced view that incorporates both knowledge of our possibilities and knowledge of our necessary limits. Enough has been said about the possibilities involved in self-knowledge; what needs to be done now is to consider two kinds of limits also involved in it. The first follows from conceptions of a good life and the second is due to the unalterable influence of permanent adversities on our character. They are alike in foreclosing certain possibilities for particular agents. They differ on account of what it is that sets limits to the possibilities. These two kinds of limits will be discussed in turn.

Suppose that we have adequate self-knowledge, and so we fit the following description of Hume's: "By our continual and earnest pursuit of character . . . we bring our own deportment and conduct frequently in review. . . . This constant habit of surveying ourselves, as it were, in reflection, keeps alive all the sentiments of right and wrong, and begets, in noble creatures, a certain reverence for themselves as well as others, which is the surest guardian of every virtue."[16] If this account applies to us, we must be

---

[13] Ibid.

[14] Iris Murdoch, *The Sovereignty of Good* (London: Routledge, 1970), 39–40.

[15] Ibid., 40.

[16] David Hume, *Enquiry concerning the Principles of Morals*, ed. L. A. Selby-Bigge, 2d ed. (Oxford: Clarendon Press, 1961), 276.

attentive to our character, that is, we must regularly describe and gauge the significance of the enduring patterns formed of desires, capacities, opportunities, values, and actions which constitute our character; we must habitually evaluate these various elements and patterns by the standard set by our conception of a good life; and we must be motivated by our description and evaluation to act appropriately.

The self-knowledge, which results from this description, evaluation, and motivation, will shape our character to be and to cause us to act in certain ways and not to be and not to act in certain other ways. The more firmly established is our character, the more set are the enduring patterns that compose it, the stronger will be this influence of self-knowledge. The ideal case, as Murdoch says, is a kind of necessity: It defines what we must and what we cannot do, what ways of being and acting are necessary and what ways are impossible for us. The necessity and impossibility are certainly not logical or conceptual; they are not imposed on us by natural or legal laws, nor are they matters of convention or custom. They follow from our having a conception of a good life and from our having identified with it so thoroughly as to make serious deviation from it unthinkable. The necessity and impossibility are dictated by our moral limits.

Deviation from these limits is certainly possible; just as we can violate legal laws, conventions, and customs, so we can live and act contrary to our moral limits. But the more firmly established those limits are, the less likely and the more psychologically damaging are their violations. This is because our moral limits depend on the most basic and most serious commitments to our conception of a good life. The ideal is to have the kind of character that spontaneously prompts us to act according to this conception and makes it unthinkable to act inconsistently with it.

The ideal, of course, rarely obtains. Saints and heroes of a certain sort exemplify it, but most of us fall short of the ideal. This has the apparent advantage of making us more flexible by being less firmly committed to our conception of a good life. The flexibility, however, is gained at the expense of doing what we ourselves think we should not. If it is understood that this is what it involves, it will not be seen as an advantage. It will be seen rather as a failure to remain faithful to our conception of a good life, especially in the face of adversity that makes it difficult to do so.

To illustrate this necessity and impossibility, consider conceptions of a good life essentially connected with belonging to a religious, cultural, or ethnic community, or with being a creative artist, a champion of a political ideal, or the defender of an institution, or with maintaining certain human relationships, such as a close marriage, a large family, or comradeship in a common cause. Such commitments determine for us what we must and must not do; they limit the area of our possibilities; they set a standard for gauging the seriousness of violations; and they put certain possibilities beyond the pale.[17]

If moral limits are borne in mind, it becomes obvious why Hampshire's account of self-knowledge as the enlargement of our possibilities by removing internal obstacles from the way of their realization cannot be right.[18] If we are committed to a conception of a good life, we are thereby committed to curtailing some of our possibilities. We must, then, recognize what is necessary and what is impossible, given our commitment. If we cultivate in ourselves aliveness to possibilities inconsistent with the necessity our commitment creates, we do not increase our control, but diminish it. Increased control shows itself not just by having more possibilities, but also by confronting some situations as leaving us with no possibilities but one, and that one as a necessity.

It does not, of course, follow from this that the enlargement of our possibilities is incompatible with living according to our conception of a good life. It is good to have a rich field of possibilities before we commit ourselves to one of them; it is also good to explore as fully as we can the possibilities left open by the conception to which we have committed ourselves; and it is similarly good to remove internal obstacles to the realization of appropriate possibilities. This is why Murdoch's account of self-knowledge as the discovery of moral necessity cannot be right. Self-knowledge should be seen as the discovery of both moral possibilities and moral limits.[19]

The second of the two kinds of limits mentioned above are those set by permanent adversities. The necessities and impossibilities just discussed are moral limits, set by our conception of a good life, and it is in our power to violate them. The limits are conditional on our moral commitments. The consequences of violating them may be psychologically destructive and morally horrible, but we *can* violate them. We usually have sufficient control over our character to decide whether to transgress moral limits by not doing what is morally necessary or by doing what is morally impossible. But there are also limits of a different kind. They do not concern what we must or must not do, given our conception of a good life, but what we must or must not do, given our character. Some of these limits are also conditional, for there are ways in which we can change our character. Some failings may be corrected; some desires may be suppressed; some in-

---

[17] For an illuminating discussion of the point, see Gerald Dworkin, "Is More Choice Better Than Less?" in *Theory and Practice of Autonomy* (Cambridge: Cambridge University Press, 1988).

[18] See Isaiah Berlin, " 'From Hope and Fear Set Free'," in *Concepts and Categories* (London: Hogarth Press, 1978), for further doubts about Hampshire's view.

[19] See Søren Kierkegaard's discussion of possibility and necessity in *The Sickness unto Death*, trans. W. Lowrie (New York: Doubleday, 1954), 168–175.

capacities may be remedied; we can train ourselves to be more perceptive or more critical about our opportunities; we can become more reflective about our values, and so on. But these ways of exercising our control are themselves limited. There are desires we cannot acquire or fail to have, capacities we irremediably lack, and others that we have only to a moderate extent and nothing we could do would improve them. These limits establish impossibilities that affect the control we have. They define the respects in which we have no control over the amount of control we have. Call these limits "personal."

Perhaps the most obvious personal limits concern cognitive capacities. Our general intelligence, specific cognitive capacities like the mathematical or language learning, memory, visual imagination, attention span, spatial orientation, and so on have upper limits beyond which it is impossible for us to go no matter how hard we try. And these limits, of course, vary from person to person. But there are limits also to what we can do, set by manual dexterity, strength, how long we can go without sleep, what our pain threshold is, the acuity of our senses, and so on. Nor are our desires free from limits. We differ in respect to what gives us sexual, musical, olfactory, culinary, or aesthetic pleasure, and we cannot make ourselves have certain desires, nor can we fail to find the satisfaction of some desires pleasurable. There are also individually variable but nevertheless absolute limits to how far we can control our fear, anger, depression, confusion, disorientation, pride, guilt, and similar emotional propensities. These limits are due to genetic inheritance, early training, the presence or absence of formative influences at propitious times, the patterns of desires and capacities with which we start out, and so forth.

It is necessary to stress that calling attention to personal limits is not intended to deny that there are many ways in which we can increase control over our character. The point is that there are inherited and acquired limits beyond which our control cannot be increased, and that there are great individual variations regarding what these limits are.

One of the tasks of self-knowledge must clearly be to learn about our personal limits. For those limits have a decisive influence on what possibilities we can make our own, and thus on what possibilities can be reasonably included in our conception of a good life. Furthermore, there are personal limits, such as low intelligence, mercurial temperament, or impoverished imagination, whose effects will be felt no matter what our conception of a good life is. Self-knowledge is needed then to conduct ourselves appropriately, given our personal limits.

Such conduct will not aim to overcome personal limits, for that cannot be done. What can be done, as Hampshire says, is to try to circumvent them. The strategies for doing so are many. We can try not to get into situations that call for resources beyond our personal limits, or to arrange for sufficient time and opportunity to try to compensate for our lack of resources, or to alter the situation so that we can use resources we have. These strategies, however, are themselves limited, not only by our personal limits but also by the extent to which their circumvention is possible. Self-knowledge is needed, therefore, not to enable us to do the impossible, but to have a realistic view of what is possible for us, given our character.

Personal limits are one of the ways in which permanent adversities present obstacles to our living a good life. They are established by the contingencies of the pre- and postnatal influences on the development of our character, by the conflicts among the values we prize, conflicts which make their joint realization totally or proportionally impossible for us, and by the evil impulses that motivate us to act, often unconsciously and unintentionally, contrary to our conception of a good life.

We can endeavor to reduce the influence of contingency, conflict, and evil on our character. But their influence may be so strong as to make our efforts unavailing. Furthermore, and more insidiously, their influence may affect us by curtailing or misdirecting the efforts we are capable of making toward controlling them. Where the limits are set by permanent adversities varies from person to person. The limits depend on the particular form and strength with which permanent adversities affect us and on the particular desires, capacities, opportunities, values, and actions that form the enduring patterns of our character.

A satisfactory account of self-knowledge must therefore aim to be more balanced than either Hampshire's, which stresses moral and personal possibilities, or Murdoch's, which stresses moral necessities. According to the present account, self-knowledge has as its objects both the moral possibilities and limits set by our conception of a good life, and personal possibilities and limits, set by our character as it is formed by permanent adversities and our own efforts.

CONCLUSION

This completes the discussion of the second mode of reflection. All three modes—moral imagination, self-knowledge, and moral depth— are ways of improving our judgment and increasing our control. Our judgment needs improvement because appropriate conduct in complex moral situations makes greater demands on our moral resources than we could have acquired from conventional morality. In our reflection on complex moral situations, we need to go beyond conventional principles and interpretations, and learn to deal with conflicts among principles; we must interpret situations not clearly covered by any principles, and respond in situations that can be reasonably interpreted in several ways. This is what judgment enables us to do.

To exercise judgment, however, we must have the required resources, and no one starts out having them. We begin with a fortuitous character, formed by genetic inheritance, early training, and conventional morality. We must then transform it, guided by our conception of a good life, into a more deliberate character that is capable of dealing with moral situations whose complexities cannot be adequately handled by conventional morality. This transformation involves increasing our control over what desires, capacities, opportunities, values, and actions form the enduring patterns of our character. It is in this way that judgment and control are connected.

Control is increased by strengthening the motivational force of our conception of a good life and by weakening the internal obstacles in our character to living according to that conception. Self-knowledge is essential to this process because it is through it that we learn what the internal obstacles are and what we can do to cope with them. The obstacles present themselves as surprises and anomalies, which may be due to remediable incoherencies in our character, or to permanent adversities that we can only, at best, cope with but never surmount. And what we can do to cope with them is to construct through self-knowledge a coherent and correct account of the significant facts of our character. That account provides our moral identity and motivates us to transform our character so as to make it less fortuitous and more deliberate. What directs this transformation is our conception of a good life. One way in which we can increase our control is to embark on this complicated process.

Increased control thus leads to improved judgment. And improved judgment makes it possible to evaluate the situations we face by bringing to them our knowledge of good and evil. In this manner, we may grow in moral wisdom by growing in our capacity to make good use of its component parts: a conception of a good life, knowledge, evaluation, and judgment.

CHAPTER EIGHT

Moral Depth:
The Third Mode of Reflection

The aim of all three modes of reflection is to improve our judgment and increase our control. As we succeed in these endeavors, we become better able to conduct ourselves in complex moral situations in accordance with our conception of a good life and to cope with obstacles created by permanent adversities and personal shortcomings. Through moral imagination we aim to surmount obstacles to our growth in breadth; through self-knowledge we attempt to do the same with obstacles to the transformation of our fortuitous character into a more deliberate one; and the obstacles we face through moral depth are to forming a reasonable attitude to the insurmountable limits placed on us by permanent adversities. These limits may be external or internal, imposed on us either by our circumstances or by our character. The discussion has been concentrating on internal obstacles, and it will continue to do so here. External obstacles will be discussed in the next chapter.

Suppose then that we have set ourselves to face the fact that permanent adversities unavoidably limit the extent to which we can increase control over our character. We endeavor to pass beyond the intellectual acknowledgment that we are both active agents and passive subjects of contingency, conflict, and evil, and we attempt to form a reasonable attitude to this lamentable fact. Such an attitude is bound to be charged with strong and perhaps contrary feelings, it is bound to inform our thinking about our past endeavors and future prospects, and so it is bound to influence our motivation and conduct. It will have these effects because it brings home to us a fact of the highest significance: No matter how reasonably and decently we endeavor to increase the control we have over our life and conduct, we are not and cannot become masters of our destiny. The fact is not merely that moral wisdom—achieved through the cultivation of the conception of a good life, knowledge, evaluation, and judgment that it comprises—is no guarantee of a good life, but the even more discouraging one that the extent to which we are able to cultivate them is itself subject to the very same obstacles we endeavor to overcome through their cultivation.

It is not surprising, therefore, if our attitude to this aspect of the human condition—and thus to our own condition—is a sense of hopelessness. If our very attempts to do as well as we can are not within our control, and if not even the success of these imperfectly controllable attempts would assure a good life, then what is the point of striving after knowledge, evaluation, and judgment? Why should we struggle on such dubious terms? We need moral depth to face this question and to find a more reasonable answer to it than that of hopelessness.

HOPELESSNESS?

Kant wrote that "All the interests of my reason, speculative as well as practical combine in the three following questions: 1. What can I know? 2. What ought I to do? 3. What may I hope?"[1] Much philosophical attention has been paid to the first two questions, while the third has been by and large neglected. But it is no less important than the others because it directs us to consider how the knowledge, evaluation, and judgment we acquire and employ will affect our prospects for living a good life.[2]

An answer to the third question may be arrived at through reflecting on the situation of Oedipus, as depicted by Sophocles first in *Oedipus the King* and later in *Oedipus at Colonus*.[3] The background of the first play is that before Oedipus was born it was prophesied that he will kill his father and marry his mother. To circumvent it, his parents arranged to have the newly born Oedipus killed. But he survived and grew into adulthood, believing himself to be the son of the King and Queen of Corinth. The prophecy was then repeated to Oedipus. To prevent it from becoming true, he left Corinth to remove himself from the proximity of his supposed parents. His prudent efforts to avoid the calamity, however, actually hastened its occurrence because it is to Thebes, to the city ruled by his real father, that his self-imposed exile brought him. On the way to Thebes, Oedipus was provoked into a fight and killed several men, not unjustifiably given the preva-

[1] Immanuel Kant, *Critique of Pure Reason*, trans. N. K. Smith (London: Macmillan, 1953), A805.

[2] The discussion in the section draws on John Kekes, *Facing Evil* (Princeton: Princeton University Press, 1990), chap. 1.

[3] Sophocles, *Oedipus the King* (*K*) and *Oedpius at Colonus* (*C*). References in the text are to the lines of these plays.

lent mores, one among whom was his unknown father. Upon arriving to Thebes, Oedipus, at great risk to himself, solved the riddle of the Sphinx, thus succeeding where many others had failed in liberating the city from her oppression. As a reward, he was made King and was given as a wife the widowed Queen, his unknown mother. As the play opens, all these events are in the past. The action concerns Oedipus's discovery that he is guilty of parricide and incest, crimes that he, in agreement with his society, finds deeply immoral. In the course of his discovery, Oedipus realizes that he unknowingly and unintentionally caused the most serious and undeserved harm to Thebes, to his wife and mother, to his children who are also his brothers and sisters, and to himself. Yet throughout his life Oedipus acted as well as can be expected of a reasonable and decent human being. He was guided by a reasonable conception of a good life; he took due account of such facts as he had; and his intentions were morally praiseworthy. Nevertheless, both he and others saw him as ruined by the evil he unknowingly and unintentionally caused.

The significant feature of Oedipus's situation for the present purposes is that he was a plaything of the gods. He had choices, and he busily made them. But the alternatives among which he could choose, the conditions in which he could do so, and his doom were all set by the gods. Oedipus was consequently only causally and not morally responsible for the evil he caused, and he did not deserve the evil he suffered. The fact is that through no fault of his own, Oedipus was manipulated by the gods for their own inscrutable purposes, and he was made to suffer a terrible fate by them. Sophocles' suggestion is that we are all liable to what befell Oedipus because it is the human condition. We all risk becoming the playthings of the gods.

The first reaction to this suggestion may well be that this cannot be the human condition because there are no such gods as Sophocles depicted. But this does not dispose of the matter because Sophocles' point need not be expressed in the vocabulary of ancient Greek polytheism. The point can just as well be expressed in terms of permanent adversities. They exist independently of us; we are all subject to them; and they can and often do make us both agents and victims of contingency, conflict, and evil, no matter what we do. Even if we are reasonable and decent, we may find ourselves in wars, revolutions, tyrannies, natural disasters, epidemics, concentration camps, crimes, and emergencies. We may find as we try to do our jobs as politicians, physicians, firefighters, officials of public health, criminal justice, or social welfare—as well as when we act in our capacities as parents, friends, or lovers—that we have to make the weightiest decisions on the basis of imperfect knowledge among noxious alternatives that circumstances force on us. Such situations are not of our own making. We have not sought to be in them. And we would gladly avoid them if we could. But we cannot. We must act. And the consequence may be that we cause unde-served suffering both to ourselves and to others. Human life is full of such suffering, and its victims may never be compensated. Reason and decency are often unavailing and go unrecognized and unrewarded, and we fre-quently do not get what we deserve.

We may come to recognize, therefore, the indifference of the scheme of things toward human merit. The good may suffer, and the wicked may flourish. And it is not just that we may enjoy undeserved benefits and suf-fer unmerited harms, but the books may not be balanced even in the long run. We have thus good reason to believe that there is no moral order in nature. The order that exists is not evil, rather than good, nor is it Mani-chean. It is indifferent. Indifference is worse than neutrality because the latter implies the presence of some witnesses who stand above the fray and remain uncommitted. That would permit some hope, for we could say that they at least know about our condition, and, perhaps, if things got really bad, their neutrality would be suspended. But there is no reason to sup-pose that this is so. There is no guarantee that what happens to us will be proportional to our merit. The attempt to answer Kant's question of what we may hope must begin with the realization that this is so.

But if we remain subject to permanent adversities no matter what we do, if the connection between what happens to us and our merit is fortuitous, then the answer to Kant's question may well be that, insofar as hope is rea-sonable, we may hope for nothing. If we allow the significance of this dis-couraging thought to sink in, it becomes very hard to justify the optimism assumed by the answers to Kant's first two questions, namely, that we should seek knowledge and strive to conform to the requirements of morality. We shall then find ourselves in the state Wordsworth described:

> . . . inwardly oppressed
> With sorrow, disappointment, vexing thoughts,
> Confusion of judgment, zeal destroyed,
> And lastly, utter loss of hope itself
> And things to hope for![4]

Kant himself avoided this discouraging state. He relied instead on ideas of faith in which "happiness stands in exact relation with morality, that is, with worthiness to be happy."[5] It seems that since reason would have led Kant to a subversive answer to his question about hope, he felt compelled

---

[4] William Wordsworth, "The Prelude," in *Poetical Works* (Oxford: Oxford University Press, 1969), Book XI, 3–7.

[5] Kant, *Critique of Pure Reason*, A810.

to seek a tamer answer outside of reason. Kant is not alone, of course, in succumbing to what may be called the transcendental temptation. A particularly clear expression of it is Hegel's: "When we see . . . the evil, the vice, the ruin that has befallen the most flourishing kingdoms which the mind of man ever created, we can hardly avoid being filled with . . . a moral sadness, a revolt of good will—if indeed it has any place within us. Without rhetorical exaggeration, a simple truthful account of the miseries that have overwhelmed the noblest nations and polities and the finest exemplars of virtue forms a most fearful picture and excites emotions of the profoundest and most hopeless sadness, counter-balanced by no consoling results. . . . But in contemplating history as the slaughter-bench at which the happiness of peoples, the wisdom of states, and the virtue of individuals have been sacrificed, a question necessarily arises: To what principle, to what final purpose, have these monstrous sacrifices been offered?"[6]

This is a clear-sighted diagnosis, and yet the assumption behind it is that there is a purpose that somehow redeems the suffering human history so amply documents. But the assumption is merely another symptom of having given in to the transcendental temptation. The hope it may give us is false hope. There is no reason to think that a purpose exists, and none for supposing that if it did, it would redeem the suffering concomitant with its realization. Do the pyramids compensate the slaves who built them? Would supernatural pyramids compensate us? Is it plausible to suppose that the new family God gave to Job compensated him for the old one God took away?

It is an odd fact in the history of ideas that Kant himself articulated one of the most serious criticisms of succumbing to the transcendental temptation. He argued in the first *Critique* that there can be no reason for postulating a purpose behind the world we know because any reason we could give must come from within that world. The most we can reasonably say about our world is that there is much in it that we do not know and there is much in what we do know that we cannot understand, explain, and control. There can be no rational warrant for going beyond this to claim knowledge of the unknown. If Kant had been consistent, he would not have done so. Be that as it may, we can derive from the first *Critique* an explanation of why hope is such a serious problem. If hope comes from the discernment of a purpose in the scheme of things, and if there is no reasonable way in which a purpose could be discerned, even if there were one, then there can be no reasonable hope.

---

[6] G. W. F. Hegel, *Reason in History*, trans. Robert S. Hartman (New York: Liberal Arts, 1953), 26–27.

FOUR STAGES OF MORAL DEPTH

Consider now how we can have a reasonably founded hope, if we acknowledge that permanent adversities put us in jeopardy, and if we refuse to entertain the false hope of a divinely ordained happy ending. Perhaps there is nothing we can do in the face of these facts, and then ignoring them may be the most reasonable course of action. A sturdy common sense may then lead us to carry on with our lives, do as well as we can, and keep out of deep waters. To do otherwise, by dwelling on the hopelessness produced by our recognition of permanent adversities, is to undermine the motivation for increasing our control to the extent we can.

The reason why it would be unreasonable to proceed in this way is that permanent adversities are not just freakish concatenations of unfavorable external circumstances, as a shallow reading of *Oedipus the King* may lead us to suppose, but daily occurrences in the lives of all of us due in part to conditions internal to our characters. To foster a self-imposed blindness about these conditions is to collude in weakening our control; it is to adopt the attitudes of sheep on the way to the slaughterhouse. There is, however, a much more promising strategy. We cannot change the fact that we are subject to permanent adversities, but we can cultivate a reasonable attitude toward it. This attitude is moral depth, and it may alleviate our sense of hopelessness.

Few would disagree that depth in general is an admirable, highly desirable, and yet rare quality. One would expect to find, therefore, that much has been written about it. But this is not so.[7] Perhaps the topic appears forbidding, because the nature of depth is itself a deep and difficult question, since it forces those who ask it to decide what is ultimately worth caring about. The antonyms of depth are shallowness and superficiality, and their prevalence is perhaps one reason why there has not been much attention paid to depth. An approximate cognate of it is profundity, whose rarity provides another reason why depth may not have been much discussed.

The discussion will concentrate on depth primarily as it may be predicated of individuals, rather than of ideas, theories, or works. Individuals may be said to possess a deep understanding of some matter, or feel deeply about a subject, or offer a deep response to some question, problem, or situation. Of these complex psychological states, understanding must be ranked as having first importance to depth, for we suspect the depth of feelings and motives, unless they are founded on understanding. If love or

[7] The only contemporary treatment of the subject is that of Anthony Savile, *The Test of Time* (Oxford: Clarendon Press, 1982), chap. 7. It contains a useful survey of some historical discussions of depth, but it concentrates on depth as an aesthetic notion. The present discussion is nevertheless indebted to Savile's.

hate, for instance, involves self-deception, then we may regard these feelings as strong or passionate, but would hesitate to ascribe depth to them. And similarly for the sorts of things people may be motivated to say or do in response to something. The same action or utterance may be deep or shallow, depending, in part, on the understanding that constitutes its background. Think of the contrast between Polonius in *Hamlet* mouthing the cliché "To thine own self be true" and Socrates repeating the Delphic injunction "Know Thyself."

An additional reason for attributing to understanding a privileged role in depth emerges by reflecting on the distinction between the appearance and reality of depth. Portentousness, gravity, seriousness of tone and mien may disguise humbug, rather than betoken depth.[8] The genuine article has a specific connection with truth, while the counterfeit lacks it. This connection is not that depth gives us direct understanding of the truth. People lack depth if their minds are cluttered with accurate information about trivial facts. And someone may possess great depth on some subject and yet be mistaken about it. Kant was wrong on just about all the central issues he discussed, but who could reasonably deny him a place among the handful of the deepest philosophers?

Depth involves discerning an underlying unity among apparently complex and unrelated phenomena. It is to see the same phenomena as many others also see, but to penetrate below their surface and construct a theory or a vision, depending on the subject matter, that leads to a possible understanding of the reality of which the appearances are manifestations. It is to possess a perspective, an organizing view that provides the foundation for understanding what was previously problematic, even if no one recognized its problems; think of Plato on love, Aristotle on virtue, Einstein on relativity, Spinoza on freedom, Marx on history, Hume on causality, Freud on the unconscious, Nietzsche on morality, and Darwin on evolution. The essential feature of these perspectives is that they provide a *possible* way of understanding a very sizable segment of the world that is, in some respect, important to us.

The depth we attribute to the authors of these perspectives is not destroyed, although it is diminished, if the proposed understanding does not survive the sustained critical attention it elicits. The world might have been like that, and if it had been, it would have been of great significance for how we live our lives. Even false perspectives may move us therefore toward understanding something important because, through rejecting the possibilities they hold out, we may be moved toward the truth.[9]

[8] See the title essay in Max Black, *The Prevalence of Humbug and Other Essays* (Ithaca: Cornell University Press, 1983).

[9] It is only in this tenuous sense that the present account agrees with Savile's claim that depth involves the approximation of truth. See Savile, *The Test of Time*, 126–127.

It is extremely unlikely, however, that depth would consist only in a purely theoretical understanding. Depth concerns important matters that bear on our lives, and it is natural for the understanding it yields to influence our emotions and motives. The more important these matters are, the more appropriate it is that understanding them should influence our emotions and motives deeply rather than superficially. It is consequently better to think of depth as having cognitive, emotive, and motivational *aspects*, rather than attempt to treat them, in isolation from one another, as being different forms of depth. There *are* different forms of depth, but the differences among them are due to subject matter, and not to the absence of some aspect of depth.

The subject matter of moral depth is the human condition. The beginning of it is a deeper cognitive understanding of the human condition. Those who succumb to the transcendental temptation also seek this understanding, but their failure makes it reasonable to look for it in a different direction. They seek it beyond nature, in a postulated supernatural world. A more reasonable approach is to take very seriously the thought that human beings are part of the natural world. Moral depth may then come from an enlarged view of the conditions of our lives that can be inferred from nature. If we are part of the natural world, then what we are and what we do, what we experience and what happens to us are also part of it. And one of the things that happens to us is that our attempt to live a good life is jeopardized by contingency, conflict, and evil. No matter how reasonable and decent we are, our endeavors may be doomed by permanent adversities. Facing this fact is the first stage of moral depth.

Moral depth begins then with descriptive knowledge of the human condition, but the knowledge will not remain merely descriptive. We are bound to care about our condition, so we are forced to realize the significance its knowledge has for our lives. The mere possession of this knowledge, therefore, carries with it an impetus toward its enlargement in the direction of incorporating emotive and motivational aspects. The emotive aspect includes our wish for success, our fear of failure, our joy when things are going well, anger, frustration, or sadness when they are not, confidence in ourselves or loss of nerve produced by understanding the odds again us.[10] The motivational aspect is responsible for our continued efforts to live according to our conception of a good life. These aspects, however, are separable only in thought. In actual life, reflection on ourselves, our projects, and our context form an indissoluble amalgam of cognitive, emotive, and motivational aspects, and they are the substance of the

[10] Some of these emotive reactions are illuminatingly discussed in Nicholas Rescher, *Ethical Idealism* (Berkeley: University of California Press, 1987), chap. 4.

knowledge, evaluation, and judgment that compose such moral wisdom as we may have.

If we are reflective, we shall have moral depth to some extent because we cannot be reflective without some understanding of the human condition. But our possession of it may only be embryonic or it may become a significant force in our character. If it becomes such a force, we shall have ground for reasonable hope.

In support of this, consider why we find Oedipus's situation so pregnant with significance. It cannot merely be because we behold Oedipus as he was manipulated into doing what he regarded as most seriously immoral. After all, sad as it is, inflicting unwitting injury on those we love, disproportionate and undeserved suffering, and self-loathing are common enough. The source of its significance is that Sophocles depicts a conflict between our understanding of the human condition and something else. This something else is not just human aspirations; it is not even human aspirations pursued reasonably and decently. It is rather the *expectation* that if we try to realize our aspirations reasonably and decently, then we shall succeed. Oedipus's situation forces those who understand it to reflect on this conflict between the human condition and our expectations, and therein lies its significance.

The expectation is that contingency, conflict, and evil will be overcome by reason and decency. Oedipus's situation shows that our expectation is disappointed. That is why we regard it as tragic. We observe the futility of human will and intellect; we watch Oedipus stumbling toward the discovery of his predicament; we see his fortunes reversed; we are moved by pity and fear; and we achieve a deeper understanding of the human condition. The result of our disappointed expectation is that we come to see Oedipus's situation as emblematic of the human condition, and we are assailed by a sense of hopelessness. To see life as some tragedies teach us to do is to see that there is no consolation, no hope. The second stage toward moral depth is to have arrived at this point.

If we continue our development toward moral depth, however, then we shall not stop at this point. We shall endeavor then to abandon this illusory expectation. The third stage of moral depth is to understand that the ground of our illusory expectation was the view we have already abandoned, namely, that reason and decency are sufficient for the realization of our aspirations. The expectation will be seen then as a lingering remnant of a stage we have left behind. We now understand that contingency, conflict, and evil may frustrate even the noblest aspirations, and that the aspiration may be ours. The effect of moral depth, then, will be that we shall be weaned from the expectation whose disappointment makes us view the human condition as hopeless. That condition will remain the same regardless of whether or not we have the illusory expectation. Moral depth, however, will change our attitude toward it by freeing us from the hopelessness that this misguided expectation produces when it runs afoul of reality.[11]

It may said against this that the possibility of developing moral depth is also subject to permanent adversities, and so it is pointless to recommend its development. But this is not so. The extent to which contingency, conflict, and evil influence our conduct varies with people and circumstances. In some cases, their influence is decisive; we are powerless to resist it; and then the recommendation *is* pointless. It would be misplaced, if not obscene, to urge people on the way to the gas chamber to develop moral depth. But not all situations are like this. In ordinary life, we can often cultivate greater depth. Oedipus could certainly have done so before calamity overtook him. The recommendation of moral depth has a point, therefore, for the vast majority of people whose lives are merely liable to, but not dominated by, permanent adversities.

The question will be pressed, however, of what good moral depth is if it does not change the facts. Why is it more reasonable to try to realize our aspirations with the understanding that we may fail no matter how hard and well we try to succeed than to have that understanding come to us as a result of failure? There is a long and a short answer. The short one is that moral depth makes us morally wiser, and contributes to making our lives better. If we have it, we shall cope with adversity better than Oedipus did. Moral depth allows us to appreciate why it is better to understand that we face permanent adversities and to live a life informed by that understanding than to be shocked into the recognition that our unrealistic expectation may well be disappointed.

This short answer, however, is general and it does not provide much guidance about how to answer the specific question that individuals will ask: What can *I* do in the face of permanent adversities to make *my* life good, given *my* character and circumstances? We all live in concrete cultural, political, and social contexts, and we are all saddled with our genetic inheritance and personal experiences which decisively influence the kind of character we have and can develop. We need a longer answer, therefore, to bring out the practical implications of this general account for our con-

---

[11] In *The Birth of Tragedy* in *Basic Writings of Nietzsche*, trans. W. Kaufmann (New York: Random House, 1968), sec. 14, Friedrich Nietzsche considers, under the label of "Socratism," an attitude very close to the one discussed here. He thinks that it is an unwarrantedly optimistic denial of the Dyonisiac foundation of tragedy. The attitude discussed here can and should take account of the facts underlying many tragedies. The attitude cannot change these facts, but it can lead to a more reasonable interpretation of them. This is the ground for some hope, but certainly not for its inflation, which, in agreement with Nietzsche, we should reject.

crete situations. How do we transform this general conception into the daily experiences of good and evil that we cause, enjoy, and suffer?

It would be a mistake, however, in searching for an answer to ignore altogether the general in favor of the concrete. For we would then deprive ourselves of the benefits provided by the accumulated experiences of those countless others who have faced the same question in concrete situations that bear various degrees of similarity to our own. Why should we not benefit from their experiences, if it would make our lives better? The fact remains, nevertheless, that the further we go in the direction of the general, the less likely it is that it will address our particular concerns. There is therefore a great need here for striking a balance between the general and the particular.

This balance depends on understanding the general conditions that affect all lives, the particular conditions that affect specific individuals in their concrete situations, and the bearing the first has on the second. Maintaining this balance is intimately connected with good lives, so it is an important matter. But its achievement is rare because it is extremely difficult. As we approach this rare, difficult, and yet important achievement so we progress toward the fourth stage of moral depth.

There is a longer answer needed then to explain how moral depth should guide our particular responses to the general human condition. The explanation is that it should do so through controlling our reactions to the understanding we have reached through the stages of moral depth. Moral depth thus requires us to pass beyond these stages to a fifth one. It yields the additional understanding that one reason why human aspirations may fail is that we react inappropriately to the understanding the first four stages of moral depth yield.

WHAT SOPHOCLES SUGGESTS

In order to do develop this answer, consider again what Sophocles says about Oedipus. One important theme running through both plays is Oedipus's development of greater moral depth. By reflecting on what Sophocles intimates about it, we will discover the elements of an extremely illuminating and much enhanced account of moral depth.

Sophocles' life spanned just about the whole of the fifth century B.C. *Oedipus the King*, generally recognized as the masterpiece of Greek tragedy, was written when Sophocles was about seventy, and *Oedipus at Colonus* was Sophocles' last play, completed shortly before his death, at the age of ninety. The first play, as has been noted, concerns Oedipus's discovery that he has unintentionally and unknowingly committed parricide and incest with his mother. He regards these acts as horrible violations of his deepest moral convictions. And when he makes his discovery, the foundation of his moral life is shattered. He loathes himself. He reacts with rage and desperation. And he blinds himself, notwithstanding the realization that he had not had the control over his actions he supposed himself to have. He nevertheless cannot escape—either in his own or in the public's eye—the sense that he is morally damaged by what he has done, even though he was not a willing and knowing agent of his own deeds. The second play shows us Oedipus as an old man facing death after many years of wandering as a blind, homeless beggar. The Oedipus of this play is a transformed man, one who has reflected on his own rise and fall and formed a well-considered judgment of himself and of what happened to him. After a lifetime of struggle and calamity, he dies at peace, having come to terms with his life.

At the beginning of the first play, Oedipus is the respected and unquestioned ruler of Thebes. His subjects tell him: "We do rate you first of men, / both in the common crises of our lives / and face-to-face encounters with the gods" (*K.* 42–44), because "you lifted up our lives" (*K.* 49). Oedipus lives the life he wants to live, and that is to be first among men. He believes that the key to it is control, and that control depends on knowledge and power. He celebrates: "O power— / wealth and empire, skill outstripping skill / in the heady rivalries of life" (*K.* 432–434). He is winning in the rivalries because of what he takes to be his superior character: "That is my blood, my nature—I will never betray it, / never fail to search" (*K.* 1193–1194). The impetus behind the ceaseless search is the passionate desire: "I must know it all, / see the truth" (*K.* 1168–1169). Then, as ominous cracks begin to appear in his life, as his control slips, Tiresias, who speaks for the gods, tells him: "you're blind to the corruption of your own life. . . . All unknowing / you are the scourge of your own flesh and blood" (*K.* 471–474). As a result, "your power ends. / None of your power follows you through life" (*K.* 1676–1677).

As the action progresses, the superficiality of Oedipus's control is revealed. It is not that he lacks the knowledge and power he believes himself to have. Rather, the knowledge and power he has are not what is required for the control he seeks. Control *is* important and knowledge and power *are* its constituents, but they are different types of knowledge and power from what Oedipus pursues. He thinks that the point of having knowledge and power is to control others, not himself. He thus fails to understand the true nature of control. Having the understanding would not save Oedipus from the calamity that befalls him—that he cannot and could not help. But he could have responded to the calamity in less self-destructive ways than he did if he had had a deeper understanding of control.

As it is, his response to his misfortune makes matters even worse. When the feebleness of his control is revealed, Oedipus responds by a desperate act of reaffirmation of the same misguided commitment to it. He reasserts his control by directing it against the only remaining subject: himself. And, in a wanton gesture, he blinds himself. When asked why he did such a horrible thing on top of all that has already happened to him, he says: "Apollo, friends, Apollo— / he ordained my agonies—these, my pains on pains! / But the hand that struck my eyes was mine / mine alone—no one else—I did it all myself" (*K.* 1467–1470). The chorus, beholding his misery, comments on his search for the wrong kind of control that shaped his self-destructive response: "Pitiful, you suffer so . . . / I wish you'd never known" (*K.* 1481–1482).

Oedipus, however, is strong, and his misfortune does not break him. He resolves to bear it and carry on because he still has a proud sense of his self: "My troubles are mine / and I am the only man alive who can sustain them" (*K.* 1548–1549), and "It's mine alone, my destiny—I am Oedipus!" (*K.* 1496). And so there he is at the end of the first play, having lost the misguided power he sought, having suffered because of the misdirected knowledge he worked so hard to acquire, and yet, for the first time, having some real control over what little is left of his previous mode of life. Implicit in the second play is the suggestion that Oedipus's control has its source in a kind of knowledge and power that is quite different from what he took them to be in the first play.

As the second play opens, many years after the end of the first, we are told: "Oedipus is no more / the flesh and blood of old" (*C.* 134–135). He has been transformed because he has acquired a deeper understanding of knowledge and power than what he had before, and because his new and better understanding allows him to control both what he does and what he does not do. As to the power that is worth having, he learns that it is not winning "in the heady rivalries of life" (*K.* 434); its beginning is in "Acceptance—that is the great lesson suffering teaches" (*C.* 6) and in "no more fighting with necessity" (*C.* 210). His attitude to knowledge also changes. The proud claims of the first play, resting on a misunderstanding of himself, "That is my blood, my nature—I will never betray it, / never fail to search" (*K.* 1193–1194) and "I must know it all, / see the truth" (*K.* 1168–1169) are replaced by "No no! Don't ask me who I am /—no more probing, testing—stop—no more!" (*C.* 225–226). Instead of using his knowledge and power as instruments for the futile effort of trying to control the world, an endeavor that almost destroyed him, he now uses them to try to control himself by understanding what he did and what happened to him and by shaping his responses to it. He says, reflecting on his past, "as time wore on / and the smoldering fever broke and died at last / and I began to feel my rage had outrun my wrongs, / I'd lashed myself too much for what I'd done, once long ago" (*C.* 486–490).

Oedipus's acceptance of necessity, his abandonment of the restless search for some key to himself outside of himself, and the beginning of his self-knowledge, however, do not incline him toward a narcissistic concentration on the fine-tuning of his soul. The moral depth he is acquiring gives him a measure of knowledge and power, and, consequently, some control, and it guides his response to the world. His knowledge concerns "the final things of life" (*C.* 656), and his power is exercised both to say "no" to the evil that comes his way and to further the cause of the good insofar as he can. The evil he rejects—indeed, excoriates—comes to him in the persons of Creon, who fraudulently attempts to enlist Oedipus's help to shore up his crumbling power (*C.* 865–910), and Polynices, Oedipus's son, who abandoned his father to a miserable old age when he could have eased his plight without much trouble (*C.* 1524–1584). His reaction to Creon and Polynices is passionate, and they show us that the transformed Oedipus is not a burnt-out wreck, but someone who controls his feelings and directs them toward appropriate expression. Oedipus also uses his power on the side of the good by bestowing on Athens "the power that age cannot destroy, / the heritage stored up for . . . Athens" (*C.* 1718–1719) that "will always form a defense . . . / a bulwark stronger than many shields" (*C.* 1724–1725).

Oedipus thus attains at the end of his life a considerable amount of control, a growing understanding of "the final things in life" (*C.* 656), and a passionate commitment to opposing the evil and supporting the good that he encounters. He resolves: "no more fighting with necessity" (*C.* 210); "acceptance—that is the great lesson suffering teaches" (*C.* 6) because resistance is futile, "there is no escape, ever" (*C.* 303). He was wrong to struggle against necessity, and yet, he sees that what happened to him was undeserved: "say my unwilling crimes against myself / and against my own were payments from the gods / for something criminal inside me . . . no, look hard, / you'll find no guilt to accuse me of—I'm innocent!" (*C.* 1101–1105). That permanent adversities impinged on his life, that they made him suffer, that his reason and will achieved the opposite of what he intended—that, he came to understand, is the human condition.

If this interpretation is correct,[12] Sophocles shows us Oedipus passing through the stages of moral depth. He understands that reason and decency may be doomed by permanent adversities, that his expectation that the human condition is otherwise is illusory. He learns to abandon this illusory expectation, to balance his general understanding of the human condition and his specific understanding of the conditions of his own life,

---

[12] The claim on behalf of this interpretation is very modest. It is only a possible interpretation of one aspect of these two plays. There are many other aspects not touched upon by this interpretation, and even of the same aspect other interpretations are possible.

and to control his inappropriate reactions to what he has thus understood and learned.

The relevance of Oedipus's life for *us* is not that we should suppose that what happened to Oedipus—the unknowing and unintentional violation of the foundation of his moral life—will happen to us too. Rather, we should understand that the very imperfect control we have over our lives makes us liable to the sort of calamity that befell Oedipus. The point is not that we are doomed, but that we are at risk. Sophocles suggests in these two plays that for us to realize our aspirations it is necessary that we come to this understanding and hold it in the focus of our attention as we live our lives.

But we still need to clarify how this understanding is going to affect our control over our lives. How can it allow us to extend the amount of control we have and thereby reduce the risk we face? There is a sense in which we cannot do either. Nothing we can do will alter permanent adversities. Once we have moral depth, we know this to be the human condition. But there is another sense in which we can extend our control, and that brings us to the fifth stage of moral depth. Obviously, we cannot reasonably hope to control what is beyond our control. But if we understand that conditions beyond our control endanger our aspirations to live good lives, then we can, to some extent, control our attitude toward this regrettable fact. This control will help us maintain our balance in the face of the realization that we are at risk and in the event misfortune actually happens to us. It will work in the first way by not allowing the understanding that we are at risk to be falsified by some form of denial, or to provoke an overreaction, or to undercut the motivation to do what we can to make our lives good. And it will work in the second way by preventing us from exacerbating through inappropriate reaction the misfortune we may come to suffer. The discussion of these pitfalls will be aided by a further consideration of how Sophocles illuminates what we have called the fifth stage of moral depth.

THE FIFTH STAGE OF MORAL DEPTH

Sophocles of course is a poet, not a philosopher. His way of showing Oedipus's development toward greater moral depth is suggestive, evocative, and it requires the reader to make an imaginative effort to appreciate the complexities of the play. For a philosophical understanding of what Sophocles tells us about moral depth, it is necessary to be more explicit and analytical.

To begin with, moral depth is an anthropocentric notion. It involves understanding the human significance of some general conditions prevailing in the world. In this respect, moral depth is different from scientific or aesthetic depth. The difference is not that the latter forms of depth are unimportant from the human point of view—all forms of depth are important for us. The difference is rather where their respective importance lies. Moral depth is important because it involves understanding the significance of permanent adversities for the human aspiration to live good lives. Scientific or aesthetic depth may affect our moral condition, but, unlike moral depth, they do not have that as their primary object.

A further difference is that originality plays an important role in scientific and aesthetic depth, but not in moral depth. To see deeply into nature is to see something *in* nature that others have not seen. And aesthetic depth usually involves the creation of new forms of sensibility, expression, or representation. Moral depth, however, concerns permanent adversities whose prevalence is hidden from no one. The facts of the human condition are not discovered by those who possess moral depth; rather, they come to appreciate the significance of these quite familiar facts. What separates moral depth from shallowness and superficiality is thus not the possession of a greater amount of factual knowledge, but the extent to which the significance of commonly possessed factual knowledge is understood.

Permanent adversities may be described *sub specie aeternitatis*, from the point of view of nowhere, as Thomas Nagel put it,[13] and *sub specie humanitatis*, from the human point of view. The first is indifferent to human welfare; the second is essentially concerned with it. From both perspectives, permanent adversities will be seen as impersonal, inexorable, and unavoidable. Sophocles refers to them as "the will of the gods." We have no comparable theological commitments, and so it seems more plausible to us to think of permanent adversities as a kind of necessity.

Sub specie aeternitatis, the significance of this necessity is metaphysical; it illuminates the forces that influence constituents of the world which roughly resemble us in size, texture, and duration. That some of these constituents are human beings is a matter of indifference from this point of view. There is a kind of necessity for beehives, snow mobiles, zebras, and paintings, as well as for human beings. What matters metaphysically is to understand the necessity, not to adopt the point of view of the particulars that are subject to it.

Sub specie humanitatis, the significance of this necessity is precisely its effect upon us. Its salient feature from the human point of view is the threat it constitutes to our aspiration to live a good life.[14] If this "effect" is under-

---

[13] Thomas Nagel, *The View from Nowhere* (New York: Oxford University Press, 1986).

[14] For an illuminating study tracing the Greek view of this notion, see Hugh Lloyd-Jones, *The Justice of Zeus* (Berkeley: University of California Press, 1983).

stood narrowly, as the force exerted on us, then it is beyond our control. But if the "effect" is understood more broadly, as that force *and* our attitude to it, then we can have some control over it since we can have some control over our attitude. And this leads to the fifth stage of moral depth, which is to avoid forming an inappropriate attitude once the human significance of the effect permanent adversities have on us has been understood.

The variety of inappropriate attitudes to the human condition is great. Discussing them would take a very long—and depressing—book, and this is not that book. It will suffice instead to discuss briefly four frequent, perhaps most typical, kinds of inappropriate attitudes: disengagement, denial, romanticism, and resignation.

Consider Nagel's wonderfully suggestive desciption: "One summer . . . a large spider appeared in the urinal of the men's room. . . . When the urinal wasn't in use, he would perch on the metal drain at its base, and when it was, he would try to scramble out of the way, sometimes managing to climb an inch or two up the procelain wall to a point that wasn't too wet. But sometimes he was caught, tumbled and drenched by the flushing torrent. He didn't seem to like it, and always got out of the way if he could. . . . Somehow he survived, presumably feeding on tiny insects attracted to the site. . . . The urinal must have been used more than a hundred times a day, and always it was the same desperate scramble to get out of the way. His life seemed miserable and exhausting."[15] If we view the human condition *sub specie aeternitatis*, we may appear as that spider. But if our perspective is truly metaphysical, this will engage our emotions and motives as little as does the spider's lot. We have then learned to cultivate the attitude of a cool, dispassionate, uncommitted observer who contemplates the spectacle while remaining disengaged from it.

The cultivation of this attitude widens the distance between ourselves as participants and ourselves as contemplators of our participation. No matter how far we succeed in widening it, however, we cannot cease to be participants because to put an end to our participation would be to put an end to ourselves. What the distance produces, therefore, is not a life of passive contemplation, for we cannot live such a life, but a life in which we cultivate a disengaged attitude to our participation. We shall not cease to do what our nature dictates, but we shall reject the naïveté of wholehearted enthusiasm toward the miserable and exhausting existence we have in *our* urinal. The result is a frame of mind in which we react to permanent adversities by teaching ourselves disengagement from the life that is endangered by them. We endeavor then to cope with the human condition by

[15] Nagel, *The View from Nowhere*, 208.

distancing ourselves insofar as we can from our humanity. And the better we succeed, the weaker will be our emotional and motivational reactions toward the human condition. "If *sub specie aeternitatis* there is no reason to believe that anything matters, then that does not matter either."[16]

All of this is predicated, however, on the assumption that we should view the human condition *sub specie aeternitatis*, and the time has come to ask why that is supposed to be desirable. If we were to adopt that point of view, then, of course, what matters *sub specie humanitatis* would not matter. But we are human, and it would be destructive of our aspirations to live a good life to adopt an attitude of disengagement from good and evil. We would worsen our condition if we responded to the realization that permanent adversities put us at risk by abandoning efforts to improve our lot. The success of those efforts *is* endangered by the risk we face. But we face only the *risk* of failure, not its certainty. Oedipus's situation *is* like the spider's in the urinal. Our situation, however, is like Oedipus's only in the sense that we are as much at risk as he was before his life collapsed. Our lives, however, have not collapsed, although they may do so. Disengagement would make collapse more likely by weakening our will and desire to exercise such control as we can.

Behind the attitude of disengagement, there is, therefore, the misjudgment of taking the state of being at risk for being doomed. Risk holds out the possibility of success, not just of failure. Excessive fear of failure may lead to a loss of nerve, and that to an attempt to extricate ourselves from the risky situation. But when the risk is integral to the human condition, we cannot extricate ourselves from it. We can only face the risk well or badly. Disengagement leads us to face it badly because it jeopardizes our chances of succeeding.

The strategy of viewing the world *sub specie aeternitatis* has notable successes to its credit. The great achievements of the physical and biological sciences have been made possible precisely by that objective, dispassionate, nonanthropocentric quest for understanding that is also behind the attitude of disengagement. From this similarity, however, no support can be derived for disengagement. The nonanthropocentric view is appropriate to understanding nature, but not the human condition. The physical and biological sciences are not *ex officio* concerned with the bearing their discoveries have on human welfare. To be sure, scientists are no less interested in our welfare than anyone else, but they are interested in their capacity as human beings, not as scientists. Disengagement, by contrast, is a deliberate turning away from the interests of humanity. It is not a phenomenological bracketing of the human condition for the purposes of in-

---

[16] Thomas Nagel, *Mortal Questions* (Cambridge: Cambridge University Press, 1979), 23.

quiry, but a conscious effort to replace, insofar as that is possible, our natural anthropocentric perspective by an alien nonanthropocentric one. The resulting disengagement is unavoidably committed, therefore, to downgrading the importance of what matters *sub specie humanitatis*. And a strategy of coping with the prospect of failure by minimizing its importance and diverting the efforts needed for success cannot help being self-defeating.

A second possible attitude toward the realization that we cannot avoid being at risk is to erect some barrier that prevents us from facing the full implications of that realization. The barrier may be conscious, involving a deliberate effort to ignore or to dismiss from our minds the disturbing truth. Or, it may be unconscious, in which case it takes the form of self-deception. We may, then, persuade ourselves that we are invulnerable to the risk other people face, or that, while the risk is there, it is so insignificant as to be negligible. This state of mind is depicted in Tolstoy's Ivan Ilych: "In the depth of his heart he knew he was dying, but not only was he not accustomed to the thought, he simply did not and could not grasp it. The syllogism he had learnt . . . 'Caius is a man, men are mortal, therefore Caius is mortal,' has always seemed to him correct as applied to Caius, but certainly not as applied to himself. . . . Caius really was mortal, and it was right for him to die, but for me . . . with all my thoughts and emotions, it's altogether a different matter. It cannot be that I ought to die. That would be too terrible."[17]

The trouble with this attitude is that it misdirects our attention and thereby increases our liability to permanent adversities that rightly focused attention might mitigate. If we keep firmly in our minds that contingency, conflict, and evil may destroy or damage us and those we love, then we shall tend to live by concentrating on what is important and not fritter away whatever opportunities we have on trivial pursuits. The denial of risk makes us more liable to it, while its acknowledgment strengthens our defenses.

Its acknowledgment, however, can also go wrong because it may elicit in us an overreaction. This can go in the direction of romantic bombast or romantic *Weltschmerz*. Both involve exaggeration, and thus a falsification of what we have to face. We may bombastically inflate our powers, or, in cosmic pessimism, overestimate the threat presented by permanent adversities. The younger Oedipus is an instructive example of one who swings back and forth between these pitfalls. He vexes bombastically: "My troubles are mine / and I am the only man alive who can sustain them" (*K.* 1548–1549), and he exaggerates in desperation that he is "the man the deathless gods

---

[17] Leo Tolstoy, *The Death of Ivan Ilych*, trans. A. Maude (New York: Signet, 1960), 121–122.

hate most of all!" (*K.* 1480). Then the combination of these inflated passions causes him to erupt in the spectacular reaction of self-blinding, which, of course, makes matters even worse than they already were.

As we face permanent adversities, realism is one of our most important resources. For our troubles are rarely so great and our destinies rarely involve so glorious Promethean struggles against overwhelming odds as they may seem to us in the throes of passion. We cannot stop ourselves from having the passions that assail us, especially not in the midst of crises which provoke them. But we can stop them from getting out of hand. If we know the emotional excesses to which we are prone, we can recognize them when they are about to occur and we can stop ourselves from being led by them to inappropriate action, like the younger Oedipus was led to self-blinding. And then, like the old Oedipus, while we still have the passions, as his responses to Creon and Polynices show, we shall also have learned to control their strength and expression: "My rage had outrun my wrongs, / I'd lashed myself too much" (*C.* 488–489). Without this control, we are liable to the risks created by the uncontrolled parts of our character, risks that add their destructive potential to those that exist beyond our control.

Yet even if we resist the temptation to deny or to overreact to our understanding of permanent adversities, there remains the lure of resignation. We may well come to wonder about the point of a wholehearted engagement in life, if the efforts we make cannot free us from contingency, conflict, and evil. The possession of this truth and the achievement of control over our feelings may just sap our will. Instinct, training, the need to earn a living, the pleasures of life, a mild curiosity about the future, and intermittent amusement afforded by being a spectator may make us carry on, but our heart will not be in it. We shall lack enthusiasm, dedication, seriousness of spirit, and our lives, then, become permeated by a languid insipidity in which nothing really matters, like J. Alfred Prufrock or the middle-aged characters of Chekhov, desultorily talking away their lives during endless barren afternoons.

The result is the very misfortune whose prospect motivated resignation. For what initially disturbs us is the fear that we shall not attain good lives despite our best efforts. If this leads us to make only minimal efforts, we collude in causing what we fear. The reasonable alternative is to make our best efforts, while understanding that they may be unavailing and disciplining ourselves not to allow our feelings to get out of hand when we face the possibility of failure. What makes this alternative reasonable is that it is the only way of making our lives good.

There may, of course, be people who do not want that. What we should say about them depends on why they do not want a good life. One possibility is that they live under barbaric conditions where their main concern must be with staying alive, and they have no energy left to wonder about the manner in which they should do so. That the vast majority of humanity has lived and is living under such conditions is a sad fact. But it does not remove the point of asking how we should live when conditions are civilized. Another possibility is that people are living in civilized conditions and yet do not want a good life because they fail to understand its nature. The appropriate response is to do what we reasonably can to make them understand it. Yet there still remain many people who live in civilized conditions, have the requisite understanding, and still do not want to have a good life. Such people are unreasonable, and they are likely to harm both themselves and others. The former is regrettable; the latter requires action. And what the action should be depends on what the appropriate reaction is to immorality.

The upshot of our discussion of the fifth stage of moral depth may be formulated either negatively or positively. Put negatively, moral depth is the mode of reflection that makes it possible to avoid forming an inappropriate attitude to what the first four stages of moral depth reveal about the human condition. In particular, it is to avoid such common ways of going wrong as disengagement, denial, romanticism, and resignation. Expressed positively, this stage of moral depth involves forming an attitude to the human condition that combines continued effort to live according to our conception of a good life, acceptance that permanent adversities endanger our success, maintaining a balanced emotional response that tilts neither toward undue pessimism nor toward foolhardy quixoticism, and an undiminished commitment to exercise fully such control as we can over our character and circumstances.

CONCLUSION

The argument in this chapter has been that we are not without resources in contending with permanent adversities. We are not doomed to a choice between false hope and hopelessness. The alternative is to cultivate moral depth composed of understanding that permanent adversities may frustrate our reasonable and decent efforts to live a good life; that the resulting sense of hopelessness is due to our unrealistic expectation that the human condition is otherwise; that abandoning the expectation is to remove the ground of hopelessness; that we must bring our general understanding of the human condition to bear on our individual condition; and that we should form an appropriate attitude to what we have thus understood.

Moral depth thus brings greater realism. It leads to the acknowledgment of the pervasive forces of contingency, conflict, and evil, and it motivates us to mitigate their destructive consequences while knowing that we may fail. This greater realism is the ground for true hope. True hope is chastened; a hope reduced, purified, and strengthened through having resisted the temptations of seeking solace by distancing ourselves from our condition, by denying the facts, by romantic self-aggrandizement or world-weariness, and by succumbing to resignation. It is a hope without the expectation of cosmic justice, and without the bitterness that the world is not more hospitable to us.

What is left is not much, but it is enough to fend off hopelessness. We may run afoul of permanent adversities, but we need not suffer this fate. And even if our lives are damaged, they need not be destroyed. Moral depth permits true hope because it saves us from the futility of hounding the unresponsive heavens to relieve our misfortune, and because it prepares us to pick up the damaged pieces, if they can be picked up, and go on. True hope does not come from a guarantee that conceptions of a good life pursued reasonably and decently will be realized. It comes from the confidence that we have done what is in our power to succeed and that if we fail despite our merits and efforts, then we need not be destroyed as a result. Moral depth does not promise good lives; it promises to make lives as free from contingency, conflict, and evil as our character and circumstances permit.

These dark thoughts are, in a currently unfashionable sense, philosophical. It is perhaps this sense that Russell had in mind when he wrote: "To teach how to live without certainty, and yet without being paralyzed by hesitation, is perhaps the chief thing that philosophy, in our age, can still do for those who study it."[18]

[18] Bertrand Russell, *A History of Western Philosophy* (New York: Simon and Schuster, 1945), xiv.

CHAPTER NINE

The Ideal of Justice

This chapter will complete the account of moral wisdom. The argument has so far been that moral wisdom has four components: a conception of a good life, knowledge, evaluation, and judgment. Knowledge is of good and evil; evaluation brings that knowledge to bear on the actual situations we face in the course of trying to live according to our conception of a good life; and judgment helps us reach a reasonable decision in complex situations whose evaluation is difficult, partly because our control over our character and circumstances is limited by permanent adversities. Moral wisdom is essentially connected therefore with increasing our control. This we may endeavor to do by improving our conception of a good life and viewing the situations we face more and more from its perspective, and by responding reasonably to the limits permanent adversities set to increasing our control. The activity of forming a reasonable response is a kind of reflection, the objects of which are both the limits internal to our character and external limits inherent in our circumstances. The discussion has just been completed of the three modes of reflection, moral imagination, self-knowledge, and moral depth, each of which concentrates on internal limits. The remaining task is to consider what response reflection prompts to external limits. The argument in this chapter aims to establish that the reasonable response is to be guided by the ideal of justice.

Socrates was the first to see and insist on the deep connection between moral wisdom and justice, and on the necessity of both to living a good life. It is appropriate, therefore, to begin the treatment of these topics by returning to the discussion in Chapter 2 of the Socratic ideal and of how an improved eudaimonistic conception of a good life differs from it.

Socrates believed that a life is good if and only if it has both moral worth and the agent is, all things considered, satisfied with it. The distinguishing mark of the Socratic ideal is the further supposition that these two components are inseparable. A life of moral worth cannot fail to be satisfying, and satisfaction with our life must be derived from its moral worth. The reason for this is that both moral worth and satisfaction derive from the same source: The extent to which our life is an approximation of what is good. Moral wisdom is to know what is good, and justice is to order our character and society to facilitate living according to it. The appearance that lives of moral worth may lack satisfaction or that satisfaction may be derived from a wicked life is taken for reality only by those who lack moral wisdom. Their mistake is symptomatic of their ignorance of the good. Those who know the good will be satisfied with their life in proportion to its moral worth.

Unlike Socrates, we, possessors of a contemporary Western sensibility, recognize the possibility that the two components of good lives may diverge. We follow Socrates in cherishing both of them, but we do not believe that lives of moral worth are bound to be satisfying or that satisfaction can be derived only from moral worth. We recognize that the good may suffer and the wicked may flourish, even in the long run, even when all things are considered. The fundamental reason that underlies this attitude is that we do not believe in cosmic justice. We do not believe that there is a moral order in reality guaranteeing that lives of moral worth will be satisfying and that wicked lives will not be. We believe, on the contrary, that permanent adversities are ineliminable features of the human condition. We deplore this fact, but recognize that it is a fact. It becomes, therefore, much the more important for us to cope with it. Human justice is our attempt to do so insofar as circumstances external to us are concerned. Our ideal of justice, consequently, is that it should be a human substitute for cosmic justice. It is a poor substitute, however, partly because the limits external circumstances impose on its realization are ineliminable. But the ideal nevertheless inspires us to do the best we can to ameliorate external obstacles to living a good life. If we follow the ideal, we increase our control, thus improve our judgment, and thus grow in moral wisdom.

THE CONCEPT OF JUSTICE

The history of philosophy abounds in theories of justice. Plato, Aristotle, Hobbes, Locke, Hume, Hegel, and John Stuart Mill, among numerous others, developed notable versions of it. And contemporary political thought is awash in controversies about justice since John Rawls's *A Theory of Justice* opened the floodgates in 1971. There is thus a vast literature on justice. But it will be largely ignored here because the way in which justice is connected with moral wisdom does not depend on the outcome of these controversies. Let it be acknowledged that justice may well be an essentially contested concept, that is, a concept open enough to allow numerous evaluatively charged and incompatible interpretations.[1] The concept nevertheless must possess some core of uncontested meaning, for without it there would be no reason to suppose that the numerous interpretations are of the same thing. Controversies about justice thus presuppose some, at least minimal, agreement among the participants regarding the subject about which they disagree.

This point may be expressed in terms of Rawls's distinction between the concept and various conceptions of justice. Rawls says, "It seems natural to think of the concept of justice as distinct from various conceptions of justice and as being justified by the role which these different . . . conceptions have in common."[2] The concern of this chapter then can be said to be with the concept of justice, and not with developing a particular conception of justice, nor with controversies concerning the respective merits of alternative conceptions of justice. The connection between justice and moral wisdom depends on the agreed upon core of justice that is encapsulated by the concept and not on the controversial aspects that lend themselves to the conflicting interpretations of different conceptions.

What then is this agreed upon core? As a start toward identifying it, we may begin with Aristotle's general formula for justice: treat equals equally and unequals unequally.[3] But this is much too vague because there is nothing that connects it specifically with justice. It is a condition of the consistent application of any principle in any context that the like cases that come under its jurisdiction should be treated alike and the different cases differently. This is as true of sorting apples, classifying fauna, diagnosing illness, judging wine, appraising antiques, and so forth, as it is of justice. This general formula, therefore, is insufficiently informative about what makes some principles principles of justice. What is needed is an account that goes beyond simple consistency and adds something that would permit the identification of particular principles as those of justice.

Considerable care must be exercised, however, about what it is that is added. It would be wrong, for instance, to add to consistency the requirement of equal treatment in respect to economic distribution. For this

---

[1] The phrase "essentially contested concepts" is William B. Gallie's; see *Philosophy and the Historical Understanding* (London: Chatto & Windus, 1964), chap. 8. In Morris Weitz, *The Opening Mind* (Chicago: University of Chicago Press, 1977), chap. 2, there is a useful account of the origins of Gallie's idea.

[2] John Rawls, *A Theory of Justice* (Cambridge: Harvard University Press, 1971), 5.

[3] Aristotle, *Nicomachean Ethics*, Book V.

would make economic equality just by definition, and that of course would be question-begging. This way of proceeding would arbitrarily identify the concept of justice with a particular conception of justice, and the result would be that conceptions of justice that allowed for economic inequality could be challenged not merely on moral or political grounds but also for being logically self-contradictory. Whatever is added to consistency, therefore, would have to be specific enough to identify some principles as principles of justice and yet remain sufficiently general to allow for conflicting conceptions of justice.

If the illusory expectation discussed in the preceding chapter is borne in mind, namely, the expectation that if we are guided by reason and morality, then we shall succeed in living a life that combines moral worth and satisfaction, it will point in the right direction toward identifying the missing core of justice. The expectation is illusory because permanent adversities may interfere and limit our chances for success in a way that no effort of ours to be more reasonable and moral could surmount. It has been argued that one stage toward moral depth involves abandoning this expectation. What needs to be discussed now is a belief that underlies the expectation and lends much strength to it.

The supposition that reasonable and moral efforts will be crowned with success rests, of course, on our belief in justice. We believe not merely that reason and morality are necessary for living a good life but also that they ought to be sufficient for it. We can be brought to see that the Socratic ideal is mistaken in claiming that reason and morality *are* sufficient, but we still hold on to the belief that even if they are not, they *ought to be* sufficient. Our belief in justice is violated if the connection between moral worth and satisfaction is severed. And if the divergence between these components of good lives is too great, if moral worth is accompanied by lifelong misery or if wickedness coexists with a life of uninterrupted enjoyment, then our belief in justice is not merely violated but outraged.

We believe that good conduct should lead to good lives, bad conduct to bad lives, and that the goodness or badness of lives ought to be proportional to the goodness or badness of the agents' conduct. This belief routinely survives the abandonment of the expectation that reality will conform to it because the belief is not primarily about how things are but about how they ought to be. Hopelessness is a product of the realization that we have limited control over making things fall less short of how we believe they ought to be.

It is necessary to press on, however, and ask why we believe that good lives should be the products of good conduct and bad lives of bad conduct. The answer finally provides the missing core of justice: People ought to get what they deserve. That is why good conduct should lead to good lives and bad conduct to bad lives. This is among our most basic moral beliefs; it is on the same level as the beliefs that we ought to act with due regard for other people's vulnerability, honor obligations we responsibly assumed, alleviate suffering, and do what we consider to be good.

If it is asked why these beliefs are to be counted among our basic moral beliefs, the answer can only be that commitment to morality must include commitment to human welfare and these beliefs are essential to it. If the question is then turned to the commitment to human welfare itself, then it is possible to answer with Hume: "I am of the opinion that tho' it be rare to meet one, who loves any single person better than himself; yet 'tis rare to meet one, in whom all the kind affections, taken together, do not overbalance all the selfish."[4] And even if we are less sanguine than the amiable Hume was about the numbers in the party of humanity, his general point still holds: "It is needless to push our researches so far as to ask, why we have humanity or a fellow-feeling with others. It is sufficient, that this is experienced to be a principle of human nature. . . . No man is absolutely indifferent to the happiness and misery of others. The first has a natural tendency to give pleasure; the second pain. This every man finds in himself."[5] We can, of course, persevere in our researches, and then we shall probably be led to an evolutionary explanation of the survival value of fellow-feeling to the species as a whole.

From the fact that we have some fellow-feeling for one another it does not follow that we shall invariably act on it. We have other motives as well, and they may be stronger than fellow-feeling; even if we act on our fellow-feeling, we may be misled by a pernicious morality; and self-deception, moral weakness, stupidity, passion, or laziness may prevent us from acting as we think we should. Hume's being right about the general human predisposition toward fellow-feeling is compatible with our acting so as to cause much evil, and even to cause a preponderance of evil over good.

It is now possible to go a little deeper in understanding the core belief of justice, namely, that people ought to get what they deserve.[6] The essen-

---

[4] David Hume, *A Treatise of Human Nature*, ed. L. A. Selby-Bigge (Oxford: Clarendon Press, 1960), 487.

[5] David Hume, *An Enquiry concerning the Principles of Morals*, ed. L. A. Selby-Bigge, 2d ed. (Oxford: Clarendon Press, 1961), 219–220. See also a survey of the psychological evidence supporting Hume's claim in Richard B. Brandt, "The Psychology of Benevolence," *Journal of Philosophy* 73 (1976): 429–453.

[6] Until about 1960, only the most cursory philosophical discussion of the nature of desert was available. This situation has changed, and the following contributions, listed in chronological order, have influenced the present discussion: Joel Feinberg, "Justice and Personal Desert," in *Nomos VI: Justice*, ed. Carl J. Friedrich and John W. Chapman (New York: Atherton, 1963); Brian Barry, *Political Argument* (London: Routledge, 1965); John Rawls, *A Theory of Justice* (Cambridge: Harvard University Press, 1971); Robert Nozick, *Anarchy, State, and Utopia* (New York: Basic Books, 1974), see the index for relevant entries; David Miller, *Social Justice* (Oxford: Clarendon Press, 1976), 83–121; Alan Zaitchik, "On De-

tial idea is not merely that desert creates a claim, but also that the claim should be based on some specific morally good or evil state, characteristic, relationship, or action that is correctly ascribed to the claimant. The claim created by desert consequently derives from some moral fact that was true of the claimant in the past. It is thus partly a backward- and partly a forward-looking claim to the effect that because of that past morally significant state, characteristic, relationship, or action someone ought to have or get something.

What is deserved varies with individuals and situations, but it may be identified in general terms as benefits or harms. Conscientious acts deserve praise; employees deserve wages from their employers; and acts of kindness deserve gratitude. Similarly, hardened criminals deserve imprisonment, incompetent physicians deserve to lose their licenses, and fraudulent claims deserve to be exposed. What is thus essential to the belief in justice is that it is good that we should receive deserved benefits and harms, and evil if we do not. And what ultimately motivates this belief is the ideal that moral worth and satisfaction should coincide.

Some of these examples may misleadingly suggest that a legitimate claim to deserving some benefit or harm always obligates some specific person or institution to provide the benefit or the harm. The claim to what we deserve may create a specific obligation, but it may also be so general as to obligate no one to do anything, as when we say that good people deserve to be happy or that wicked people do not deserve robust health or riches. There is still a claim, but it is against the scheme of things. It amounts to saying that it would be a good thing if the world were such as to assure the coincidence of moral worth and satisfaction, as well as of wickedness and dissatisfaction.

The progress made so far toward clarifying the concept of justice may be summed up by the claim that the essential element that needs to be added to consistency is desert. The concept then contains the core idea that like cases should be treated alike and different cases should be treated differently in respect to our getting the benefits and harms we deserve. And deserved benefits and harms are to be understood as satisfactions and dissatisfactions commensurate with our moral worth or the lack of it. This understanding of the concept allows for the existence of many conceptions of justice, which will depend on what states, characteristics, relationships,

---

serving to Deserve," *Philosophy and Public Affairs* 6 (1977): 371–388; William A. Galston, *Justice and the Human Good* (Chicago: University of Chicago Press, 1980), 170–191; Michael Sandel, *Liberalism and the Limits of Justice* (Oxford: Blackwell, 1984), see the index for relevant entries; George Sher, *Desert* (Princeton: Princeton University Press, 1987); and John Kekes, *Facing Evil* (Princeton: Princeton University Press, 1990), chap. 3.

or actions are thought to be morally significant and thus appropriate grounds of claim for desert and on what benefits and harms are taken to satisfy the claim.

There is a contemporary tendency, however, to doubt that desert should be included in the core of the concept of justice. A case in point is Rawls's claim that "there is a tendency for common sense to suppose that . . . the good things in life . . . should be distributed according to moral desert. . . . Now justice as fairness [i.e., Rawls's theory] rejects this conception."[7] The reason being that "desert presupposes the existence of [a] . . . cooperative scheme."[8] According to this view, desert depends on institutional arrangements; consequently claims of desert cannot be as basic to justice as is supposed here.

Rawls is right in thinking that what specific grounds are taken to create a claim for desert and what specific benefits and harms are taken to satisfy the claim do depend on prevailing institutions. He is wrong, however, in overlooking the fact that one of the reasons for having institutions is to assure that we get what we deserve. Since institutions regulate the allocation of desert, desert must be prior to the institutions that regulate its allocation, although *honoring* specific claims to specific deserved benefits and harms may depend on them. The following considerations will strengthen this point.

First, if claims of desert were not basic because they presupposed institutions, then one of the strongest reasons for criticizing institutions would have to be abandoned. A very good criticism of an institution is that it is unjust because it causes undeserved harm to people. If desert were a product of institutions, then, provided only that the institution functioned in accordance with its own rules of allocation, it could not fail to be just, it could not fail to allocate to people what they deserve, because its rules define what counts as desert and justice. The standard practice of criticizing institutions on precisely these grounds shows that desert is more fundamental to justice than institutional arrangements.

Second, if desert were not part of the core of justice, what would occupy its place? The historically favored alternatives are basic needs, human rights, important wants, true interests, and appropriate merits. But in each case, it is reasonable to ask why we should favor whatever they turn out to be. And the answer must ultimately be that we value people and that we are committed to their welfare, and so we think that in normal circumstances they deserve to have their needs, rights, wants, interests, or merits honored.

Third, it may be supposed that placing desert at the core of justice overstates the case. Why should the core of justice not simply be the allocation

---

[7] Rawls, *A Theory of Justice*, 310.
[8] Ibid., 103.

of benefits and the protection against harms, without making any mention of desert at all? Because it would assume an overly simple view of benefits and harms. Harming people may actually be beneficial because, like amputation, it may prevent greater harm; benefits may be obtained criminally, and then they are unjust; and it may be just to harm people even without the prospect of avoiding greater harm in the future, such as punishing repentant serial killers. Justice requires therefore more than the mere allocation of benefits and protection against harms: benefits and harms must be deserved, if their allocation is to be just.

Fourth, a further reason why desert is at the core of justice is that justice is concerned with how we should conduct ourselves toward other people, and desert is a consideration central to that. Their connection is so basic and obvious as to be almost tautological. Morality must include commitment to other people's welfare; hence it must include justice. Justice is concerned with allocating benefits and harms so as to promote human welfare. This involves benefiting those who contribute to it and harming those who violate it, as well as making benefits and harms proportional to the contributions to or the violations of human welfare. That people should get what they deserve—the core of justice—is simply an expression of this idea.

Doubts about the centrality of desert to justice are often due to some misinterpretation of this idea. The connection between the allocation of desert and human welfare does not imply any form of consequentialism, although it is compatible with it. A just system for allocating benefits and harms may be instrumental to human welfare, but it may also be constitutive of it. The relation may be means to end, or it may be part to whole, aspect to figure, content to form, and so forth. The justification of the allocation of desert need not, therefore, be in terms of the consequences it produces.

Nor does the centrality of desert mean that morality invariably requires giving people what they deserve. There are other, perfectly legitimate, moral motives. Love, generosity, and gratitude may justifiably lead us to benefit people more than they deserve; and mercy, forgiveness, and pity may be reasonable grounds for inflicting less than deserved harm. Justice is an important moral value, but there are also other important moral values. Desert is one moral consideration, therefore, while there are others, and they may conflict with, mitigate, or override it.

It is now possible to formulate two conclusions that have emerged from the discussion of the concept of justice. First, the lack of cosmic justice forces us to recognize that moral worth and satisfaction, may diverge. Their divergence is morally objectionable because it creates an imbalance that ought not to exist. The purpose of justice is to reduce this imbalance by making them diverge less from each other. This should be done by allocating benefits and harms in proportion to the recipients' contribution to or violation of human welfare. As a shorthand formula, it may be said that justice is the human substitute for cosmic justice in the allocation of desert.

Second, the concept of justice sets a minimum standard that all reasonable conceptions of justice must meet: No reasonable conception of justice can be inconsistent with the concept of justice. The justification of this minimum standard is that since conceptions of justice are elaborations of the concept of justice, they cannot reasonably contradict that of which they are elaborations. Any inconsistency of this type conclusively establishes the failure of the attempted elaboration.

The reason for calling attention to this minimum standard is that egalitarian conceptions of justice that ignore the centrality of desert, such as Rawls's, fail to meet it. The concept of justice requires that all benefits and harms be allocated proportionally to what their recipients deserve. But egalitarian conceptions require that at least some important benefits and harms be allocated equally, independently of what their recipients deserve. Such conceptions therefore cannot be reasonable elaborations of the concept of justice.

It may be said in reply that egalitarian conceptions of justice are not inconsistent with the concept of justice because on a fundamental level people are equally deserving. If we bear in mind, however, that desert is created by contribution to human welfare, then we can see that this defense is committed to the indefensible view that people contribute equally to human welfare.

Or the rejoinder may be that morality requires that everyone should enjoy certain basic benefits and not be subject to certain basic harms, regardless of what he or she deserves. Not even if this were true could it be used to defend an egalitarian conception of *justice* since justice is to allocate benefits and harms proportionally to desert. Guaranteeing certain basic benefits and the absence of certain basic harms independent of desert may be required by decency, altruism, solidarity, benevolence, charity, or pity, but it cannot be required by justice. Human suffering is great and it offends our moral sensibility. The hope of alleviating it, however, is diminished rather than enhanced by basing it on a misinterpretation of justice.

MAKING LIVES MORE JUST

The concept of justice understood in this sense is an ideal, not a description of any individual, society, or institution. The ideal will not be realized because there are insurmountable limits in its way. These limits may be internal or external to the agents who aim at justice. When reflection is directed toward finding a reasonable response to the understanding that there are these limits, then the deep connection between justice and moral wisdom becomes apparent. Justice and moral wisdom have the common object of making good lives possible. Justice aims at this object by developing institutions and characters so that they will more closely approximate the ideal of making satisfaction proportional to moral worth. Moral wisdom aims at the same object by developing our conception of a good life, knowledge, evaluation, and judgment so that we can live a life that is satisfying and has moral worth. Both justice and moral wisdom are based on the assumption that good lives depend on maintaining a balance between moral worth and satisfaction. But they differ because justice concentrates on one aspect of this necessary endeavor, the allocation of desert, while moral wisdom includes the general nature of the conception of a good life, knowledge, evaluation, and judgment that are required for that balance. It may be said then that justice is an aspect of moral wisdom.

The emerging concept of justice is so far largely formal. Justice does require the allocation of desert, but it is still necessary to know how that should be done. Sophocles' *Antigone* is a profound treatment of this problem.[9] The center of this play is the conflict between Creon and Antigone. Creon is the King of Thebes. Antigone is a young woman, the daughter of Oedipus, who was Creon's predecessor on the throne before tragedy befell him and he was exiled by Creon. The conflict between Creon and Antigone has several sources, but the one that bears on justice is political. Creon and Antigone are committed to incompatible conceptions of justice, and they are led by their commitments to a confrontation in which neither is willing to compromise. The conflict turns on Creon's decree that the corpse of Polynices, one of Antigone's brothers, be subjected to an obscenely humiliating treatment, while her other brother, Eteocles, was to be buried with all honors due to a hero. Antigone cannot accept the humiliation of Polynices, disobeys the decree, and performs symbolic rites honoring her brother. This brings about the confrontation between Creon and Antigone:

[9] Sophocles, *Antigone*. References are to the lines of this play. The interpretation here proposed follows one of several traditional ways of reading the play. See for instance Anne Paolucci and Henry Paolucci, eds., *Hegel on Tragedy* (New York: Harper, 1962), see the index for relevant passages on *Antigone*; Bernard M. W. Knox, *The Heroic Temper* (Berkeley: University of California Press, 1964), chaps. 3–4; and Martha C. Nussbaum, *The Fragility of Goodness: Luck and Ethics in Greek Tragedy and Philosophy* (Cambridge: Cambridge University Press, 1986), chap. 3, which contains a survey of the literature, as well as of competing interpretations.

Creon: Do you deny you did this, yes or no?
                                        (491)

Antigone: Of course I did it. It wasn't Zeus, not in the least
                who made this proclamation—not to me.
                Nor did that Justice, dwelling with the gods
                beneath the earth, ordain such laws for men.
                Nor did I think that your edict had such force
                that you, a mere mortal, could override the gods,
                the great unwritten, unshakable traditions.
                                        (499–506)

To appreciate what is at stake between them, it is necessary to look beyond the simple-minded interpretation that Creon is a tyrant abusing his
authority and Antigone is heroically resisting him. The conflict is not between injustice and justice. Creon and Antigone agree that what justice requires ought to be done. They disagree about what that is. Both are
concerned with treating Polynices as he deserves to be treated. Creon
thinks, however, that Polynices deserves humiliation for being a traitor,
while Antigone thinks that he deserves a decent burial, regardless of what
he did. Their conflict is about the requirements of justice.

It is crucial to appreciating their conflict that both protagonists have a rea-
soned case. Antigone's is better, and it is shown to be better, but only a superficial reading of the play would lead one to dismiss Creon's case out of
hand. According to Creon, justice consists of man-made rules. The power to
make them belongs to the ruler. As Creon says: "I now possess the throne
and all its powers, / . . . ruling the people, / making laws" (193–197). This
power must be exercised in the interest of the city, and places "the awesome
task of setting the city's course" (199) upon the ruler. The city's welfare must
come before all other considerations in ruling because "our city *is* our
safety" (211). The ruler is the protector of that safety, hence

                            . . . that man
            the city places in authority, his orders
            must be obeyed, large and small,
            right and wrong. Anarchy—
            show me a greater crime in all the earth!
            She, she destroys cities, rips up houses,
            breaks the ranks of spearmen into headlong rout.
            But the ones who last it out, the great mass of them
            owe their lives to discipline. Therefore
            we must defend the men who live by law.
                                        (748–757)

Friendship, family ties, the decencies and affections of civilized existence presuppose the rule of law and the absence of anarchy: "whoever places a friend / above the good of his country, he is nothing . . . nor could I ever make that man a friend of mine / who menaces our country" (209–210). From this it follows that

> Eteocles, who died fighting for Thebes,
> excelling all in arms: he shall be buried,
> crowned with a hero's honors.
> (218–220)

> But as for his blood brother, Polynices,
> . . . who thirsted to drink
> his kinsmen blood and sell the rest to slavery
> . . . he must be left unburied, his corpse
> a carrion for birds and dogs to tear,
> an obscenity for the citizens to behold!
> (222–231)

According to Creon's conception then justice depends on the ruler, who has the power to make rules, and who ought to exercise it for the protection of the community.

Antigone rejects Creon's conception. She thinks that Creon "has no right to keep me from my own" (59). The rule he made violated a deeper conception of justice. It had no

> . . . such force
> that you, a mere mortal, could override the gods,
> the great unwritten, unshakable traditions.
> They are alive, not just today or yesterday:
> they live forever.
> (503–508)

Creon mocks this conception as he sentences Antigone to death: "Let her cry for mercy, sing her hymns / to Zeus who defends all bonds of kindred blood" (734–735). But Creon cannot sustain his conception in the face of the forces uniting against him and siding with Antigone: the chorus speaking for Theban elders says: "Yours is the power Zeus, what man on earth / can override it, who can hold it back?" (678–680); his son Haemon tells him: "I see my father offending justice . . . trample down the honors of the gods" (833–835); the prophet Tiresias warns: "This is violence / you have forced upon the heavens" (1192–1193); and finally

Creon, ground into submission, concedes: "No more fighting a losing battle with necessity" (1230); "It's best to keep the established laws" (1237). Antigone's conception of justice is thus shown to prevail, while Creon's is shown to lose.

It may seem at first sight that Sophocles is telling us that Antigone's case is stronger because it appeals to a conception of justice as divinely ordained rules, while Creon's case is weaker because it rests on a conception of justice as man-made. But this is not so. Antigone's case *is* stronger and Creon's *is* weaker, but what makes them so is more subtle than it first appears.

No one in the play doubts that Creon is right in believing that justice ought to protect the community; nor is there any challenge to the notion that the power to make rules belongs to the ruler. Furthermore, Antigone's adherence to what she regards as divinely ordained rules brings her nothing but suffering, and the same is true of her defenders; so there is no suggestion that divine justice will somehow compensate Antigone and others when man-made justice miscarries.

What Creon is faulted for is poor judgment and lack of moral wisdom in exercising the power that rightly belongs to him. We are told about Creon that "it's terrible when the one who does the judging / judges things all wrong" (366–367), that his are "empty, mindless judgments" (845), and that "he shows the world that of all the ills / afflicting men the worst is lack of judgment" (1372–1373). But Antigone is not praised either; she is upbraided: "Why rush to extremes?" (80); "You're in love with impossibility" (104); she is "passionate, wild" (525); and there is a "wild passion / raging through the girl" (1022–1023). She herself comes to see that "once I suffer I will know that I was wrong" (1018), and she suffers.

Creon and Antigone are alike in having bad judgment. Each has a case, but each case is ruined by being taken to the extreme. In placing the protection of the community unequivocally over family ties, Creon is undone by coming to feel the force of those very ties. Analogously, for the love of her dead brother, Antigone pits herself against legitimate authority and against Ismene, the one living member of her immediate family. Both Creon and Antigone are blinded by intransigence. It is, therefore, not the lesson of this play that a conception of justice as divinely ordained rules is better than a conception of justice as man-made rules. Its lesson is rather that human justice ought not to ignore the objective conditions of human existence, conditions to which all reasonable conceptions of a good life must conform.

Creon sees that whoever rules must make rules of justice for protecting the community, but he does not see that the will of the ruler must conform to objective conditions, that the rules cannot be arbitrary if they are indeed to protect the community and make good lives possible. Creon was right to stress against Antigone his responsibility as a lawmaker; he was wrong, however, in the way in which he discharged that responsibility. Antigone rightly objected to that. Antigone was right to base her objection on Creon's rule being contrary to the objective conditions of human existence, but she was wrong in being impatient and contemptuous of man-made laws. Creon was blinded by power; Antigone was blinded by purity. Both are extremely dangerous in politics, as the cases of Stalin and Robespierre illustrate.

The play shows the connection between justice, good judgment, and moral wisdom by showing how their lack leads the protagonists to tragedy. Its lesson is articulated by two witnesses to the tragic events. Tiresias the prophet tells us, "A sense of judgment, wisdom / is the greatest gift we have" (1165–1166); and the chorus concludes, "The mighty words of the proud are paid in full / with mighty blows of fate, and at long last / these blows will teach us wisdom" (1468–1470).

The conclusion of the play suggests that justice requires going beyond the formal conditions encapsulated by the concept of justice that like cases be treated alike and unlike ones differently in respect to the allocation of desert. It is necessary to develop a conception of justice to specify what we should do to make moral worth and satisfaction coincide. The play warns against two ways in which we can go wrong in trying to accomplish this. According to one, justice depends entirely on the ruler, who may be an individual, an elite, or the majority, but who determines what justice is. According to the other, justice is inherent in the objective conditions under which we live; just rules need to be discovered, not made, and if we inquire reasonably enough, then we shall know what they are. Sophocles suggests, by contrast, that an adequate conception of justice requires us to use judgment and moral wisdom to make rules that will enable us to pursue our conceptions of a good life within the limits set by the special circumstances of our society and the objective conditions of human existence. In Sophocles' words:

> Man the master, ingenious beyond all measure
> past all dreams, the skills within his grasp—
> he forges on, now to destruction
> now again to greatness. When he weaves in
> the laws of the land, and the justice of the gods
> that binds his oaths together
> he and his city rise high—
> but the city casts out
> that man who weds himself to inhumanity.
>
> (406–414)

Creon came to grief because he ignored the justice of the gods, or, as we would say, the objective conditions of human existence, and Antigone suffered the same fate because she ignored the laws of the land. It remains an enduring problem how they can be woven together so as to approximate the ideal of making satisfaction proportional to moral worth. The *ideal* of justice requires that they be woven together. The analysis of the *concept* of justice shows that doing so depends on allocating desert to make satisfaction proportional to moral worth. And competing *conceptions* of justice represent different ways of trying to meet this requirement.

SOME LIMITS OF JUSTICE

Suppose that we learn from the mistakes of Creon and Antigone and develop a conception of justice that rightly commands the allegiance of people committed to reason and morality. This conception will embody a system of man-made rules that regulate three aspects of justice: the distribution of desert, the rectification of undeserved distribution, and the adjudication of conflicts caused by disagreements about what is deserved. The rules will pay due regard to the objective conditions affecting human welfare; they will be based on an understanding of good and evil from the human point of view; and they will reflect the conceptions of a good life that have evolved in the moral tradition of the society that possesses the system of rules. The rules in that context, therefore, express what is regarded as beneficial and harmful, what benefits and harms are deserved, and how deserved benefits and harms are to be distributed, undeserved distribution rectified, and conflicts about what is deserved adjudicated, so as to make satisfaction proportional to moral worth.

The unsettling fact whose significance must now be considered is that even if such a conception of justice has been successfully developed, there can be no reasonable expectation of success in implementing it. One already familiar reason for this is that the ideal aimed at would require surmounting internal limits, created by contingency, conflict, and evil, to the aspiration to live a good life. These limits, however, are insurmountable because one of their main sources is within ourselves. The only available remedy of them is thus infected with the disease it is intended to cure. Given the previous discussion of permanent adversities and of what moral wisdom can do about them, it will suffice to note here that justice is as beset by permanent adversities as are other aspects of our aspiration to live a good life. There is, however, a hitherto unconsidered second reason why not even the most reasonable and morally commendable conception of justice could be successfully implemented. The reason is that external limits also stand in the way: scarcity limits just distribution; disproportionality limits just rectification; and the intractability of nature limits just adjudication.

The most obvious way in which scarcity limits just distribution is through the insufficiency of material resources. No matter how reasonable and morally commendable is a conception of justice, and no matter how strong is the commitment to implementing it, if there is not enough money, food, medicine, prison space, police protection, or hospital care that could be distributed, then people cannot have what they deserve. It is not only material resources, however, that may be scarce, but also the expertise needed to create and deliver them. Physicians, teachers, administrators, or research scientists may be as scarce as food, shelter, and medicine.

The distribution of scarce resources among those who deserve them necessarily results in injustice because it must be decided who among the deserving will get them, and whatever is decided, some people will not get what they deserve. It is useless to try to avoid such injustice by distributing scarce resources equally among all deserving people because the equal distribution of scarce resources will result in the even greater injustice of no one getting what he or she deserves. If there are not enough oxygen tanks, it does not help to ration the suffocating to the same brief periods of breathing. Furthermore, there are numerous scarce resources whose equal distribution is impossible. Medical specialists, inspiring teachers, or first-rate administrators must restrict their activities to particular contexts, but if there are not enough of them, deserving people outside of those contexts will not get the treatment, education, or efficient service they deserve.

It would be a mistake to underestimate the seriousness of scarcity as a limit on just distribution by thinking that a more efficient system of distribution could overcome it. Improved efficiency may ameliorate some aspects of economic scarcity, but not all scarcity is economic. Scarcity often stems from the human condition, and no improvement in efficiency could ameliorate it. We often have to choose between the good things we deserve because there is not enough time, energy, or opportunity to enjoy all of them. Concentration on creative work may be incompatible with cultivating satisfying friendships; early retirement in order to take pleasure in reading and traveling excludes going on with a highly satisfying job; continued growth in depth of some specialized knowledge makes the desired breadth of appreciation ranging over numerous fields unlikely; the price of reflectiveness is diminished spontaneity; carefree enjoyment of well-earned pleasures cannot go with dedication to political activism; and so forth.

Scarcity forces such choices not only on the level of individual action, but also on the social level, where the choices are among incompatible public policies. Should limited funding go to support deserving artistic or scientific talent? Are the worst off more or less deserving of scarce resources than those who generate future resources? Do the old deserve to hold on to the jobs they do well or do the young deserve them so that they can have a start in life? Furthermore, liberty and order, justice and patriotism, the free market and high culture, private life and political power are often so related that the more there is of one, the scarcer will the other be. Regardless of its causes, the effect of scarcity is that it prevents people from getting what they deserve because there is not enough of it. Since a reasonable and morally commendable conception of justice must be committed to distribution according to desert, and since scarcity makes it impossible to implement that commitment, scarcity imposes an unavoidable limit on justice.

The rectificatory aspect of justice is concerned with correcting undeserved distribution. People may not have what they deserve either because past systems of distribution were unjust or because fortuitous advantages and disadvantages independent of any deliberate system of distribution cause the failure of benefits and harms to be proportional to what their recipients deserve. The purpose of rectification is to redress this imbalance and make benefits and harms proportional to desert. This endeavor, however, is limited by the disproportionality that is an insurmountable obstacle to rectification. The most serious reason for this is that some forms of undeserved harm cannot be rectified.

The simple idea guiding rectification is that of balance. Justice is thought to require that the benefits and harms caused ought to equal the benefits and harms received. If there is an imbalance, rectification consists in adding or removing the right amount of benefit or harm so that the balance will be reestablished. It complicates this simple idea that justice is thought to be satisfied if the balance is achieved within a lifetime because temporary imbalance is not always sufficient to support the claim that injustice has been done. The idea is, however, that, insofar as it is possible, the balance should be maintained throughout a life. The most frequently employed forms of rectification are compensation and punishment. The former normally involves adding benefits to balance past undeserved harms, while the latter consists either in adding harms or in removing benefits so that the sum total of undeserved benefits will be appropriately reduced.

This idea, however, is too simple to be realistic. It rests on a mistaken assumption that benefits and harms can be measured by some scale common to them all. Only if this were true would it make sense to speak of adding or removing benefits and harms so as to achieve a balance. Whether the common scale is based on measuring benefits and harms in terms of some objective units, like money, or in terms of subjective judgments based on pairwise comparisons, makes no theoretical difference to the point that the assumption is false because different types of benefits and harms are often incommensurable. There are some undeserved harms for which no benefits can compensate the victim, and there are also undeserved harms for whose infliction no punishment can redress the balance.

Consider compensation first. What could compensate people who sacrificed their lives for a noble cause, who were blinded or disfigured in an accident for which they were not responsible, who were forced to spend the best years of their lives in concentration camps on trumped-up charges, or who contracted AIDS through blood transfusion? Take punishment next. What is the proportional punishment for mass murderers, torturers, or fanatics who destroy great works of art? There is no conceivable compensation or punishment that could redress such imbalances because no benefit or harm could be commensurate with what created them. Disproportionality, therefore, unavoidably limits efforts at rectification. As scarcity often makes it impossible to have a just system of distribution, so disproportionality frequently places rectification beyond our reach.

To appreciate the limit the intractability of nature imposes on the adjudicative aspect of justice it is necessary to return to the idea that a reasonable and morally commanding conception of justice would be a human substitute for cosmic justice. If there were no man-made justice, the allocation of benefits and harms would be entirely fortuitous, and satisfaction would not be proportional to moral worth. The connection between living a good life and moral worth would then be purely accidental, as would be the connection between bad lives and wickedness. We find this morally repugnant, and so we aim to enlarge the sphere wherein our conception of justice may prevail. The extent to which we are able to do this is the extent of civilized life. The boundary of one is the boundary of the other. Beyond it lies barbarism, an amoral world in which good and evil have no foothold. These efforts to enlarge the sphere of justice may, of course, miscarry. But there is no reasonable alternative to making them because the good we aim to achieve and the evil we want to avoid require it.

The distinction between civilization and barbarism does not coincide with the distinction between humanity and nature. Human nature is part of nature, and no matter how far we go in our efforts, we cannot assume complete control over our nature since the efforts we can make are subject to the conditions that prevail in nature. And, as it has been argued, contingency, conflict, and evil are among these conditions.

There is another reason, however, why the two sets of distinction do not coincide. We have been quite successful in enlarging the sphere of civilized life due to the lasting and continuing contribution of science and technology. They help us extend the limits of civilized life by making a larger portion of our lives accessible to justice. Once we learn how to cure a disease or increase the yield of a crop, we can also endeavor to allocate the new benefits and the remaining burdens justly.

We must not, however, allow ourselves to succumb to a self-congratulatory optimism. The enlargements of the civilized world merely add a plank to our raft bobbing on a vast and uncertain ocean with no safe haven available. Uncivilized forces continue to affect us in the most fundamental ways. Our genetic inheritance, susceptibility to hundreds of species of viruses, the natural resources of the planet, the future of the solar system and the galaxy, the boundaries of human life expectancy, the finite capacity of our brain to assimilate information, the fragility of the conditions required for sustaining human life, and so on, keep us vulnerable in ways that we may ameliorate around the margins but cannot realistically hope to control.

It must be recognized therefore that there are vast areas of nature that crucially influence civilized life and remain intractable to our conception of justice, no matter how reasonable and morally commanding it is. The image we should have of our efforts of assuring the just allocation of benefits and harms is not that of humanity as a benign colonizer of an uninhabited continent, gradually learning to cultivate more and more of its resources. It is much closer to the truth that our efforts are like Gulliver's in trying to free himself from one of the thousands of bonds by which Lilliputians are holding him down, except that the bonds against which we struggle are of Brobdingnagian proportions.

The implication of this for the adjudicative aspect of justice is that the conflicts that prevent the just allocation of desert are not merely between people with different conceptions of justice, not even between people who are committed to justice and those who reject it altogether, but also between humanity and nonhuman forces. This latter type of conflict is by far the most serious because no appeal to reason and morality or to some shared ground could possibly ameliorate it, because the antagonists on one side are brute, barbaric, impersonal, and nonconscious forces, which cannot consider the human case for justice. There are, therefore, conflicts about justice that are not open to adjudication.

The practical significance of the imperfections of justice is that efforts to make life more just must be directed largely toward alleviating injustice. Injustice, however, is always a specific offense against specific individuals who suffer specific undeserved harm in specific contexts. Injustice is alleviated to the extent to which specific remedies are found to specific injuries. It is useless, therefore, to approach the question of how life can be made more just by attempting to construct an abstract conception of justice. Even if such a conception were to succeed in commanding the assent of reasonable people, it could not be used to alleviate the imperfections of justice because the conception would lack the essential concrete detail.[10]

Our efforts to construct a system of justice as a substitute for nonexistent cosmic justice must be seen, therefore, as possible only within limits imposed by external conditions. These limits are unavoidable because scarcity, disproportionality, and the intractability of nature cannot be eliminated from our lives. Part of moral wisdom is to understand the significance of this and to develop a reasonable attitude toward it.

JUSTICE AND MORAL WISDOM

If this analysis of justice is correct, it follows that the human substitute for cosmic justice is unavoidably imperfect. Reflection on this disheartening fact discloses yet another respect in which our control is bound to fall short of what is needed to make our lives good. Moral wisdom and justice motivate us to do what we can to make moral worth and satisfaction proportional to each other, but we must face the fact that this ideal is unattainable. The two components of good lives will diverge not merely because of internal limits set by permanent adversities but also because of external limits inherent in our circumstances.

Moral wisdom prompts a twofold attitude to what reflection reveals about the significance of the imperfection of justice. It involves, on the one hand, a reaffirmation of the ideal of justice. The reason why justice is an ideal worth pursuing is that good lives require it. That the ideal is shown on reflection to be unattainable does not mean that our lives could not be made better by making them more just. The pursuit of perfect justice is doomed to failure. But the pursuit of justice, imperfect as it is bound to be, will make our lives better, or at least less bad, because it is better to come closer to a life in which people get what they deserve than to abandon the pursuit and thereby make injustice more likely. So part of the attitude that moral wisdom prompts will strengthen the motivational force of the ideal of justice by cleansing it of the false hope based on the illusory expectation that it will be achieved. It is reason enough for the pursuit of justice that it will make our lives better. And it is a bad reason for weakening our commitment to justice that what is gained from its pursuit is not as good as it might be if the human condition were other than it is.

---

[10] It is hard to see, therefore, how Rawls's conception of justice could yield the political program that his second thoughts on the subject claim that it was meant to do. See John Rawls, *Political Liberalism* (New York: Columbia University Press, 1993).

The other part of the attitude moral wisdom prompts helps us react appropriately to our own experience of injustice. One source of injustice is the familiar fact of immorality. But this kind of injustice does not call into question the very ideal of justice itself; on the contrary, it provides a good reason for reaffirming the ideal. The sources of injustice that have been considered in this chapter, however, do raise questions about the ideal, and it is partly for answering them that we need moral wisdom. If justice is indeed imperfect, then we shall encounter the consequences of scarcity, disproportionality, and the intractability of nature in our lives. We ourselves, the people we love, and the institutions to which we feel allegiance will suffer injustice, and suffer not merely because of the immorality of some people but because of the injustice inherent in the scheme of things. It is particularly difficult—and particularly important—to control our reactions when things go badly for us. Resentment, anger, vindictiveness, despair, self-deception, guilt, capitulation, and cynicism are some of the reactions against which we have to guard.

We can do so by keeping firmly in mind what reflection on injustice has disclosed both about the point of justice and about injustice being bound to occur. The point of justice is to order the human world so as to decrease the naturally occurring gap between moral worth and satisfaction. The imperfect system we have created to this end is the bulwark between a barbaric existence in which we get what we deserve only by chance and civilized life where we can try to do our inadequate best to allocate desert justly. That the bulwark is continually besieged both internally by permanent adversities and externally by scarcity, disproportionality, and the intractability of nature does not change the fact that the possibility of living good lives depends on defending it. If we can remain reasonable in the face of assaults on justice in general and on our own opportunity to enjoy deserved benefits and escape undeserved harms, then we shall want to protect the system of justice, even though it has allowed the very injustice to occur that now threatens us. For reason will show that the alternative will further weaken the system and produce more injustice.

It is, of course, extraordinarily difficult to remain committed to justice when we are victims of injustice. Part of the difficulty is that our emotional reactions tend to be stronger than the control we can exert over them. If we bear in mind, however, that injustice is bound to occur, then we can weaken our inappropriate emotional reactions and strengthen our control over them. Doing so involves reminding ourselves of two considerations. The first is that the injustice we are experiencing is not directed at us personally. To be sure, we are its victims. But not because of anything having to do with us. We simply happened to be the persons to whom injustice occurred, but its occurrence signifies no ill will toward us. It is just a natural process into whose path we have unwittingly stumbled. The second is that as we bear the impersonality of injustice in mind, so the inappropriateness of our emotional reactions to it will emerge. These reactions direct our outrage either outward or inward. We seek someone who could be blamed, and the choice is between other people and ourselves. There is, however, no one who can properly be blamed either for permanent adversities or for scarcity, disproportionality, and the intractability of nature. If we understand that much injustice is due to the intrinsic imperfections of our systems of justice, then we shall see the inappropriateness of our emotional reactions. This will not dissolve them. But it will weaken them, and thus make controlling them easier.

The attitude to injustice moral wisdom helps us develop will, therefore, allow us to increase our control. We learn to reject the misguided expectation of perfect justice and strengthen our commitment to the ideal of justice, even though reflection has led us to understand its imperfection. We bring ourselves to understand that the source of much of the injustice we suffer is not ill will toward ourselves, for there is nothing personal meant by the misfortune that befalls us. The realization that there is no one to blame for much injustice will make injustice easier to bear by increasing our control over the inappropriate emotional reactions that exacerbate the damage already done.

CONCLUSION

No amount of moral wisdom can eliminate injustice. But the more moral wisdom we have, the less we shall allow injustice to undermine the possibility of living a good life. To have more moral wisdom, rather than less, we need reflective understanding of the insurmountable external and internal limits on our efforts to live a good life; preparedness to face the threats these limits present; unwillingness to seek or accept illusory consolation; clarity about our own motivation and circumstances; self-control; constancy in adversity; and steadfast allegiance to the irremediably flawed institution of human justice, which is still the only way of approximating the ideal of justice. These are rare achievements, and rarer still in combination. It will perhaps be obvious by now that they are nevertheless worth aiming at because, given the human condition, good lives are very unlikely without them.

CHAPTER TEN

Growing in Moral Wisdom

The aim of this chapter is to gather together the threads of the discussion. This will be done in two steps. The first is an overall account of moral wisdom, which derives from the preceding consideration of its various constituents. The second is an account of the development of moral wisdom. It should not be supposed, however, that the first step is a description of the state of being morally wise as the end toward which the development of moral wisdom tends and that the second is a description of the means required for its achievement. Moral wisdom is essentially tied to certain sorts of activities, but they should not to be understood as efforts to cross some threshold beyond which lies moral wisdom. They consist rather in a lifelong engagement in specific tasks. The tasks all concern the development of moral wisdom, and growth in moral wisdom is growth in the consistency with which we keep ourselves engaged in the appropriate tasks and the success with which we manage to perform them. The two steps toward an overall description of moral wisdom are separable, therefore, only artificially, for the purposes of exposition. The structural description that emerges from the first must be conjoined with the developmental description provided by the second.

MORAL WISDOM AS AN ATTITUDE TO LIFE

The possession of any virtue necessarily affects our character. Some ways of being affected, however, are far more important than others. All the virtues are good to have, but there still are major and minor ones. Courage, moderation, and justice are major; tact, cheerfulness, and efficiency are minor. The major virtues are more important because they have a formative influence on our moral standing. To face adversity coura-geously, to satisfy desires moderately, or to deal with people justly is to re-spond to features of our lives which cannot fail to be important. What makes them so is that the good and evil that corresponding actions cause to ourselves or others are usually much more serious than those caused by our being or not being tactful, cheerful, or efficient. Adversity, desires, and other people constantly and unavoidably demand our moral attention, while manner, mood, and organization are more likely to form the back-ground against which the important events in a life normally occur.

Moral wisdom is certainly a major virtue, but it has a claim to be even more: the most important of all the virtues. All the other virtues, both major and minor, are concerned with good conduct in some specific area of life. Good conduct, however, requires knowing what the good generally is in that specific area, how to evaluate the particular situation we face in the light of that general knowledge, and how to judge complex situations in which knowledge and evaluation are difficult. And these, of course, are precisely the capacities moral wisdom provides. One reason for thinking, then, that moral wisdom is the most important virtue is that other virtues presuppose it. There is ample support for this view in the works of Plato and Aristotle, but we should nevertheless be cautious in embracing it. Un-derstanding the reason why caution is warranted will lead to a centrally im-portant feature of moral wisdom.

There are many simple moral situations in which what good and evil conduct would be is obvious. We normally need no further knowledge than anybody familiar with a moral tradition already has; the evaluation of the situation is so straightforward as to make it unnecessary for normal people even to pause over it, and so there is no need to exercise judgment. Just as native speakers of a language do not need to reflect on how to ex-press themselves in many routine communicative contexts, so agents raised in a moral tradition do not need to reflect on how to conduct them-selves in many simple moral contexts. And when there is no need for re-flection, then there is no need for moral wisdom. What the courageous, moderate, or just action would be in many particular situations is perfectly obvious. The exercise of virtues in simple moral situations does not, there-fore, presuppose moral wisdom, and so it cannot be regarded as the most important virtue. It is no doubt a major one because some moral situations are complex and there is need for reflection in them, but that need is only an occasional feature of life.

Moral wisdom and reflection would be generally dispensable if three conditions were felicitously met. The first is that there exists a robust moral tradition in a society. It commands and has for a long time com-manded the allegiance of the vast majority of people living there. It is rich enough to incorporate a sufficient variety of conceptions of a good life, so that people do not feel seriously thwarted or frustrated by what seem to them to be arbitrary restrictions. It is flexible, so that it can accommodate itself to inevitable changes in social conditions. And it is generally and without much deep questioning recognized as authoritative. It makes no difference to meeting this condition whether the authority of the moral tradition is due to its intrinsic merits, to the absence of attractive alternatives, to the persuasiveness of its advocates, or to the lack of critical spirit in the people who live according to it. What matters is that the moral tradition is in place and people feel allegiance to it.

The second condition is that people should have adopted a conception of a good life for themselves from among the alternatives their moral tradition makes available. As they try to live according to it, they can, therefore, count on the support of their tradition for their endeavors. They see their tradition as the source of worthwhile possibilities and as the bulwark defending them in their efforts to realize them. And the participating agents, in turn, appear from the point of view of the tradition as worthy of respect and support in their struggles to live some form or another of a traditionally accredited life.

The third condition is that they are succeeding in living the life they want to live. They find that the anticipated rewards are forthcoming and that they are indeed rewarding. To be sure, there are obstacles in their way—living a good life is never easy—but reason and morality prove sufficient to overcome them. People living such blessed lives have not fallen afoul of permanent adversities. They have not, of course, ceased to be liable to them, but they have so far escaped the risks they present.

If these conditions are met, then the moral situations people encounter will appear simple to them. They know the point of view from which they should evaluate them; their knowledge and evaluation are backed by the moral tradition to which they give their willing allegiance; their lives are flourishing; contingency, conflict, and evil do not seriously impinge on them; and so they rarely face the need to make difficult judgments requiring the sort of reflection that moral wisdom provides.

Perhaps there were some idyllic periods and lives in human history in which these conditions were actually met. Even so, however, they were surely rare and unrepresentative of the normal conditions of our existence. Plenty of historical attempts had been made to establish moral orthodoxies, but very few of them gave sufficient scope to human possibilities, and those that escaped internal challenges by knowledgeable critics and external challenges by able advocates of competing alternatives were rarer still. As a result, harmony between a moral tradition and individual conceptions of a good life is the exception, not the rule. It is normally hard for individuals to commit themselves wholeheartedly to a moral tradition because its defects are apparent and because there usually are attractive alternatives beckoning just around the corner. Conceptions of a good life, therefore, rarely escape being in some respects at odds with the moral tradition from which they derive many of their elements. Some degree of moral alienation is a standard human experience.

The difficulties in the way of meeting these conditions, however, are exacerbated by permanent adversities. There may be some human lives that escape serious accidents, grief, injustice, illness, social unrest, physical, psychological, or social insecurity, persecution, exploitation, discrimination, and similar contingencies; lives that are not beset by deep conflicts among the plurality of values to which their agents have committed themselves; and lives that are free from unconscious and unintentional evil motives and patterns of corresponding actions which are inimical to the moral tradition and the conceptions of a good life that define the good for the agents. Such lives, however, are highly unusual. Most human lives are affected by contingency, conflict, and evil, and we can avoid taking notice of them as little as we can ignore our dissatisfactions with our moral tradition and the difficulties we encounter in trying to live according to our conception of a good life. And that, of course, is why we need judgment, reflection, and moral wisdom.

To return now to the question of whether moral wisdom is indeed the most important of the major virtues, or merely one among them, the answer will be seen to depend on what the balance is taken to be between simple moral situations, in which moral wisdom is not needed, and complex ones, in which it is. Both kinds of situations occur in all contexts, but the question is whether complex ones occur so frequently as to make dealing with them necessary for living a good life. To this question there is no general answer. The reasonable answer depends on the historical and social context of a moral tradition, on the character and circumstances of individuals trying to live according to the conceptions of a good life they derive from their moral tradition, and on the extent to which permanent adversities impinge on individual lives.

There can be no serious doubt, however, about what the answer is in *our* context, that is, in the contemporary Western world whose moral tradition is an unstable compound of classical, Judeo-Christian, and Enlightenment influences to which have been added, among others, the influences of the scientific, industrial, and sexual revolutions, vast technological changes, the population and communication explosions, and two world wars. The authority of our moral tradition is in tatters, and alternatives and challenges to it are numerous. The plurality of values in it are in constant conflict. Its conflict-resolving principles and hierarchies are as controversial as the values whose conflicts they are meant to resolve. There are also very few generally acknowledged limits to what a permissible conception of a good life may be. There is, therefore, often no clear moral guidance derivable from our moral tradition on which reasonable and morally motivated individuals can count. The balance between simple and complex moral situations has been shifting, and will continue in the foreseeable future to shift, toward complex ones. Whatever may have been true of other times, circumstances, and moral traditions, we need judgment, reflection, and moral wisdom now to cope with the ever-increasing number of complex moral situations we must face.

This need is sufficiently pressing to make moral wisdom the most important virtue for us. To make this claim about moral wisdom is not to minimize the need for or the intrinsic importance of other virtues. It is rather to restate for our times the eudaimonistic view that the other virtues presuppose moral wisdom because the knowledge, evaluation, and judgment their exercise depends on in the complex moral situations we face are provided, if at all, by moral wisdom. If we know what our moral tradition and conception of a good life call for, then we know how to evaluate and judge complex situations. And then the exercise of courage, moderation, and justice becomes a matter of applying our knowledge to make the right effort, in the right circumstances, in the right way. We know then what dangers we ought to face, what desires we ought to control, and what we owe to other people. The reason then why moral wisdom is the most important virtue for us is that its possession removes reasonable doubts about the course of action that best reflects the values of our moral tradition and conceptions of a good life.

This way of thinking about moral wisdom discloses the centrally important feature of it that was mentioned but not discussed earlier. It is that moral wisdom is needed when doubts about good lives are appropriate. And doubts are appropriate when the obstacles to living well are created not merely by our rational and moral shortcomings but also by our moral tradition, conceptions of a good life, and character. The doubts that call for moral wisdom, therefore, are occasioned precisely by those constituents of good lives that in simple moral situations can be relied on to guide us. Coping with these doubts requires standing back from our life and activities and reflecting on them. Because the objects of this reflection are the moral tradition which we have made our own, the conception of a good life that inspires us, and the character that we have to rely on to enable us to live as we think we should, moral wisdom, which prompts the reflection, is a reflexive and a second-order virtue. Through its reflexive aspect we reflect on ourselves and on how the external world affects us. And through its second-order aspect we reflect on how to cope with our reasonable doubts about what it is that we ought to do. This is why moral wisdom is the virtue of reflection and why the activities proper to it aim to change us internally.

The exercise of moral wisdom, therefore, takes place during a disruption of the process of deliberation leading from our conception of a good life to a particular action in a particular situation. This process may be disrupted by any number of obstacles, but when the obstacles are permanent adversities which undermine the very moral resources on which we have to rely to cope with them, then it is that we need moral wisdom. It helps us come as close as possible to reestablishing the smooth flow of our life. But since the obstacles are created by permanent adversities which act through ourselves and which cannot be removed, moral wisdom can meet our need only by redirecting the flow. And that involves changing ourselves, by adjusting our conception of a good life and character to the world, rather than changing the world.

The extent of that adjustment, however, needs to be tailored to the severity of the disruption permanent adversities cause in our life. The ideal is to have a conception of a good life and a character that need no adjustment at all. It would be realized if there were no obstacles to our acting as our conception of a good life prescribes and if we would find our life good when we regularly and characteristically act that way. Adjustments are needed because this ideal is rarely realized.

If we understand, however, why the adjustments are needed and what is involved in making them, then we shall aim to change our conception of a good life and character only as much as is necessary to cope with permanent adversities. The necessary change, of course, may be very considerable. It may be so great as to require the drastic measure of abandoning our conception of a good life or changing our character in fundamental ways. And then we may not want to make it. This is the theme of tragedy. Part of moral wisdom is to adjust our conception of a good life and character in a way that makes it less rather than more likely that permanent adversities would force on us the tragic choice between taking such a drastic measure and going under.

Making this adjustment depends on increasing our control by developing a reasonable conception of a good life and bringing our actions in conformity with it. The reason for wanting to exercise control is the realization that the meaning, purpose, and goodness of our lives, as well as our moral identity, depend on living according to our conception of a good life. The motivational force of this realization derives from the central importance of success and from the destructive consequences of failure. So that when permanent adversities disrupt the smooth flow of life whereby our conception of a good life is translated into particular actions in particular situations, then the function of control is to strengthen the motivational force of our conception of a good life by reminding us of the great benefit of success and the great cost of failure. This will not tell us what we should do about the permanent adversities we face, but it will make us want to do something, and it will make us reflect on what it is that we could do.

What we could do is to reflect on the internal and external obstacles permanent adversities present and to change ourselves in order to reduce their severity. The amelioration of internal obstacles depends on the three modes of reflection: moral imagination, self-knowledge, and moral depth. Coping with external obstacles created by the imperfections of justice depends on forming our reactions to them in the light of a reflective understanding of the reasons why the ideal of justice is unattainable.

The general problem that all modes of reflection involved in increasing our control attempt to answer is: How can we change ourselves so as to cope with the effects of permanent adversities on us? And the answer must recognize, first, that we cannot change permanent adversities themselves, and, second, that the extent to which we can change ourselves without doing great damage is limited by the need to remain faithful to our conception of a good life and by the psychological risks involved in a radical transformation of our character.

The answer we can derive from moral imagination is that one way of coping with the obstacles permanent adversities present to the realization of the possibilities required by our conception of a good life is to enlarge our field of possibilities. This depends on changing our conception of a good life and character by cultivating greater breadth than we had before. We thereby make available to ourselves a richer variety of possibilities. So that if permanent adversities foreclose some possibilities, we shall still have others left. Moral imagination thus helps us cope with permanent adversities by leading us to recognize and correct the narrowness of our vision of a good life. The greater breadth we have, the less disastrous it will be if permanent adversities make some of the possibilities we desire unrealizable.

Self-knowledge is the second mode of reflection through which we can increase control. The object of self-knowledge and of the control we can exercise in possession of it is our character. We all start out with a fortuitous character formed by our genetic inheritance, early experiences, and education into the conventions of our society. As we form a conception of a good life, so we come to view our fortuitous character from its point of view. This involves a description and an interpretation of the relevant autobiographical facts with a view of constructing a coherent account of our life. Such an account provides the means for the evaluation of our fortuitous character. The evaluation will be at least partly adverse because we realize that some of the obstacles to living according to our conception of a good life are internal to ourselves. This realization will motivate us to transform our fortuitous character into a more deliberately shaped one so that the internal obstacles to living as we think we should would be rendered less formidable. The transformation begins with the construction of a coherent account, but it must go beyond it because the facts on which the account is based have a life of their own. They are our desires, hopes, fears, aversions, memories, fantasies, plans, disappointments, and so on, which form the content of our unruly emotions and imagination. They often surprise us. They present anomalies that refuse to fit into the account we are trying to impose on them, and they exert a strong influence on what our limits are and what possibilities are options for us. Adequate self-knowledge must be based on a continuous revision of the initial account by doing justice to these surprises, anomalies, possibilities, and impossibilities.

Some of the facts we come to know about ourselves, however, cannot be brought within our control because they are the effects of permanent adversities that lie beyond our capacity to alter. They establish some of what we can and cannot do. One purpose of the control we can exercise through self-knowledge is to construct our conception of a good life so as to take account of them, and to transform our fortuitous character into a deliberate one by aiming to realize possibilities only within these limits.

Self-knowledge helps us cope with permanent adversities, therefore, by providing a realistic account of ourselves which enables us to understand and evaluate our past and to take from it intimations about the direction in which we can and cannot develop in the future. Self-knowledge thus defines our moral identity, and by doing so it sets a standard that we can use to assess the seriousness of internal obstacles to living according to our conception of a good life. It is thus an inventory of our moral resources and a necessary condition of marshalling them. Its aim is not to overcome the effects of permanent adversities on our character and conception of a good life, but to help us live as well as possible given the limits and possibilities they present.

When we learn from self-knowledge that permanent adversities unavoidably limit the extent to which we can increase our control, it is bound to have a strong influence on how we feel about our prospects of living a good life. For what we learn is that our best efforts to adhere to reason and morality are insufficient to guarantee the goodness of our lives. This is not a neutral piece of information which we can contemplate *sub specie aeternitatis*. It will provoke in us feelings of despair, cynicism, helpless anger, self-pity, or some other manifestation of hopelessness. And hopelessness will threaten to undermine our motivation to make our best efforts. If our best efforts are not good enough, we shall be tempted to wonder what the point is of struggling to make them, especially since they are so hard. The third mode of reflection, moral depth, aims to alleviate this sense of hopelessness and thus to shore up our weakening motivation.

Moral depth combines the realization that we are subject to permanent adversities, the abandonment of the illusory expectation that reality is hospitable to our endeavors and that at least in the long run our best efforts will bear fruit, and the correction of our misguided emotional reactions to the view of life that emerges from the realization and from giving up the illusory expectation. Moral depth helps us cope with permanent adversities, then, by bringing us to acknowledge their effects on us and yet not allowing this to result in emotional overreaction or in sapped motivation. We learn from it that the best course of action in face of the risk in which we stand is not to allow knowledge of our vulnerability to interfere with doing what we can to avoid the risk, transform our character, and to live a good life.

The obstacles to living a good life are, of course, not only internal, but also external. The latter exist independent of our characters and conceptions of a good life, but they may prevent us from living a good life by making it impossible to get what we deserve. Since the aim of justice is to assure that we do get what we deserve, external obstacles may be identified as instances of injustice. Injustice may be caused by human irrationality or immorality, but it may also be due to permanent adversities. In the latter case, injustice occurs because not even perfect rationality and morality could bring it about that we get what we deserve. The deserved benefits may be scarce and no system of distribution could satisfy all just claims. The rectification of past injustice may be impossible because no benefit or harm could be proportional to what is deserved. And the intractability of nature puts beyond our control a wide range of benefits that we deserve but cannot have and harms that we do not deserve but nevertheless have to endure.

The task of reflection that moral wisdom directs toward these externally occurring permanent adversities is to formulate a reasonable response to our understanding of their causes and unavoidability. This response will reaffirm our commitment to the ideal of justice because its unattainability does not remove the reason for trying to come as close to it as possible. And it will also prevent our personal experience of injustice to deter us from living according to the human system of justice. Motivating this response is the reflective understanding moral wisdom yields that imperfect human justice—our substitute for the myth of cosmic justice—is still the bulwark that separates civilized life from barbarism. It is very hard to keep this in mind and to act according to it when we have fallen afoul of injustice. Even so, it remains the policy that reason and morality dictate.

The view of moral wisdom which emerges from our consideration of the difficulties requiring the increase of control reveals it as a virtue whose exercise is called for when the smooth flow of life is interrupted. These interruptions force us to stand back and reflect on their sources and on what we can do to cope with them. This is why moral wisdom is the virtue of reflection, and not of action. To be sure, moral wisdom is an aid to action, and, in complex situations, an indispensable aid, but it aids us only indirectly. It is not, like so many of the other virtues, a disposition to act appropriately in the appropriate situation, but a disposition to reflect on how to act appropriately when doing so is rendered difficult by conditions over which we have no control. The exercise of moral wisdom occurs, therefore, privately, inwardly, at one remove from active participation in life.

Moral wisdom is not merely a virtue, but also an attitude of life formed in response to adversity. It consists in the successful combination of two essential tendencies that nevertheless move us in opposite directions. One is the tendency of active engagement, the struggle to do what we can to make our life good. We may describe this as natural. But there is also the tendency to form a realistic view of our prospects, to assess the difficulties we face, to take stock of the limits and possibilities we have. This does not occur naturally; it has to be cultivated, and it will be cultivated only when the adversities we face are serious enough to drive us to it. Because when that happens the adversities are bound to have disrupted our active engagement, the temptation of disengagement, of distancing ourselves from our troubles, of resigning ourselves to them by adopting the perspective of detached reflection rather than that of active engagement is ever-present. Moral wisdom combines these two tendencies, the one natural, the other forced on us by adversities. And by combining them, it acts to correct the deficiencies from which each standing alone suffers. Unreflective continuation of active engagement when adversities make a good life unattainable and detached reflection on the adversities without actively contending with them are both self-defeating, if it is a good life that we want. Moral wisdom combines the perspectives of detached reflection and of active engagement so that both are retained and employed to aid us in living a good life.

MORAL WISDOM AS THE LOSS OF INNOCENCE

The reason why moral wisdom involves not merely detached reflection but also action is that it is not a natural trait but a difficult achievement toward which we must develop gradually if we want to live a good life. Moral wisdom can be developed only through active engagement. Nevertheless, even if we were to achieve such great success in its development as to make further effort in that direction unnecessary, its connection with activity would still remain because having moral wisdom consists in exercising it. To the question of how moral wisdom can be developed, a number of complementary answers have already been given in the course of the preceding arguments. Its development may be described as increasing our control, or transforming our fortuitous character into a more deliberate one, or making the complex situations we encounter into simple ones through reflection. These alternative descriptions should be recognized as having the same subject; they differ only because they are given from different points of view. But to these descriptions, it may now be added the new one that the development of moral wisdom may also be viewed as the process of losing our innocence.

The previous descriptions of the development of moral wisdom required a vocabulary, various distinctions, and they ended up presupposing a fairly complex philosophical analysis. Even if they succeeded in being as they were meant to be, accurate, revealing, and inviting enough to motivate us to make them fit our own case, they would be unlikely to spring to our lips when we try to describe the significant events that form their subject matter. It is otherwise, however, with the loss of innocence. As we are growing in moral wisdom, we may well come to see the process as a particular way of losing our innocence. And it is the description of this process that will now be added to the ones already given.

"Innocence" may mean either a state falling on a continuum somewhere between guiltlessness and purity, or an open, simple, trusting, guileless, spontaneous manner of conduct that is lacking in artifice and calculation. The two senses are connected, of course, because one natural explanation of innocent conduct is that it stems from a state of innocence. The discussion will nevertheless concentrate on "innocence" used in the second sense. Its approximate cognates are "purity" and "simplicity" in one of their own several senses.[1] Within the second sense, Montaigne insightfully

[1] The literature on innocence, or its cognates, is meager. Michel de Montaigne makes a few very illuminating remarks about it in "Of Cruelty," in *The Complete Works of Montaigne*, trans. Donald M. Frame (Stanford: Stanford University Press, 1958); Søren Kierkegaard's *Purity of Heart*, trans. D. V. Steere (New York: Harper & Row, 1948), is a somewhat perfervid and religiously oriented discussion; Nicolai Hartmann's *Ethics*, trans. S. Coit (London: Allen & Unwin, 1932), vol. 2, chapter 18 is devoted to it; Frances Myrna's "Purity in Morals," *Monist* 66 (1983): 283–297, is a good critical examination of Hartmann's views; Konstantin Kolenda's *Philosophy in Literature* (Totowa, N.J.: Barnes & Noble, 1982), chapters 3–4 treats the holy innocents of Melville's Billy Budd and Dostoyevsky's Prince Myshkin and Alyosha Karamazov; Herbert Morris's "Lost Innocence," in *On Guilt and Innocence* (Berkeley: University of California Press, 1976), is perhaps the best thing on the subject, and the present discussion is indebted to it; see also Elizabeth Wolgast's "Innocence" *Philosophy* 68 (1993): 297–306, which does not take into account the complexities of the subject, nor much of the literature available on it; and John Kekes, "Constancy and Purity," *Mind* 92 (1983): 499–518,

distinguishes between three kinds of innocence. The first is "to be simply provided with a nature easy and affable.... [This] makes a man innocent, but not virtuous.... [It is] an innocence that is accidental and fortuitous ... a childish innocence: little vigor and no art."[2] The source of innocence in this childlike state is the lack of a certain kind of knowledge. It is ignorance that makes the resulting conduct simpleminded, pure, and innocent. People possessing it are like Adam and Eve were before they ate the apple from the Tree of Knowledge.[3]

The second is to exert control "by main force, and, having let oneself be surprised by the first commotions of passions, to arm and tense oneself to stop their course and conquer them." The agent has "himself strengthened by perpetual constancy, and always remain[s] in the plan he ... set himself."[4] The source of this kind of innocence is that the agents have acquired the relevant knowledge, and they conduct themselves according to it. Their innocence shows in their simple, pure, unquestioning adherence to a conventional plan of life. They are confident in their knowledge of right and wrong, and constant in their corresponding actions. But they do not understand the larger context of their knowledge and actions. They do not understand, that is, that there are alternatives to what they claim to know, that in saying "yes" they are also saying "no" to numerous possibilities, and that there are great complexities of which they remain unaware. The purity and innocence of their conduct is a sign of simplification, which, being due to insufficient understanding, is oversimplification. Creon and Antigone both exemplify this kind of innocence.

The third and best kind of innocence is possessed by agents who have "so perfect a habituation ... that it has passed into their nature. It is no longer ... laborious ... or ... formed by the ordinances of reason and maintained by a deliberate stiffening of the soul; it is the very essence of their soul, its natural and ordinary gait. They have made it so by ... long exercise ... coming upon a fine rich nature."[5] These agents possess the relevant knowledge and understand its significance. They are aware of the larger context, of the alternatives, and of the fact that in having committed

---

"Purity and Judgment in Morality," *Philosophy* 63 (1988): 453–469, and *The Morality of Pluralism* (Princeton: Princeton University Press, 1993), chapter 10. Innocence is also discussed in the context of politics. The question there is about the extent to which moral innocence is compatible with political engagement. See Stuart Hampshire's *Innocence and Experience* (Cambridge: Harvard University Press, 1989), which transcends the political context, and Peter Johnson's *Politics, Innocence, and the Limits of Goodness* (London: Routledge, 1988); the latter has a useful bibliography.

[2] Montaigne, "Of Cruelty," 310, 311, 313.

[3] Morris's "Lost Innocence" is a highly suggestive reflection on this myth.

[4] Montaigne, "Of Cruelty," 310 and 309.

[5] Ibid., 310.

themselves to some possibilities, they have excluded others. They have worked their way through these complexities; they are aware of the significance of their conduct; and they have achieved sufficient clarity about what they are doing and why. The innocence of their conduct is the hardwon result of the sort of struggle and reflection in which agents possessing one of the two previous kinds of innocence are not yet capable of engaging. These three kinds of innocence may be called "prereflective," "unreflective," and "reflective."

"Innocence" is clearly an evaluative term in all of its uses, but it is less clear whether the evaluation is moral and whether it is favorable or unfavorable. The morally evaluative uses of "innocence" are those in which the knowledge or ignorance that is attributed to the agents has good and evil as its objects. The present discussion, of course, focuses on the connection between the moral senses of prereflective, unreflective, and reflective innocence, on the one hand, and moral wisdom, on the other. And the connection is that the development of moral wisdom proceeds from prereflective innocence through unreflective innocence to reflective innocence. The kinds of innocence, therefore, whose loss is concomitant with the development of moral wisdom are prereflective and unreflective. Reflective innocence, by contrast, is a highly desirable frame of mind that is one of the great internal goods gained from the possession and exercise of a sufficient degree of moral wisdom.

It needs now to be considered what the moral modes of prereflective and unreflective innocence are, why it is good to lose them, and how their loss involves the development of moral wisdom. Prereflective innocence is characterized by ignorance of good and evil. Agents possessing such ignorance lack a moral dimension, consequently there are no moral considerations motivating or restraining their conduct. They innocently and simplemindedly act on their desires, which rule them. If their desires are benign, they may unintentionally conform to moral standards; if their desires are malevolent, they may unthinkingly violate them. This is the typical mentality of young children before moral education forces them to learn to control their desires. Moral education, however, does not always take, and there may actually be some exceptional people who do not need it. In the former case, we encounter adults who are brutes or psychopaths; in the latter, we find the holy innocents whose desires are uniformly benign and who are not subject to the urges that moral education helps the rest of us resist. But whether for good or for evil, prereflectively innocent people do not control their desires. The human condition being what it is, desires need to be controlled because reasonable conceptions of a good life require it and because adversities force it on us. The loss of prereflective innocence, therefore, is not a regrettable part of growing up, but a positive requirement imposed on us by rationality and morality.

Unreflective innocence involves knowledge of good and evil, but the knowledge is not deep enough. The agents endeavor to control their conduct so as to conform to their understanding of the good and to avoid what they understand to be evil, but they have not reflected sufficiently to recognize the permanent adversities they face and their significance for their endeavors. Unreflectively innocent agents are typically committed to some conventional view of good and evil that happens to prevail in their moral tradition. And then, with various degrees of consistency, they conduct themselves in conformity to it. Insofar as the situations they face are simple, there is no reason why they could not live good lives. As it has been argued, however, conceptions of a good life that depend on moral situations remaining simple are very unlikely to be reasonable, for contingency, conflict, and evil are going to disrupt most lives in most contexts, and they are going to make many moral situations complex.

If this happens to unreflectively innocent agents, they will be left without moral resources to cope with the complexities they have encountered. They will be forced to choose either to reaffirm in increasingly dogmatic terms their conventional commitments or to abandon the moral tradition and conception of a good life that provides their moral identity, and the meaning and purpose of their lives. The former cannot help them because it is precisely the oversimplifications implicit in their commitments that make the complexities they face intractable, and the latter destroys everything they value.

This was just the choice both Creon and Antigone were forced to make, as shown in the preceding chapter. They both chose to reaffirm their commitments in the face of challenges to them. Because they were both exceptionally strong and intransigent, their destructive insistence on treating the situation as if it were simple took on heroic proportions. Their willful blindness to the complexities of their shared predicament eventually resulted not only in their own destruction, but also in that of many others who were caught up in the tragedy.

What is it then that is lacking from the knowledge of good and evil that characterizes unreflective innocence? What should Creon and Antigone have known which could have mitigated the tragedy? The first missing element is the understanding that knowledge of good and evil and being motivated by it to pursue the good and avoid what is evil are not enough because of our vulnerability to permanent adversities. Unreflective innocence creates the illusion that if we have the right knowledge and if we act on it the right way, then life will go well for us. But contingency, conflict, and evil may derail us no matter what we do.

The second missing element is the understanding that the reason why permanent adversities are such formidable obstacles to good lives is that we are not only their potential victims but also their potential agents. Contingency, conflict, and evil permeate our character and conceptions of a good life, and that is the reason why our vulnerability to them is as great as it is. For the adversity they present invades all the resources we have for trying to overcome it.

Unreflective innocence nurtures the illusion that if we face adversity stalwartly, then, although we may be defeated by it, we have at least maintained our purity and integrity, and we can take solace in having acted reasonably and morally well. This illusion is destroyed, however, by the understanding that the internal defects of our character and conceptions of a good life are partly responsible for our defeat. And as we come to this understanding, it dawns on us that what we took to be reasonable and morally good action has involved a great oversimplification of the demands of rationality and morality. We thus have to suffer not only the calamitous consequences of the adversity we face, but also the collapse of our self-esteem.

If this is applied to Creon and Antigone, the following interpretation suggests itself. By the end of the play, Creon is forced to the understanding that his conception of a good life, that of being a good ruler, is deficient, and so also is his character. He was right in thinking that ruling consists in the exercise of power, but he was wrong in not realizing that it must be exercised within the limits set by human nature and moral tradition. He violated these limits, and so he came to grief. But he was led to violating them by his character defects, by his stubborn, intransigent obsession with having others unquestioningly bow to his authority, and it was that realization that finally destroyed him.

Antigone, by contrast, was both better and worse off. Her oversimplification was not as bad as Creon's because she recognized the limits Creon was violating. But her conception of a good life was nevertheless faulty. She failed to see that social life involves compromises, that her obsession with purity, with absolute obligation, and her utter disregard of the need to harmonize the conflicting requirements of purity and obligation make it impossible for people to live together. She was in one respect worse off than Creon because Creon came to recognize his own faults, while Antigone did not. It is of course an achievement of doubtful value to die knowing one's faults rather than to die in the grip of misplaced self-esteem. It must be remembered, however, that the play is for *our* reflection, so that *we* can learn from it to live better, and not for the benefit of Creon or Antigone, who are the means, not the objects, of instruction.

The reason, therefore, why it is good to lose unreflective innocence is to prevent tragic choices being forced on us. We learn to do that by developing a reflective understanding of our vulnerability to permanent adversities, by forming our character and conceptions of a good life in the light of that understanding, and by jettisoning the illusion that the right efforts made in the right way will free us from permanent adversities. Learning these matters, however, amounts to growing in moral wisdom, and that is why describing the loss of prereflective and unreflective innocence is the same as describing ourselves growing in moral wisdom.

This understanding may be deepened by noticing that the loss of innocence is a loss of illusions and a gain in inwardly directed reflectiveness. The illusion that permeates prereflective innocence is an attitude to other people and to the physical world that regards them as instrumental to the satisfaction of our desires. It projects onto the scheme of things the importance we attribute to our desires. The satisfaction of desires is accepted as a matter of course, and each instance of it serves to reinforce the illusion. Frustrated desires are regarded as a violation of the natural order, and they are greeted with various degrees of anger, dismay, and sadness. Responsibility for frustration is attributed to external causes. For in the grip of the illusion that society and the physical world were meant to satisfy our desires, there is little room left for entertaining the idea that there may be something wrong with the desires themselves.

This illusion, of course, is quite unlikely to survive the numerous frustrations exposure to reality inevitably brings. As the illusion wanes, so we begin to evaluate our desires. We learn to identify them as trivial or important, immediate or long-term, socially acceptable or unacceptable, harmful and beneficial, and we learn to think about the overall balance and coherence of our various desires. Thus we are brought to increased reflectiveness by the idea that replaces the illusion, namely, that since society and the physical world frustrate our desires, the best chance we have of satisfying them is to control them so as to escape their frustration. There enters the growing realization that there is a cleavage between ourselves, on the one hand, and other people and the world, on the other, and that the satisfaction of our desires depends on taking stock of both. We are thus forced out of the childish illusion characteristic of prereflective innocence that our desires are the pivot on which everything turns, and we become receptive to standards that may guide their control.

Some saints and monsters may not have to exert the control that exposure to the world forces on the rest of us. But understanding the exceptional circumstances that make control for them dispensable reinforces the accuracy of our description for the vast majority of unexceptional lives. The desires of born saints need not be altered because they are so moderate and benign to begin with that they naturally conform to the appropriate standards. And the people who are monstrous genetically may be so successful in satisfying their desires by manipulating other people as to make their control unnecessary. Such cases, if any, are bound to be very rare, and most of us need help in learning to control our desires.

This help is normally supplied, indeed it is pressed on us, by our moral tradition, which we receive in the form of moral education. We internalize the prevailing conventions and use them as standards for evaluating our desires. And so we pass on to unreflective innocence. The illusion that infuses this frame of mind is the expectation that desires favorably evaluated by the prevailing standards will be satisfied. If the expectation is met, the illusion is strengthened. If it is disappointed, we blame either the standards or our defects in conforming to them. Improvement is assumed to be possible in either case, and it is seen to depend on revising the standards or on overcoming our defects. Whichever it is, however, the illusion persists that provided improvements are made, our desires will be satisfied.

Doubt on this score enters if we realize that permanent adversities often make it impossible to effect many necessary improvements. And if further reflection allows us to realize that we ourselves may also be among the agents through whom permanent adversities create obstacles to the satisfaction of our favorably evaluated desires, then we ascend to a new level of reflectiveness. Part of the enduring significance of Sophoclean tragedies is that they motivate those who understand them to seek this enhanced reflection. They bring us to see that just as prereflective innocence was shattered by our discovery of the cleavage between ourselves, on the one hand, and the social and physical world, on the other, so unreflective innocence cannot survive the discovery of the cleavage within ourselves between our rational pursuit of a good life through the satisfaction of our favorably evaluated desires and contingency, conflict, and evil, which also permeate our character.

The loss of innocence, involving the corollary processes of loss of illusion and gain in reflectiveness, is painful. We lose something that was a great comfort to have, and what we acquire in its place is a considerable burden. The comfort we forego is being able to afford to be forgetful of our self. If we are not divided from the world by frustrated or condemned desires, we can afford to relax. We do not then have to think critically about our desires, curb them, or make great efforts to control them; we can just easily, trustingly, unquestioningly amble along life's way and serenely take our blessings for granted. The burden that replaces the comfort is the need for constant reflection involving an effort to understand the complexities we face, assess our resources, and use control to mediate between our desires and actions. There is much, therefore, that stands in the way of our willingness to lose our innocence, and there *are* reasons for nurturing our illusions and for fending off the disclosures of inwardly directed reflection.

But there are reasons also on the other side. The first is that our frustrations undermine the comforts of innocence and incline us toward the acceptance of the burden of reflection. We discover that the world is not the idyllic place we expected it to be in the security of childhood or in the safe conformity to prevailing conventions. The notice we are forced to take of the obstacles to living as we think we should will tend to make us acknowledge them, and as we do, so we lose our innocence. The second reason is that the possibility of control, of being masters of our fate is for us a powerfully motivating ideal. Innocence stands in its way because it nurtures the illusion that living a good life is much easier than it is and so control is dispensable. The illusion disguises from us the adversities we face, and thus it enlists our collusion in succumbing to them. Understanding this will lead us to want to lose the illusion. The third reason is that the loss of innocence is the loss only of prereflective and unreflective innocence. There is also reflective innocence which enables us to regain some of the lost comfort and to shed some of the acquired burden.

REFLECTIVE INNOCENCE AND MORAL WISDOM

The loss of prereflective and unreflective innocence is a necessary first stage toward the development of reflective innocence. It is a stage from which it is possible to see, as Stuart Hampshire points out, that the "virtues that bring great political achievements and civic glory have their cost in the loss of integrity and in the loss of the virtues and the satisfactions of friendship and fair dealing. The virtues that are essential to an admirable private life, such as loyal friendships and a sense of personal honour and of integrity, have their cost in political powerlessness. A weak and philosophically confused person cannot understand that every kind of human excellence comes from a strong concentration of energies and it always has its consequent cost. Such a person dissipates his energies and falls short of any form of human excellence. All virtue, like all genuine learning, results from a specialisation of human powers."[6] To see this is to see that contingency, conflict, and evil inescapably limit human possibilities. "Life, and liveliness, within the soul and within society, consists in perpetual conflicts between impulses and ideals. . . . Harmony and inner consensus come with death. . . . To correct Plato's analogy: justice within the soul may be seen as the intelligent recognition and acceptance of conflicting and ambivalent elements in one's own imagination and emotions—not the suppression of conflicts by a dominant intellect for the sake of harmony, but rather their containment through some means of expres-

[6] Hampshire, *Innocence and Experience*, 165.

sion peculiar to the individual. . . . [T]he life of the soul is a series of compromise formations, which are evidently unstable and transient, just as every successive state of society is evidently unstable and transient."[7]

There is, therefore, a second stage beyond the loss of the two lesser kinds of innocence: the containment of contingency, conflict, and evil within our character through some means of expression peculiar to the individual. That expression involves constructing and living according to a reasonable conception of a good life—a conception formed by reflection on the possibilities and limits afforded by our character, moral tradition, and the realities of the physical world. Such a conception *may* make the containment of permanent adversities possible by increasing our control over them through exercising sufficient attraction to appeal to our intellect, imagination, and emotions, and through disallowing our character defects to exacerbate the obstacles permanent adversities will present.

Living according to a reasonable conception of a good life, however, is no guarantee that the life will be good. The third stage of development toward reflective innocence is reached only when the life lived according to a reasonable conception actually succeeds in being good. As Herbert Morris writes: "To appreciate that there is [contingency, conflict, and] evil in the world, to hold no illusions about it, to be serious about it, to have experienced many of its manifestations, to have seen as well as [contingency, conflict, and] evil what allows for . . . [their] being overcome, to see all that makes for good and to give it due weight—these seem among the essential components of . . . wisdom. They link closely with lost innocence." But, in addition, "We operate with a conception of worth of human beings that leads to our esteeming more highly those who are not just moral persons but morally wise persons. They have . . . not been crushed by what they have confronted, but have emerged . . . victorious, capable, despite and because of knowledge [of permanent adversities], of affirming rather than denying life."[8]

Reflective innocence is reached, then, by those who succeed in passing through the stages of losing lesser forms of innocence, living according to a reasonable conception of a good life, and knowing and coping with permanent adversities. Such people enjoy the comforts of higher innocence and carry a reduced burden of reflection. Both of these benefits are traceable to the same source: the achievement of simplicity, which derives neither from simple-mindedness, nor from oversimplification. The simplicity of reflective innocence is the possession of those who have developed their character and conception of a good life and used them to work their way

---

[7] Ibid., 189.
[8] Morris, "Lost Innocence," 161.

through the complexities that would baffle others, who have freed themselves from the illusions that disguise or minimize permanent adversities, and who have achieved clarity about their limits and possibilities. This kind of simplicity is the product of firm control, of sufficient reflection, and of having developed a second nature that makes spontaneity once again possible. Reflective innocence is innocence regained, innocence free of illusions, a well-earned reward of maturity, an attitude of openness to the world which is maintained with full knowledge of one's vulnerability to permanent adversities. It is the attitude in which

> We shall not cease from exploration
> And the end of all our exploring
> Will be to arrive were we started
> And know the place for the first time.[9]

The conduct that spontaneously flows from reflective innocence may be indistinguishable from that which is prompted by prereflective and unreflective innocence. The difference between them need not be in what is done; it concerns primarily the conception of a good life, knowledge, evaluation, and judgment that form the background to what is done. And this background, of course, is moral wisdom, while the background of prereflective and unreflective innocence is its lack. Reflective innocence, then, is the great internal good that follows from having a reasonable conception of a good life, knowledge of good and evil, facility in evaluating the actual situations we face in the light of that knowledge, and good enough judgment to render simple the complex situations whose evaluation is difficult.

The fact remains, however, that permanent adversities may ruin a life no matter how much moral wisdom the person living it has. If that happens, then the sign of moral wisdom will not be reflective innocence, since the conditions in which it is appropriate will be lacking. Its sign will then be to bear the misfortune. It will be made more bearable by the knowledge that we have done what we could to prevent it, that it is not due to our defects or to being singled out for maltreatment by malevolent forces, and that what we endure is just the accident of having stumbled into the path of the blind, impersonal, indifferent juggernaut of the natural world.

[9] T. S. Eliot, "Four Quartets," in *The Complete Poems and Plays* (New York: Harcourt, 1971), 145.

Works Cited

Adkins, Arthur W. H. *Merit and Responsibility: A Study in Greek Values.* Oxford: Clarendon Press, 1960.

Arendt, Hannah. *Eichmann in Jerusalem: A Report on the Banality of Evil.* New York: Viking, 1964.

Aristotle, *Metaphysics.* Translated by W. D. Ross. In *The Complete Works of Aristotle,* edited by Jonathan Barnes. Princeton: Princeton University Press, 1984.

———. *Nicomachean Ethics.* Translated by W. D. Ross, revised by J. O. Urmson. In *The Complete Works of Aristotle,* edited by Jonathan Barnes. Princeton: Princeton University Press, 1984.

———. *Poetics.* Translated by I. Bywater. In *The Complete Works of Aristotle,* edited by Jonathan Barnes. Princeton: Princeton University Press, 1984.

———. *Rhetoric.* Translated by Rhys Roberts. In *The Complete Works of Aristotle,* edited by Jonathan Barnes. Princeton: Princeton University Press, 1984.

Barry, Brian. *Political Argument.* London: Routledge, 1965.

Bencivenga, Ermanno. *The Discipline of Subjectivity.* Princeton: Princeton University Press, 1990.

Berlin, Isaiah. *Four Essays on Liberty.* Oxford: Oxford University Press, 1969.

———. " 'From Hope and Fear Set Free'." In *Concepts and Categories.* London: Hogarth Press, 1978.

Black, Max. *The Prevalence of Humbug and Other Essays.* Ithaca: Cornell University Press, 1983.

Brandt, Richard B. "The Psychology of Benevolence and Its Implications for Philosophy." *Journal of Philosophy* 73 (1976): 429–453.

———. "Traits of Character: A Conceptual Analysis." *American Philosophical Quarterly* 7 (1970): 23–37.

Brann, Eva. *The World of Imagination.* Chicago: University of Chicago Press, 1986.

Cioffari, Vincenzo. "Fortune, Fate, and Chance." In *Dictionary of the History of Ideas,* edited by Philip P. Wiener. New York: Scribner's, 1973.

Collingwood, Robin G. *An Essay on Metaphysics.* Oxford: Clarendon Press, 1940.

Cooper, John M. "Aristotle on the Goods of Fortune." *Philosophical Review* 94 (1985): 173–196.

——. *Reason and Human Good in Aristotle.* Cambridge: Harvard University Press, 1975.

Douglas, Mary. *Implicit Meanings.* London: Routledge, 1975.

Drengson, Alan R. "The Virtue of Socratic Ignorance." *American Philosophical Quarterly* 18 (1981): 237–242.

Dworkin, Gerald. "Is More Choice Better than Less?" In *Theory and Practice of Autonomy.* Cambridge: Cambridge University Press, 1988.

Eliot, T. S. "Four Quartets." In *The Complete Poems and Plays.* New York: Harcourt, 1971.

Feinberg, Joel. "Justice and Personal Desert." In *Nomos VI: Justice,* edited by Carl J. Friedrich and John W. Chapman. New York: Atherton, 1963.

Fischer, John M., ed. *Moral Responsibility.* Ithaca: Cornell University Press, 1986.

Frankfurt, Harry G. "Freedom of the Will and the Concept of a Person." In *The Importance of What We Care About.* Cambridge: Cambridge University Press, 1988.

——. *The Importance of What We Care About.* Cambridge: Cambridge University Press, 1988.

Gadamer, Hans-Georg. *Truth and Method.* Translated by Garrett Barden and John Cumming. New York: Seabury Press, 1975.

Gallie, William B. *Philosophy and the Historical Understanding.* London: Chatto & Windus, 1964.

Galston, William A. *Justice and the Human Good.* Chicago: University of Chicago Press, 1980.

Geertz, Clifford. "Found in Translation: On the Social History of Moral Imagination." In *Local Knowledge.* New York: Basic Books, 1983.

——. "'From the Native's Point of View': On the Nature of Anthropological Understanding." In *Local Knowledge.* New York: Basic Books, 1983.

——. *The Interpretation of Cultures.* New York: Basic Books, 1973.

——. *Local Knowledge.* New York: Basic Books, 1983.

Goffman, Erving. *The Presentation of Self in Everyday Life.* New York: Doubleday, 1959.

Gowans, Christopher, ed. *Moral Dilemmas.* New York: Oxford University Press, 1987.

Griswold, Charles. *Self-Knowledge in Plato's Phaedrus.* New Haven: Yale University Press, 1986.

Grube, Georges M. A. *Plato's Thought.* Boston: Beacon Press, 1964.

Gunn, Giles. *The Culture of Criticism and the Criticism of Culture.* New York: Oxford University Press, 1987.

Hamlyn, David W. "Self-Knowledge." In *Perception, Learning, and the Self.* London: Routledge, 1983.

Hampshire, Stuart. *Freedom of the Individual.* Expanded edition. Princeton: Princeton University Press, 1975.

——. *Innocence and Experience.* Cambridge: Harvard University Press, 1989.

——. *Morality and Conflict.* Cambridge: Harvard University Press, 1983.

——. "Subjunctive Conditionals." In *Freedom of Mind.* Oxford: Clarendon Press, 1972.

——. *Thought and Action.* London: Chatto & Windus, 1960.

Hardie, William F. R. *Aristotle's Ethical Theory.* Oxford: Clarendon Press, 1980.

Hartmann, Nicolai. *Ethics.* Translated by S. Coit. London: Allen & Unwin, 1932.

Hegel, G. W. F. *Reason in History.* Translated by Robert S. Hartman. New York: Liberal Arts, 1953.

Hiley, David R. *Philosophy in Question.* Chicago: University of Chicago Press, 1988.

Hollis, Martin, and Steven Lukes, eds. *Rationality and Relativism.* Oxford: Blackwell, 1982.

Hume, David. *An Enquiry concerning the Principles of Morals.* Edited by L. A. Selby-Bigge. 2d ed. Oxford: Clarendon Press, 1961.

——. *A Treatise of Human Nature.* Edited by L. A. Selby-Bigge. Oxford: Clarendon Press, 1960.

Irwin, Terence. *Plato's Moral Theory.* Oxford: Clarendon Press, 1977.

James, William. *Psychology: Briefer Course.* New York: Henry Holt, 1922.

——. "The Will to Believe." In *The Will to Believe.* New York: Dover, 1956.

Johnson, Mark. *Moral Imagination: Implications of Cognitive Science for Ethics.* Chicago: University of Chicago Press, 1993.

Johnson, Peter. *Politics, Innocence, and the Limits of Goodness.* London: Routledge, 1988.

Kant, Immanuel. *Critique of Pure Reason.* Translated by Norman Kemp Smith. London: Macmillan, 1953.

——. *Groundwork of the Metaphysics of Morals.* Translated and analysed by H. J. Paton. New York: Harper, 1964.

Kaufmann, Walter. *Nietzsche.* 4th ed. Princeton: Princeton University Press, 1974.

Kekes, John. "Constancy and Purity." *Mind* 92 (1983): 499–518.

——. *Facing Evil.* Princeton: Princeton University Press, 1990.

——. *The Morality of Pluralism.* Princeton: Princeton University Press, 1993.

——. *Moral Tradition and Individuality.* Princeton: Princeton University Press, 1989.

——. "Purity and Judgment in Morality." *Philosophy* 63 (1988): 453–469.

Kidd, I. G. "Socrates." In *The Encyclopedia of Philosophy,* edited by Paul Edwards. New York: Macmillan, 1967.

Kierkegaard, Søren. *Purity of Heart.* Translated by Douglas V. Steere. New York: Harper & Row, 1948.

——. *The Sickness unto Death.* Translated by Walter Lowrie. New York: Doubleday, 1954.

Knox, Bernard M. W. *The Heroic Temper.* Berkeley: University of California Press, 1964.

Kolenda, Konstantin. *Philosophy in Literature.* Totowa, N.J.: Barnes & Noble, 1982.

Krausz, Michael, ed. *Relativism: Interpretation and Confrontation.* Notre Dame, Ind.: University of Notre Dame Press, 1989.

Krausz, Michael, and Jack W. Meiland. eds. *Relativism: Cognitive and Moral.* Notre Dame, Ind.: University of Notre Dame Press, 1982.

Kupperman, Joel. *Character.* New York: Oxford University Press, 1991.

——. "Character and Self-Knowledge." *Aristotelian Society Proceedings* 85 (1984/85): 219–238.

Lloyd-Jones, Hugh. *The Justice of Zeus.* Rev. ed. Berkeley: University of California Press, 1983.

Lovibond, Sabina. *Realism and Imagination in Ethics.* Minneapolis: University of Minnesota Press, 1983.

MacIntyre, Alasdair. *After Virtue.* Notre Dame, Ind.: University of Notre Dame Press, 1981.

Marcel, Gabriel. *The Decline of Wisdom.* Translated by Manya Harari. London: Harvill, 1954.

Margolis, Joseph. *The Truth about Relativism.* Oxford: Blackwell, 1991.

Matson, Wallace I. and Adam Leite. "Socrates' Critique of Cognitivism." *Philosophy* 66 (1991): 145–167.

Mill, John Stuart. *Autobiography.* Indianapolis: Bobbs-Merrill, 1957.

——. *On Liberty.* Indianapolis: Hackett, 1978.

Miller, David. *Social Justice.* Oxford: Clarendon Press, 1976.

Montaigne, Michel de. *The Complete Works of Montaigne.* Translated by Donald M. Frame. Stanford: Stanford University Press, 1958.

Morris, Herbert. "Lost Innocence." In *On Guilt and Innocence.* Berkeley: University of California Press, 1976.

Murdoch, Iris. *The Fire and the Sun.* Oxford: Clarendon Press, 1977.

——. *The Sovereignty of Good.* London: Routledge, 1970.

——. "The Sovereignty of Good over Other Concepts." In *The Sovereignty of Good.* London: Routledge, 1970.

Myrna, Frances. "Purity in Morals." *Monist* 66 (1983): 283–297.

Nagel, Thomas. "Moral Luck." In *Mortal Questions.* Cambridge: Cambridge University Press, 1979.

——. *The View from Nowhere.* New York: Oxford University Press, 1986.

Nehamas, Alexander. *Nietzsche: Life as Literature.* Cambridge: Harvard University Press, 1985.

Nietzsche, Friedrich. *The Birth of Tragedy.* In *Basic Writings of Nietzsche.* Translated and edited with commentaries by Walter Kaufmann. New York: Random House, 1968.

——. *Ecce Homo.* In *Basic Writings of Nietzsche.* Translated and edited with commentaries by Walter Kaufmann. New York: Random House, 1968.

North, Helen. *Sophrosyne: Self-Knowledge and Self-Restraint in Greek Literature.* Ithaca: Cornell University Press, 1966.

Novitz, David. *Knowledge, Fiction, and Imagination.* Philadelphia: Temple University Press, 1987.

Nozick, Robert. *Anarchy, State, and Utopia.* New York: Basic Books, 1974.

Nussbaum, Martha C. "The Discernment of Perception: An Aristotelian Conception of Private and Public Rationality." In *Love's Knowledge.* New York: Oxford University Press, 1990.

——. *The Fragility of Goodness: Luck and Ethics in Greek Tragedy and Philosophy.* Cambridge: Cambridge University Press, 1986.

Paolucci, Anne, and Henry Paolucci, eds. *Hegel on Tragedy.* New York: Harper, 1962.

Paton, H. J. *The Categorical Imperative.* Philadelphia: University of Pennsylvania Press, 1971.

Plato. *The Apology.* Translated by Hugh Tredennick. In *Plato: The Collected Dialogues,* edited by Edith Hamilton and Huntington Cairns. Princeton: Princeton University Press, 1961.

——. *Crito.* Translated by Hugh Tredennick. In *Plato: The Collected Dialogues,* edited by Edith Hamilton and Huntington Cairns. Princeton: Princeton University Press, 1961.

——. *Euthydemus.* Translated by W. H. D. Rouse. In *Plato: The Collected Dialogues,* edited by Edith Hamilton and Huntington Cairns. Princeton: Princeton University Press, 1961.

——. *Meno.* Translated by W. K. C. Guthrie. In *Plato: The Collected Dialogues,* edited by Edith Hamilton and Huntington Cairns. Princeton: Princeton University Press, 1961.

——. *Phaedo.* Translated by Hugh Tredennick. In *Plato: The Collected Dialogues,* edited by Edith Hamilton and Huntington Cairns. Princeton: Princeton University Press, 1961.

——. *Phaedrus.* Translated by R. Hackforth. In *Plato: The Collected Dialogues,* edited by Edith Hamilton and Huntington Cairns. Princeton: Princeton University Press, 1961.

——. *Protagoras.* Translated by W. K. C. Guthrie. In *Plato: The Collected Dialogues,* edited by Edith Hamilton and Huntington Cairns. Princeton: Princeton University Press, 1961.

——. *The Republic.* Translated by Georges M. A. Grube. Indianapolis: Hackett, 1974.

Polanyi, Karl. *Personal Knowledge.* New York: Harper, 1958.

Rawls, John. *Political Liberalism.* New York: Columbia University Press, 1993.

——. *A Theory of Justice.* Cambridge: Harvard University Press, 1971.

Rescher, Nicholas. *Ethical Idealism.* Berkeley: University of California Press, 1987.

Rorty, Amélie, ed. *Essays on Aristotle's Ethics.* Berkeley: University of California Press, 1980.

Rosenblum, Nancy L., ed. *Liberalism and the Moral Life.* Cambridge: Harvard University Press, 1989.

Russell, Bertrand. *A History of Western Philosophy.* New York: Simon and Schuster, 1945.

Sandel, Michael, ed. *Liberalism and Its Critics.* Oxford: Blackwell, 1984.

Santayana, George. *Interpretations of Poetry and Religion.* New York: Harper, 1957.

Savile, Anthony. *The Test of Time.* Oxford: Clarendon Press, 1982.

Shakespeare, William. *King Lear.* In *The Complete Works of William Shakespeare,* edited by W. J. Craig. London: Oxford University Press, 1954.

Sher, George. *Desert.* Princeton: Princeton University Press, 1987.

Sherman, Nancy. *The Fabric of Character.* Oxford: Clarendon Press, 1989.

Sinnott-Armstrong, Walter. *Moral Dilemmas.* Oxford: Blackwell, 1988.

Sophocles. *Ajax.* Translated by John Moore. In *The Complete Greek Tragedies: Sophocles II,.* edited by David Grene and Richmond Lattimore. Chicago: University of Chicago Press, 1969.

——. *Antigone.* In *The Three Theban Plays,* translated by Robert Fagles. New York: Viking, 1982.

——. *Oedipus at Colonus.* In *The Three Theban Plays,* translated by Robert Fagles. New York: Viking, 1982.

——. *Oedipus the King.* In *The Three Theban Plays,* translated by Robert Fagles. New York: Viking, 1982.

——. *Philoctetes.* Translated by David Grene. In *The Complete Greek Tragedies: Sophocles II,* edited by David Grene and Richmond Lattimore. Chicago: University of Chicago Press, 1969.

Sternberg, Robert J., ed. *Wisdom: Its Nature, Origin, and Development.* New York: Cambridge University Press, 1990.

Stocker, Michael. *Plural and Conflicting Values.* Oxford: Clarendon Press, 1990.

Taylor, Charles. "Responsibility for Self." In *The Identities of Persons,* edited by Amélie Rorty. Berkeley: University of California Press, 1976.

Tolstoy, Leo. *The Death of Ivan Ilyich.* Translated by A. Maude. New York: Signet, 1960.

Trilling, Lionel. "Why We Read Jane Austen." In *The Last Decade.* New York: Harcourt, Brace, 1979.

Urmson, John O. *Aristotle's Ethics.* Oxford: Blackwell, 1988.

Versenyi, Laszlo. *Socratic Humanism.* New Haven: Yale University Press, 1963.

Vlastos, Gregory. *Socrates, Ironist and Moral Philosopher.* Ithaca: Cornell University Press, 1991.

Warnke, Georgia. *Gadamer.* Stanford: Stanford University Press, 1987.

Warnock, Mary. *Imagination* London: Faber and Faber, 1976.

Watson, Gary. "Free Agency." In *Free Will.* Edited by Gary Watson. Oxford: Oxford University Press, 1982.

——. ed. *Free Will.* Oxford: Oxford University Press, 1982.

Weitz, Morris. *The Opening Mind.* Chicago: University of Chicago Press, 1977.

White, Nicholas P. *A Companion to Plato's Republic.* Indianapolis: Hackett, 1979.

Whitman, Cedric H. *Sophocles: A Study of Heroic Humanism.* Cambridge: Harvard University Press, 1951.

Wiggins, David. "Deliberation and Practical Reason." In *Needs, Values, Truth.* Oxford: Blackwell, 1987.

——. "Truth, Invention, and the Meaning of Life." In *Needs, Values, Truth.* Oxford: Blackwell, 1987.

Williams, Bernard. "Conflicts of Values." In *Moral Luck.* Cambridge: Cambridge University Press, 1981.

——. "Moral Luck." In *Moral Luck.* Cambridge: Cambridge University Press, 1981.

Wittgenstein, Ludwig. *Philosophical Investigations.* Translated by G. E. M. Anscombe. Oxford: Blackwell, 1968.

Wolf, Susan. *Freedom within Reason.* New York: Oxford University Press, 1991.

Wolgast, Elizabeth. "Innocence." *Philosophy* 68 (1993): 297–306.

Wollheim, Richard. *The Thread of Life.* Cambridge: Harvard University Press, 1984.

Wordsworth, William. "The Prelude." In *Poetical Works.* New revised edition by Ernest de Selincourt. Oxford: Oxford University Press, 1969.

Wright, Georg Henrik von. *The Varieties of Goodness.* London: Routledge, 1963.

Zaitchik, Alan. "On Deserving to Deserve." *Philosophy and Public Affairs* 6 (1977): 371–388.

Index